TEACHINGS OF LORD KAPILA

The Son of Devahūti

Other BBT Publications

Books by His Divine Grace A.C. Bhaktivedanta Swami Prabhupāda

Bhagavad-gītā As It Is
Śrīmad-Bhāgavatam, Cantos 1-12 (18 vols.)
Śrī Caitanya-caritāmṛta (17 vols.)
Teachings of Lord Caitanya
The Nectar of Devotion
The Nectar of Instruction
Śrī Īśopaniṣad
Easy Journey to Other Planets
Kṛṣṇa Consciousness: The Topmost Yoga System
Kṛṣṇa, the Supreme Personality of Godhead
Perfect Questions, Perfect Answers
Teachings of Lord Kapila, the Son of Devahūti
Teachings of Queen Kuntī
The Path of Perfection
Kṛṣṇa, the Reservoir of Pleasure
The Science of Self-Realization
Preaching Is the Essence
Life Comes From Life
The Perfection of Yoga
Beyond Birth and Death
On the Way to Kṛṣṇa
Rāja-vidyā: The King of Knowledge
Elevation to Kṛṣṇa Consciousness
Kṛṣṇa Consciousness: The Matchless Gift
Back to Godhead magazine (founder)

available from

The Bhaktivedanta Book Trust
P.O. Box 324
Borehamwood, Herts.
WD6 1NB, U.K.

The Bhaktivedanta Book Trust
P.O. Box 262
Botany, N.S.W.
2019, Australia

The Bhaktivedanta Book Trust
3764 Watseka Ave.
Los Angeles
CA 90034, USA

TEACHINGS OF LORD KAPILA

The Son of Devahūti

His Divine Grace
A.C. Bhaktivedanta Swami Prabhupāda
FOUNDER-ĀCĀRYA OF THE INTERNATIONAL SOCIETY FOR KRISHNA CONSCIOUSNESS

THE BHAKTIVEDANTA BOOK TRUST

Readers interested in the subject matter of this book
are invited by the International Society for Krishna Consciousness
to correspond with its Secretary.

International Society for Krishna Consciousness
3764 Watseka Avenue
Los Angeles, California 90034
USA

ISKCON
P.O. Box 324, Borehamwood
Herts. WD6 1NB
England
Telephone: 01-905 1244

First Printing, 1977: 50,000 copies
Second Printing, 1988: 3,000 copies
Third Printing, 1990: 80,000 copies

Printed in Germany

Library of Congress Cataloging in Publication Data

Puranas. Bhāgavatapurāna. English. Selections.
Teachings of Lord Kapiladeva.

Bibliography: p.
Includes index.
I. Bhaktivedanta Swami, A.C., 1896-1977
II. Title.
BL1135.P7A22 1977 294.5'925 77-11077
ISBN 0-89213-008-3

Contents

Foreword

Kapila Muni, a renowned sage of antiquity, is the author of the philosophical system known as Sāṅkhya, which forms an important part of India's ancient philosophical heritage. Sāṅkhya is both a system of metaphysics, dealing with the elemental principles of the physical universe, and a system of spiritual knowledge, with its own methodology, culminating in full consciousness of the Supreme Absolute. Kapila, however, is not an ordinary philosopher or sage. According to Vedic tradition, the tradition of India's ancient scriptural literature, He Himself is an *avatāra* (incarnation) of the Supreme Absolute Truth.

Kapila's teachings are originally inscribed in the *Śrīmad-Bhāgavatam*, or *Bhāgavata Purāṇa*, one of the most important scriptural documents of Vedic theism. Within the *Bhāgavatam*, Kapila's teachings comprise Chapters Twenty-five through Thirty-three of the Third Canto. This book, *Teachings of Lord Kapila, the Son of Devahūti*, is based on a unique series of lectures presented in Bombay, India, in the spring of 1974, by His Divine Grace A. C. Bhaktivedanta Swami Prabhupāda. In this series, Śrīla Prabhupāda spoke from the Twenty-fifth Chapter, which contains the beginning of Lord Kapila's teachings. Śrīla Prabhupāda is the author of a celebrated multivolume translation and commentary on the entire text of the *Bhāgavatam*, and at the time of the Kapila lectures he had already completed his written commentary on the section of the *Bhāgavatam* dealing with Kapiladeva's teachings. In these special lectures, however, Śrīla Prabhupāda went into significantly greater detail in elucidating the verses and shed an even broader light upon these fascinating teachings.

The text begins with the words of Śaunaka, the foremost of the sages of Naimiṣāraṇya, the vastly learned sages to whom *Śrīmad-Bhāgavatam* was originally spoken some thousands of years ago. The sages have already heard about Lord Kapiladeva from Sūta Gosvāmī, an exalted spiritual master, and it is clear from Śaunaka's words that they accept Kapila Muni as being an incarnation of the Lord Himself and as therefore being the highest authority on *yoga* and transcendental knowledge. In recounting the history of Lord Kapila, Sūta Gosvāmī, in accordance with Vedic principles for presenting spiritual knowledge, refers to discourse by great spiritual masters who have previously discussed this same subject. In this case, Sūta Gosvāmī refers to a discussion between Vidura and the great sage Maitreya, who was a friend of Vyāsadeva, the original compiler of the Vedic literature.

As Sūta Gosvāmī has already described, Lord Kapila appeared in this world as the son of Kardama Muni, a master of mystic *yoga*, and his wife, Devahūti. Both Kardama Muni and Devahūti were aware of the divinity of their son. Indeed, even before Kapila's birth, Lord Brahmā himself, the chief created person in this universe, had appeared before Devahūti and revealed to her that her son was to be an incarnation of the Supreme Lord and that this incarnation would enlighten her with spiritual knowledge.

According to the Vedic social system, a man with a grown son may accept the order of *sannyāsa*, thus renouncing all connections with his family and worldly life, and entrust his wife to the care of his son. Kardama Muni, of course, knew that his son was an incarnation of the Supreme Lord, yet to honor this Vedic system and emphasize its importance, he too eventually accepted *sannyāsa*, entrusting his wife, Devahūti, to the care of his divine son, Kapiladeva. Therefore, as Sūta Gosvāmī begins to answer Śaunaka's request to hear further about Lord Kapiladeva, the sages have already been informed of how Kardama Muni departed for the forest, leaving Kapiladeva behind with Devahūti.

After Kardama Muni's departure, Devahūti, remembering the prophetic words of Lord Brahmā, approaches her divine son and humbly expresses her desire for spiritual enlightenment: "My Lord, I have fallen into the abyss of ignorance. Your Lordship is my only means of getting out of this darkest region of ignorance because You are my transcendental eye, which, by Your mercy only, I have attained after many, many births. . . . Now be pleased, my Lord, to dispel my great delusion . . . You are the ax which can cut the tree of material existence. I therefore offer my obeisances to You, who are the greatest of all transcendentalists, and I inquire from You as to the relationship between man and woman and between spirit and matter." (*Śrīmad-Bhāgavatam* 3.25.7–11) Pleased by His mother's pure desire for spiritual enlightenment, and feeling great compassion for her, Kapila begins to speak on the Sāṅkhya philosophy.

Now, what is Sāṅkhya? Insofar as Sāṅkhya deals with the elemental categories or principles of the physical universe, Sāṅkhya is what

Western scholars generally refer to as "metaphysics." The term *sāṅkhya* literally means "to count." This name is used because Sāṅkhya philosophy enumerates principles of cosmic evolution by rational analysis. The etymological meaning of the word *sāṅkhya* is "that which explains very lucidly by analysis of material elements." Philosophically, this term is used because the Sāṅkhya system expounds analytical knowledge that enables one to distinguish between matter and spirit. This understanding culminates in *bhakti*, devotion for and service to the Supreme. It may be said, therefore, that Sāṅkhya and *bhakti* form two aspects of the same process, *bhakti* being the ultimate goal or ultimate aspect of Sāṅkhya.

It is interesting to note, at this point, that long after Lord Kapila's descent, an imitation Kapila appeared on the Indian subcontinent and propounded a nontheistic Sāṅkhya. That which is generally studied as Sāṅkhya in the contemporary academic context is actually this later, nontheistic, materialistic Sāṅkhya. The Sāṅkhya philosophy, propounded by the original Kapila, is practically unknown in the West. *Teachings of Lord Kapila, the Son of Devahūti* (along with Śrīla Prabhupāda's complete commentary on Kapila's Sāṅkhya in his edition of *Śrīmad-Bhāgavatam*) is probably the first major exposition in the English language on the original, theistic Sāṅkhya. It should therefore be of considerable interest to scholars in this field.

Because the basic principle and the ultimate goal of Lord Kapiladeva's Sāṅkhya philosophy is *bhakti*, this is the subject with which Lord Kapiladeva begins His instructions to Devahūti. Consequently, because this volume, *Teachings of Lord Kapila, the Son of Devahūti*, is Śrīla Prabhupāda's commentary on the beginning of Lord Kapila's teachings, it is chiefly concerned with the science of *bhakti-yoga*—the process of linking with God (*yoga* means "linking") through *bhakti* (devotion).

As the actual history begins, Devahūti approaches her son, Kapila, and with deep humility expresses her sincere desire for spiritual enlightenment. In response, Lord Kapila delineates "the path of the transcendentalists, who are interested in self-realization." Concisely summarizing the actual process of self-realization, Kapila defines consciousness in both the conditioned and liberated states. He describes the psychology of pure consciousness, delineates the symptoms and characteristics of a *sādhu*, holy person, and stresses the importance of *sādhu-saṅga*, association with those who are saintly. Kapiladeva then explains that liberation is merely a stage preliminary to the attainment of *bhakti* and that one who attains *bhakti* automatically achieves liberation. One who engages in *bhakti*, devotional *yoga*, automatically transcends material desires and ultimately crosses beyond birth and death.

According to later descriptions in *Śrīmad-Bhāgavatam*, Devahūti ultimately attains full enlightenment in transcendental knowledge by hearing and understanding the sublime philosophical teachings of her great son.

—The Publishers

CHAPTER ONE

The Purpose of Lord Kapila's Advent

TEXT 1

śaunaka uvāca
kapilas tattva-saṅkhyātā
bhagavān ātma-māyayā
jātaḥ svayam ajaḥ sākṣād
ātma-prajñaptaye nṛṇām

TRANSLATION

Śrī Śaunaka said: Although He is unborn, the Supreme Personality of Godhead took birth as Kapila Muni by His internal potency. He descended to disseminate transcendental knowledge for the benefit of the whole human race.

PURPORT

The word *ātma-prajñaptaye* indicates that the Lord descends for the benefit of the human race to give transcendental knowledge. Material necessities are quite sufficiently provided for in the knowledge given in the Vedic literatures, which offer a program for good living and gradual elevation to the platform of *sattva-guṇa*, the mode of goodness. Once one is situated in *sattva-guṇa*, one's knowledge expands. On the platform of passion there is no knowledge, for passion is an impetus to enjoy material benefits. On the platform of ignorance there is neither knowledge nor enjoyment but simply animalistic living.

The *Vedas* are intended to elevate one from the mode of ignorance to the platform of goodness. When one is situated in the mode of goodness, he is able to understand knowledge of the self, or transcendental knowledge. Such knowledge cannot be appreciated by any ordinary man;

therefore a disciplic succession is required. This knowledge is expounded either by the Supreme Personality of Godhead Himself or by His bona fide devotee. Śaunaka Muni also states here that Kapila, the incarnation of the Supreme Personality of Godhead, took birth or appeared simply to disseminate transcendental knowledge. To understand that one is not matter but spirit soul (*ahaṁ brahmāsmi:* "I am by nature Brahman") is not sufficient for understanding the self and his activities. One must be situated in the activities of Brahman. Knowledge of those activities is explained by the Supreme Personality of Godhead Himself. Such transcendental knowledge can be appreciated in human society but not in animal society, as clearly indicated here by the word *nṛṇām*, "for the human beings." Human beings are meant to lead a regulated life. By nature, there is regulation in animal life also, but that is not like the regulative life described in the scriptures or by the Vedic authorities. Only when one's life is regulated according to the *Vedas* can one understand transcendental knowledge.

For the propagation of this transcendental knowledge, Kapiladeva, the incarnation of the Supreme Personality of Godhead, gave instructions in Sāṅkhya philosophy to His mother, Devahūti. Later, another Kapiladeva appeared who expounded atheistic Sāṅkhya philosophy, which dealt with the twenty-four elements but gave no information about God. The original Kapila is called the Devahūti-putra Kapila, and the other is called the atheist Kapila. Concerning Kapiladeva, Śaunaka Ṛṣi says, *kapilas tattva-saṅkhyātā.* Kapila is the Supreme Person; therefore He can explain the Absolute Truth. Actually only Bhagavān can know the true position of the ultimate truth. No one else can know it. Bhagavān, Kṛṣṇa or His incarnation, occasionally visits the earth to give humanity information about the aim of life. Thus the Supreme Lord descended as Kapiladeva, *tattva-saṅkhyātā.* The word *saṅkhyātā* means "expounder," and *tattva* means "the Absolute Truth." The Absolute Truth is Bhagavān Śrī Kṛṣṇa Himself. We cannot understand the Absolute Truth or the Supreme Person by mental speculation, especially when we are under the influence of the three modes of material nature (*sattva-guṇa*, *rajo-guṇa* and *tamo-guṇa*). Only those who are situated in *sattva-guṇa* (the mode of goodness) are fit to understand the Absolute Truth. According to *Bhagavad-gītā* (18.42), those possessing brahminical qualifications are situated in *sattva-guṇa.*

śamo damas tapaḥ śaucaṁ
kṣāntir ārjavam eva ca
jñānaṁ vijñānam āstikyaṁ
brahma-karma svabhāvajam

"Peacefulness, self-control, austerity, purity, tolerance, honesty, wisdom, knowledge and righteousness—these are the qualities by which the *brāhmaṇas* work."

According to the Vedic conception, there must be men in society who are factually *brāhmaṇas*, capable of expounding the real truth. If everyone becomes a *śūdra*, the Absolute Truth cannot be understood. It is said that at the present moment in Kali-yuga everyone is a *śūdra* (*kalau śūdra-sambhavāḥ*), and it is very difficult in this age to find qualified *brāhmaṇas*, for they are very rare. There is practically not a single qualified *brāhmaṇa* in this age.

prāyeṇālpāyuṣaḥ sabhya
kalāv asmin yuge janāḥ
mandāḥ sumanda-matayo
manda-bhāgyā hy upadrutāḥ

"O learned one, in this iron age of Kali men have but short lives. They are quarrelsome, lazy, misguided, unlucky and, above all, always disturbed." (*Bhāg.* 1.1.10) The people in this age are very short-lived and slow in understanding spiritual life. Actually human life is meant for understanding spiritual values, but because everyone in this age is a *śūdra*, no one is interested. People have forgotten life's real purpose. The word *manda* means both slow and bad, and everyone in this age is either bad or slow or a combination of both. People are unfortunate and disturbed by so many things. According to *Śrīmad-Bhāgavatam* there will eventually be no rain and consequently a scarcity of food. The governments will also levy very heavy taxes. The characteristics of this age predicted by *Śrīmad-Bhāgavatam* are already being experienced to some degree. Since Kali-yuga is a very miserable age, Caitanya Mahāprabhu, who is Śrī Kṛṣṇa Himself, advises everyone simply to chant Hare Kṛṣṇa.

harer nāma harer nāma
harer nāmaiva kevalam

kalau nāsty eva nāsty eva
nāsty eva gatir anyathā

"In this age of Kali there is no alternative, there is no alternative, there is no alternative for spiritual progress than the holy name, the holy name, the holy name of the Lord." (*Bṛhan-nāradīya Purāṇa*) This process is not Caitanya Mahāprabhu's invention, but is advised by the *śāstras*, the *Purāṇas*. The process for this Kali-yuga is very simple. One need only chant the Hare Kṛṣṇa *mahā-mantra*. Since everyone in this age is an unintelligent, unfortunate and disturbed *śūdra*, how can anyone understand the Absolute Truth or the aim of life? As stated by the Lord Himself in *Bhagavad-gītā* (4.7):

yadā yadā hi dharmasya
glānir bhavati bhārata
abhyutthānam adharmasya
tadātmānaṁ sṛjāmy aham

"Whenever and wherever there is a decline in religious practice, O descendant of Bharata, and a predominant rise of irreligion—at that time I descend Myself."

Some hundreds and thousands of years ago Lord Kṛṣṇa appeared as Devahūti-putra Kapiladeva. His father's name was Kardama Muni. After Kapiladeva grew up, His father, according to the Vedic system, retired, took *sannyāsa* and left home to cultivate spiritual life. It is not that one should rot in this material world throughout one's whole life. *Pañcāśordhvaṁ vanaṁ vrajet.* According to the Vedic injunctions, there are four *āśramas* and four *varṇas*, and these used to be followed very strictly. After his son grew up, Kardama Muni, being a strict follower of the *Vedas*, left home and put his wife in the charge of his grown son, Kapiladeva.

It is said of Kapiladeva: *kapilas tattva-saṅkhyātā bhagavān.* Lord Kapila is Bhagavān. Nowadays Bhagavān is taken very cheaply because the word is misused, but actually Bhagavān is not an ordinary man. *Avajānanti māṁ mūḍhāḥ:* because Bhagavān Śrī Kṛṣṇa appeared as a human being, fools and rascals (*mūḍhas*) consider Kṛṣṇa an ordinary human. As Kṛṣṇa Himself states in *Bhagavad-gītā* (7.13):

tribhir guṇamayair bhāvair
ebhiḥ sarvam idaṁ jagat
mohitaṁ nābhijānāti
mām ebhyaḥ param avyayam

"Deluded by the three modes (goodness, passion and ignorance), the whole world does not know Me, who am above the modes and inexhaustible."

Yet there are *mahātmās*, great souls, who can understand Kṛṣṇa. Arjuna could understand that although Kṛṣṇa was playing the part of his friend, He was nonetheless the Supreme Personality of Godhead. Arjuna was in perfect knowledge, yet Kṛṣṇa instructed him for our benefit. Arjuna requested Kṛṣṇa's instructions, which are set forth for all human society. After hearing *Bhagavad-gītā*, Arjuna addressed Kṛṣṇa as *paraṁ brahma paraṁ dhāma*, "the Supreme Brahman and supreme abode."

Every person is actually Brahman, spirit soul. We are not actually the body. Awareness of *ahaṁ brahmāsmi* ("I am Brahman") is actual self-realization. According to Vedic culture, one must understand that he is Brahman, not the body. We should not remain in ignorance like cats and dogs, thinking, "I am this body, I am American, I am Indian, I am *brāhmaṇa*, I am *kṣatriya*, I am Hindu, I am Muslim," and so on. These are all bodily designations. When one comes to spiritual understanding, he understands *ahaṁ brahmāsmi*, "I am Brahman." This is called Brahman realization. It is not that we become Brahman by some practice. Gold is gold, even if it is covered with some dirt, which can certainly be removed. Similarly, we are all Brahman, spirit soul, but somehow or other we have come in contact with these material elements (*bhūmir āpo 'nalo vāyuḥ*), and we have acquired bodily coverings. Consequently we think, "I am this body." This is ignorance, and unless one is enlightened by spiritual knowledge, he remains animalistic.

Understanding one's spiritual identity is called *dharma*. The ultimate goal of *dharma* is enunciated by Śrī Kṛṣṇa Himself in *Bhagavad-gītā* (18.66) . *Sarva-dharmān parityajya mām ekaṁ śaraṇaṁ vraja:* "Abandon all varieties of religion and just surrender unto Me." On this earth we have created so many *dharmas*—Hindu *dharma*, Muslim *dharma*, Christian *dharma*. These are all manufactured *dharmas*, but real *dharma* is attained when we come to the conclusion that Śrī Kṛṣṇa is everything. Again, in the words of Śrī Kṛṣṇa in *Bhagavad-gītā* (7.19):

bahūnāṁ janmanām ante
jñānavān māṁ prapadyate
vāsudevaḥ sarvam iti
sa mahātmā sudurlabhaḥ

"After many births and deaths, he who is actually in knowledge surrenders unto Me, knowing Me to be the cause of all causes and all that is. Such a great soul is very rare."

The Kṛṣṇa consciousness movement is meant for the propagation of this message. We are not preaching a particular sectarian religious system but a real religion, *dharma. Dharmaṁ tu sākṣād bhagavat-praṇītam:* no one actually knows what *dharma* is, and no one can manufacture *dharma. Dharma* is the order of the Supreme Being. No one can manufacture state laws; they are given by the government. The simplest definition of *dharma* is that *dharma* is the order of the Supreme Being. Since the Supreme Being, God, is one, His order must be one. How, then, can there be different *dharmas?* It is not possible. Different *dharmas* are created due to ignorance, which causes people to think in terms of Hindu *dharma*, Muslim *dharma*, Christian *dharma*, this *dharma* or that *dharma*. No. Gold is gold. If a Christian possesses some gold, does it become Christian gold? Gold is gold whether possessed by a Hindu, a Muslim or a Christian. According to the order of the Supreme Personality of Godhead, *dharma* means surrendering unto that Supreme Being. This is *bhāgavata-dharma*, and everyone should be taught how to surrender unto God. God is one; there cannot be two Gods. When there is competition, there is no God. Presently there is a different God on every street, but Kṛṣṇa is not that kind of God. He is the Supreme God. As Kṛṣṇa Himself states in *Bhagavad-gītā* (7.7):

mattaḥ parataraṁ nānyat
kiñcid asti dhanañjaya
mayi sarvam idaṁ protaṁ
sūtre maṇi-gaṇā iva

"O conqueror of wealth [Arjuna], there is no truth superior to Me. Everything rests upon Me, as pearls are strung on a thread."

The purpose of this Kṛṣṇa consciousness movement is to inform everyone that no one is superior to Kṛṣṇa, God. Because many young Americans and Europeans are fortunate and know nothing of any hodgepodge god, they have taken this bona fide Kṛṣṇa consciousness movement seriously. *Kṛṣṇas tu bhagavān svayam:* Bhagavān, God, means Śrī Kṛṣṇa. We have simply presented this information, saying, "Here is God. Śrī Kṛṣṇa." Because they have taken this seriously, many young Americans and Europeans are advancing in Kṛṣṇa consciousness. Consequently many people are surprised to see how Americans and Europeans have become such great devotees and are dancing in ecstasy. How is it they are so advanced? They have taken the information seriously: *kṛṣṇas tu bhagavān svayam.* Whether one touches fire blindly or knowingly, fire will burn. It is not that because the fire is touched by a child, fire will not burn. These young Westerners have touched fire, and consequently it is acting as fire.

Ācāryopāsanam: this information (*kṛṣṇas tu bhagavān svayam*) is not concocted, but is accepted by the *ācāryas* in the disciplic succession. Although an impersonalist, Śaṅkarācārya has accepted Kṛṣṇa as the Supreme Personality of Godhead. So have Rāmānujācārya, Madhvācārya, Viṣṇusvāmī, Nimbārka and Śrī Caitanya Mahāprabhu and His followers. They all accept Kṛṣṇa as the Supreme, just as Arjuna himself did. This is the simplest method. There is no need to speculate, "What is God? Where is God?" Why foolishly go on searching? Here is God—Kṛṣṇa. We may think that Kṛṣṇa cannot be seen, but Kṛṣṇa can appear in the form of His energy. Of course, a stone is not God, but a stone is another one of God's energies. Heat and light are not fire, but without fire there cannot be heat or light. In that sense, heat and light are nondifferent from fire. This material world is like the heat and light of the supreme fire.

ekadeśa-sthitasyāgner
jyotsnā vistāriṇī yathā
parasya brahmaṇaḥ śaktis
tathedam akhilaṁ jagat

"Just as a fire is situated in one place, but spreads illumination all around, the Supreme Personality of Godhead, Parabrahman, spreads His energies throughout this universe." (*Viṣṇu Purāṇa* 1.22.53)

The sun is situated in one place, and its light and heat expand throughout the entire solar system. As soon as we perceive light and heat, we can understand that the sun is there. Since light and heat can be perceived by everyone, Kṛṣṇa says in *Bhagavad-gītā* (7.8), *prabhāsmi śaśi-sūryayoḥ:* "I am the light of the sun and the moon." People are saying, "Can you show me God?" while not realizing that they are seeing God daily at every moment. Because people are foolish in this age, they cannot understand that when we perceive the energy of the Lord, we can feel the presence of the Lord.

The young devotees in the Kṛṣṇa consciousness movement are presently worshiping Kṛṣṇa. What are the signs of a devotee? The actual sign of a devotee is that he is no longer interested in material enjoyment: *bhaktiḥ pareśānubhavo viraktir anyatra ca* (*Bhāg.* 11.2.42). The disciples of this Kṛṣṇa consciousness movement do not go to cinemas, restaurants or clubs, and they do not smoke or drink. In European and American countries all these things are available and are very cheap, but these young people are not interested in them. They are simply interested in sitting on the floor and learning about Kṛṣṇa consciousness. Why is this? They have actually rejected the material world. When one comes to detest material enjoyment, one can understand that he has advanced spiritually. Spiritual life does not mean taking *sannyāsa* and then smoking or drinking tea. One must actually come to detest material life. One comes to lose interest in material activities and becomes interested only in the understanding of God, the Supreme Being, and His service. As enjoined in *Śrīmad-Bhāgavatam* (5.5.1):

nāyaṁ deho deha-bhājāṁ nṛloke
kaṣṭān kāmān arhate viḍ-bhujāṁ ye

"Of all the living entities who have accepted material bodies in this world, one who has been awarded this human form should not work hard day and night simply for sense gratification, which is available even for the dogs and hogs that eat stool." The word *viḍ-bhujām* means "stool-eaters." Hogs work hard day and night simply eating stool, and because stool contains chemicals, hydrophosphates, the hog gets strength, becomes very fat and enjoys sex. In any case, human life is meant not for imitating the life of a hog but for *tapasya*, austerity:

tapo divyaṁ putrakā yena sattvaṁ
śuddhyed yasmād brahma-saukhyaṁ tv anantam

"Rather, my dear boys, one should engage in penance and austerity to attain the divine position of devotional service. By such activity, one's heart is purified, and when one attains this position, he attains eternal, blissful life, which is transcendental to material happiness and which continues forever." (*Bhāg.* 5.5.1)

This is the meaning of Vedic civilization. The society of *varṇāśrama-dharma*—composed of *brāhmaṇas, kṣatriyas, vaiśyas, śūdras, gṛhasthas, vānaprasthas, brahmacārīs* and *sannyāsīs*—is meant to elevate people gradually to the perfect stage of understanding God. The whole aim of the different *varṇas* and *āśramas* is the worship of the Supreme Lord. One can attain this understanding through this social system, which admits of gradations. When one goes to school, he begins with the first grade, then progresses to the second, third and so forth. In this way one makes progress.

When human society accepts *varṇāśrama-dharma*, it can gradually come to the understanding of Brahman. By birth, everyone is a *śūdra;* therefore everyone has to be educated. The word *dvija* means "twice-born." One is first born through the womb of a mother, and one's next birth is given by the spiritual master and Vedic knowledge. Vedic knowledge is the mother, and the spiritual master is the father. When one is twice-born (*dvija*), he receives a sacred thread from the spiritual master and begins to learn about spiritual life. He is then allowed to read the Vedic literatures. In this way one becomes a son of Vedic literature. *Nigama-kalpa-taror galitaṁ phalam: Śrīmad-Bhāgavatam* is the essence of Vedic culture. It is a wish-fulfilling tree, and we can take whatever we want from it. Vedic knowledge is perfect, and if we want to come to know it, we must take shelter of a bona fide *guru* (*tad-vijñānārthaṁ sa gurum evābhigacchet*).

Unfortunately, in this age everything is mismanaged. People forget the aim of life, and at such a time the Supreme Lord Himself comes. The Supreme Lord descends out of compassion because He is more anxious to have us return home, back to Godhead, than we are to go. Because we are in ignorance, we do not know anything about the kingdom of God. We know nothing about how to get there or how to become happy. We have forgotten all this. Therefore Kṛṣṇa comes at intervals or sends His representative, the pure devotee. Sometimes He comes personally, and sometimes He sends His incarnation.

Kapiladeva is an incarnation of the Supreme Person, Kṛṣṇa. Therefore it is stated: *kapilas tattva-saṅkhyātā bhagavān ātma-māyayā*. The word *māyā* means not only "illusion," but also "affection" and "energy." When Kṛṣṇa comes, all His energies also come. It is not that He is forced to come. We have to accept a certain type of body because we are forced to do so, but this is not the case with Śrī Kṛṣṇa. Presently I may have a human form, but in the future I cannot demand a human form. We receive bodies in the next life according to *karma*, not will. One cannot demand to be a high-court judge unless one has been educated for the job. First of all, one must become qualified. If one qualifies himself, one may become a *devatā*, a demigod like Indra or Candra, or one can become a dog or a cat. That depends on one's *karma*, or activities (*karmaṇā daiva-netreṇa*). When Kṛṣṇa or His incarnation come, they do not depend on *karma* for their bodies. The Supreme Lord is above *karma* and is fully independent. It is therefore said, *ātma-māyayā*. The Supreme Lord comes by His own energy, not by the external energy or by force. When the governor visits the prison, he is not forced to do so. He is not to be considered a condemned person; rather, he goes by his own good will just to see how things are going on. However, it is understood that when an ordinary person is placed in jail, he is sent there by force because he has been proven a criminal. A criminal may think that he and the governor are one, just as rascals and fools think that Kṛṣṇa is one of them. *Avajānanti māṁ mūḍhā mānuṣīṁ tanum āśritam*. A knowledgeable person knows that when Kṛṣṇa or His incarnation descends upon the material world, the Supreme Lord maintains His transcendental position. He is not an ordinary man, nor is He forced into the material world due to *karma*. The Supreme Lord comes by His own good will. *Paraṁ bhāvam ajānantaḥ*. Rascals cannot understand what Kṛṣṇa is; therefore they think that Kṛṣṇa is a human being. As Kṛṣṇa Himself states in *Bhagavad-gītā* (7.3):

manuṣyāṇāṁ sahasreṣu
kaścid yatati siddhaye

yatatām api siddhānāṁ
kaścin māṁ vetti tattvataḥ

"Out of many thousands among men, one may endeavor for perfection, and of those who have achieved perfection, hardly one knows Me in truth."

Understanding Kṛṣṇa is therefore not so easy. As stated by Kṛṣṇa, out of many thousands one person may become a *siddha,* a self-realized being. And out of many *siddhas,* one may be able to understand Kṛṣṇa. It is our great fortune that Śrī Caitanya Mahāprabhu, Kṛṣṇa Himself, has appeared and given us a very easy process by which we can understand Kṛṣṇa. What is that process? We need only hear about Kṛṣṇa. That's all. We have therefore opened all these centers of Kṛṣṇa consciousness throughout the world.

śṛṇvatāṁ sva-kathāḥ kṛṣṇaḥ
puṇya-śravaṇa-kīrtanaḥ
hṛdy antaḥ-stho hy abhadrāṇi
vidhunoti suhṛt satām

"Śrī Kṛṣṇa, the Personality of Godhead, who is the Paramātmā [Supersoul] in everyone's heart and the benefactor of the truthful devotee, cleanses desire for material enjoyment from the heart of the devotee who has developed the urge to hear His messages, which are in themselves virtuous when properly heard and chanted." (*Bhāg.* 1.2.17)

If we hear about Kṛṣṇa, we become purified. Hearing about Kṛṣṇa means associating with Kṛṣṇa. In this way we may perfect our lives.

CHAPTER TWO

The Transcendental Master and Supreme Yogī

TEXT 2

na hy asya varṣmaṇaḥ puṁsāṁ
varimṇaḥ sarva-yoginām
viśrutau śruta-devasya
bhūri tṛpyanti me 'savaḥ

TRANSLATION

Śaunaka continued: There is no one who knows more than the Lord Himself. No one is more worshipable or more mature a yogī than He. He is therefore the master of the Vedas, and to hear about Him always is the actual pleasure of the senses.

PURPORT

In *Bhagavad-gītā* it is stated that no one can be equal to or greater than the Supreme Personality of Godhead. This is confirmed in the *Vedas* also: *eko bahūnāṁ yo vidadhāti kāmān.* He is the supreme living entity and is supplying the necessities of all other living entities. Thus all other living entities, both *viṣṇu-tattva* and *jīva-tattva*, are subordinate to the Supreme Personality of Godhead, Kṛṣṇa. The same concept is confirmed here. *Na hy asya varṣmaṇaḥ puṁsām:* among living entities, no one can surpass the Supreme Person because no one is richer, more famous, stronger, more beautiful, wiser or more renounced than He. These qualifications make Him the Supreme Godhead, the cause of all causes. *Yogīs* are very proud of performing wonderful feats, but no one can compare to the Supreme Personality of Godhead.

Anyone who is associated with the Supreme Lord is accepted as a first-class *yogī.* Devotees may not be as powerful as the Supreme Lord, but by constant association with the Lord they become as good as the Lord Himself. Sometimes the devotees act more powerfully than the Lord. Of course, that is the Lord's concession.

Also used here is the word *varimṇaḥ*, meaning the most worshipful of all *yogīs*. To hear from Kṛṣṇa is the real pleasure of the senses; therefore he is known as Govinda, for by His words, by His teachings, by His instruction—by everything connected with Him—He enlivens the senses. Whatever He instructs is from the transcendental platform, and His instructions, being absolute, are nondifferent from Him. Hearing from Kṛṣṇa or His expansion or plenary expansion like Kapila is very pleasing to the senses. *Bhagavad-gītā* can be read or heard many times, but because it gives great pleasure, the more one reads *Bhagavad-gītā* the more he wants to read and understand it, and each time he gets new enlightenment. That is the nature of the transcendental message. Similarly, we find that transcendental happiness in the *Śrīmad-Bhāgavatam.* The more we hear and chant the glories of the Lord, the more we become happy.

In the previous verse, the incarnation of the Supreme Personality of Godhead as Devahūti-putra Kapiladeva has been explained as *bhagavān ātma-māyayā.* The word *bhaga* means "opulence," and *vān* means "one who possesses." All the opulences of the creation are present in Bhagavān. As stated in the *Vedas* (*Kaṭha Upaniṣad* 2.2.13):

nityo nityānāṁ cetanaś cetanānām
eko bahūnāṁ yo vidadhāti kāmān

Nitya, Bhagavān, is the singular, and *nityānāṁ* are the plural *jīvas,* or living beings. *Nityo nityānāṁ:* we are many, but God is one. There is no limit to the *jīvas;* no one can count them. The word *ananta* means that they are without limit. All these *jīvas,* living entities, are being maintained by the Supreme One. We cannot conceive how many living entities are being maintained by the Supreme Lord. All the great elephants, all the small ants, all the 8,400,000 species of life are maintained by Bhagavān. Why do we worry that He will not maintain us? Those who are devotees of the Lord and have taken shelter at His lotus feet, leaving everything aside simply to render service unto Him, will certainly be cared for. In our Kṛṣṇa consciousness movement, we have over a hundred centers, and Kṛṣṇa is maintaining them all. None of our devotees are employed for independent incomes, yet they are all being maintained. In *Bhagavad-gītā*, Kṛṣṇa never says, "Do this or that, and I will then maintain you." Rather, He states that not only will He maintain us, but He will also protect us from the results of sin, from sinful *karma* (Bg. 18.66). All of this assurance is there.

Tasyaiva hetoḥ prayateta kovidaḥ. The word *kovidaḥ* means "intelligent." An intelligent person should try to attain shelter at the lotus feet of Kṛṣṇa. Human life is actually meant for getting in touch with the lotus feet of Kṛṣṇa. That should be our only business. The word *upari* indicates the higher planetary systems. There are seven higher planetary systems, and we are in the middle system, in Bhūrloka. Within this one universe, there are fourteen planetary systems, and the living entities are wandering in different bodily forms on different planets. According to *karma*, the living entity sometimes goes up and sometimes goes down. He wanders in this way, thinking how he can become materially happy and satisfy his senses. The *śāstras* say that we should not do this, that we should endeavor to understand Kṛṣṇa. We should not worry about eating and sleeping, for the needs of the body are already arranged. We do not have to work independently to maintain the body.

tal labhyate duḥkhavad anyataḥ sukhaṁ
kālena sarvatra gabhīra-raṁhasā

Our actual endeavor should be to attain happiness; that is our real struggle for existence. According to the *śāstras: tal labhyate duḥkhavat.* The word *duḥkhavat* indicates that although we do not want misery, misery comes anyway. We don't have to endeavor separately for misery. No one says, "Let there be a fire in my house" or "Let my child die." No one aspires after these things, yet they happen. Everyone is thinking, "May my child live happily" or "May I get so much money." We do not ask or pray for catastrophes, yet they come without invitation. Similarly, whatever happiness is there for our enjoyment will also come without our asking for it. The conclusion is that we should not endeavor for so-called happiness or distress, but should try to attain that position whereby we can understand Kṛṣṇa and get shelter at His lotus feet. This should be the real human endeavor.

It was Caitanya Mahāprabhu who said to Rūpa Gosvāmī:

brahmāṇḍa bhramite kona bhāgyavān jīva
guru-kṛṣṇa-prasāde pāya bhakti-latā-bīja

"The living entity is wandering up and down, from one planet to another, and he is very fortunate if by the mercy of the spiritual master and Kṛṣṇa Himself he can get the seed of devotional service to Kṛṣṇa." (Cc. *Madhya* 19.151) The Kṛṣṇa consciousness movement is an attempt to make people fortunate. In this age, everyone is unfortunate (*manda-bhāgyāḥ*), but now we are trying to reverse the situation.

Throughout the world there are problems everywhere. One country has one type of problem, and another country has another. There is strife within governments themselves, and even presidents are fraught with problems. Sometimes we may think we are very fortunate, just as President Nixon was thinking, "I am very fortunate. I have become the president of the United States." Then he soon realized that he was most unfortunate. Actually this is the situation for everyone. We should not think that the only apprehended culprit is President Nixon and that we are safe. There is a Bengali proverb: Dry cow dung is used for fuel, and it is said that when the dry cow dung is being burned, the soft cow dung is laughing, saying, "Oh, you are being burned, but I am safe." It does not know that when it dries out, it will be thrown into the fire too. We may laugh because President Nixon is in trouble, and we may think ourselves very safe because we have a big bank balance, but actually no one is safe. Eventually everyone will dry up and be thrown in the fire. That is a fact. We may survive for a few years, but we cannot avoid death. In fact, it is said, "As sure as death." And what is the result of death? One loses everything—all honor, money, position and material life itself. Kṛṣṇa states in *Bhagavad-gītā* (10.34), *mṛtyuḥ sarva-haraś cāham:* "I am all-devouring death." Kṛṣṇa comes as death and plunders everything—bank balance, skyscrapers, wife, children and whatever. One cannot say, "My dear death, please give me some time to adjust." There is no adjustment; one must immediately get out.

Foolish people are unaware of the miserable conditions of material life. Kṛṣṇa says in *Bhagavad-gītā* (13.9), *janma-mṛtyu-jarā-vyādhi-duḥkha-doṣānudarśanam.* Real knowledge means knowing that however great one may be, the four principles of material life are present: birth, old age, disease and death. These exist in the highest planetary system (Brahmaloka) and in the lowest (Pātālaloka).

tasyaiva hetoḥ prayateta kovido
na labhyate yad bhramatām upary adhaḥ
tal labhyate duḥkhavad anyataḥ sukhaṁ
kālena sarvatra gabhīra-raṁhasā

"Persons who are actually intelligent and philosophically inclined should endeavor only for that purposeful end which is not obtainable even by wandering from the topmost planet down to the lowest planet. As far as happiness derived from sense enjoyment is concerned, it can be obtained automatically in course of time, just as in course of time we obtain miseries even though we do not desire them." (*Bhāg.* 1.5.18)

When Dharmarāja asked Mahārāja Yudhiṣṭhira what the most wonderful thing in the world was, Mahārāja Yudhiṣṭhira replied: *ahany ahani bhūtāni gacchantīha yamālayam.* "Every moment people are dying, but those who are living are thinking, 'My friend has died, but I shall live forever.' " (*Mahābhārata, Vana-parva* 313.116) Soft cow dung thinks the same way. This is typical of conditioned beings.

Bhagavān, the Supreme Lord, is not in this position. It is therefore said: *bhagavān ātma-māyayā.* We come onto this planet to enjoy or suffer life for a few days—fifty or a hundred years—but Bhagavān, the Supreme Personality of Godhead, does not come for that purpose (*na māṁ karmāṇi limpanti*). It is further stated, *na hy asya varṣmaṇaḥ:* "No one is greater than Him." No one is greater than Bhagavān or equal to Him. Everyone is inferior. According to *Caitanya-caritāmṛta* (*Ādi* 5.142), *ekale īśvara kṛṣṇa, āra saba bhṛtya.* There is only one master—Kṛṣṇa. All others are subservient, beginning with Lord Brahmā, Viṣṇu, Maheśvara, Indra, Candra and all the demigods (there are thirty-three million demigods) and the middle and lower species. Everyone is *bhṛtya,* or servant. When Kṛṣṇa orders, "My dear Mr. So-and-So, now please give up your place and leave," one must go. Therefore everyone is a servant. This is the position of Lord Brahmā and the ant as well. *Yas tv indragopam athavendram aho sva-karma.* From

Lord Indra to *indragopa*, an insignificant insect, everyone is reaping the consequences of his *karma*. We are creating our own *karma*, our next body, in this life. In this life we enjoy or suffer the results of our past *karma*, and in the same way we are creating further *karma* for our next body. Actually we should work in such a way that we will not get another material body. How can this be done? We simply have to try to understand Kṛṣṇa. As Kṛṣṇa says in *Bhagavad-gītā* (4.9):

janma karma ca me divyam
evam yo vetti tattvataḥ
tyaktvā dehaṁ punar janma
naiti mām eti so 'rjuna

"One who knows the transcendental nature of My appearance and activities does not, upon leaving the body, take his birth again in this material world, but attains My eternal abode, O Arjuna."

This sounds very simple, but actually understanding Kṛṣṇa is very difficult. If we become devotees of Kṛṣṇa, understanding Kṛṣṇa is easy. However, if we try to understand Him by *jñāna*, *karma* or *yoga*, we will be frustrated. There are many types of *yogīs*, but he who is devoted to Kṛṣṇa is the topmost *yogī*. Śrī Kṛṣṇa is far above all yogic processes. In India there are many *yogīs* who can display some magical feats. They can walk on water, make themselves very light or very heavy and so forth. But what is this compared to Kṛṣṇa's yogic mystic powers? By His potencies, great planets are floating in space. Who can manage to float even a small stone in the air? Sometimes a *yogī* may show a little mystic power by manufacturing some gold, and we are so foolish that we accept him as God. However, we forget that the real *yogī*, the Supreme Lord Himself, has created millions of gold mines and is floating them in space. Those who are Kṛṣṇa conscious are not befooled by *yogīs* who claim to be Bhagavān. A Kṛṣṇa conscious person wants only to serve the foremost *yogī*, Yogeśvara (*varimṇaḥ sarva-yoginām*). Because we are trying to become His devotees, we accept the Supreme Lord, Yogeśvara, as the Supreme Personality of Godhead. Kṛṣṇa Himself states in *Bhagavad-gītā* (18.55):

bhaktyā mām abhijānāti
yāvān yaś cāsmi tattvataḥ

tato māṁ tattvato jñātvā
viśate tad anantaram

"One can understand the Supreme Personality as He is only by devotional service. And when one is in full consciousness of the Supreme Lord by such devotion, he can enter into the kingdom of God."

This process is actually very simple. One must first of all realize that the first problem is the conquest of death. Presently we consider death compulsory, but actually it is not. One may be put into prison, but actually prison is not compulsory. It is due to one's work that one becomes a criminal and is therefore put in jail. It is not compulsory for everyone to go to jail. As living entities, we have our proper place in Vaikuṇṭhaloka.

paras tasmāt tu bhāvo 'nyo
'vyakto 'vyaktāt sanātanaḥ
yaḥ sa sarveṣu bhūteṣu
naśyatsu na vinaśyati

avyakto 'kṣara ity uktas
tam āhuḥ paramāṁ gatim
yaṁ prāpya na nivartante
tad dhāma paramaṁ mama

"There is another nature, which is eternal and is transcendental to this manifested and unmanifested matter. It is supreme and is never annihilated. When all in this world is annihilated, that part remains as it is. That supreme abode is called unmanifested and infallible, and it is the supreme destination. When one goes there, he never comes back. That is My supreme abode." (Bg. 8.20–21)

Everything is present in Vaikuṇṭhaloka. There we can have an eternal, blissful life full of knowledge (*sac-cid-ānanda*). It is not compulsory for us to rot in this material world. The easiest way to go to the Vaikuṇṭhalokas is: *janma karma ca me divyam evaṁ yo vetti tattvataḥ.* Simply try to understand Kṛṣṇa. Why does He come? What are His activities? Where does He come from? Why does He come in the form of a human being? We only have to try to understand this and study Kṛṣṇa as

He explains Himself in *Bhagavad-gītā.* What is the difficulty? God personally explains Himself as He is, and if we accept *Bhagavad-gītā* as it is, we shall no longer have to transmigrate. *Tyaktvā dehaṁ punar janma naiti.* We shall no longer have to endure birth and death, for we can attain our spiritual bodies (*sac-cid-ānanda-vigraha*) and live happily in Kṛṣṇa's family. Kṛṣṇa is providing for us here, and He will also provide for us there. So we should know that our happiness is in returning home, back to Godhead, where we can eat, drink and be merry in Kṛṣṇa's company.

CHAPTER THREE

How to Understand the Lord's Activities

TEXT 3

yad yad vidhatte bhagavān
svacchandātmātma-māyayā
tāni me śraddadhānasya
kīrtanyāny anukīrtaya

TRANSLATION

Therefore please precisely describe all the activities and pastimes of the Personality of Godhead, who is full of self-desire and who assumes all these activities by His internal potency.

PURPORT

The word *anukīrtaya* is very significant. *Anukīrtaya* means "to follow the description"—not to create a concocted mental description, but to follow. Śaunaka Ṛṣi requested Sūta Gosvāmī to describe what he had actually heard from his spiritual master, Śukadeva Gosvāmī, about the transcendental pastimes that the Lord manifested by His internal energy. Bhagavān, the Supreme Personality of Godhead, has no material body, but He can assume any kind of body by His supreme will. That is made possible by His internal energy.

We can understand the pastimes of the Lord by following one or some of the authorized devotional processes.

śravaṇaṁ kīrtanaṁ viṣṇoḥ
smaraṇaṁ pāda-sevanam

arcanaṁ vandanaṁ dāsyaṁ
sakhyam ātma-nivedanam

"Hearing, chanting and remembering the holy name, form, pastimes, qualities and entourage of the Lord, offering service according to the time, place and performer, worshiping the Deity, offering prayers, always considering oneself the eternal servant of Kṛṣṇa, making friends with Him and dedicating everything unto Him—these are the nine processes of devotional service." (*Bhāg.* 7.5.23)

There are nine basic processes of devotional service—hearing and chanting about the Supreme Lord, remembering Him, serving His lotus feet, worshiping Him, offering prayers to the Lord, acting as His servant, becoming His friend, and surrendering everything to Him. The beginning is *śravaṇaṁ kīrtanam,* hearing and chanting. One must be very eager to hear and chant. As stated in *Bhagavad-gītā* (9.14):

satataṁ kīrtayanto māṁ
yatantaś ca dṛḍha-vratāḥ
namasyantaś ca māṁ bhaktyā
nitya-yuktā upāsate

"Always chanting My glories, endeavoring with great determination, bowing down before Me, the great souls perpetually worship Me with devotion."

We have to speak or chant about the holy activities of the Supreme Personality of Godhead, but first we have to hear about them. This *Śrīmad-Bhāgavatam* was recited by Śukadeva Gosvāmī and heard by Parīkṣit Mahārāja, and we in turn have to hear about Kṛṣṇa and then chant about Him (*śravaṇaṁ kīrtanaṁ viṣṇoḥ*). When we speak of Viṣṇu, we mean Kṛṣṇa. Kṛṣṇa is the origin of the *viṣṇu-tattva*—that is, Viṣṇu is an expansion of Kṛṣṇa. When we speak of Viṣṇu, we understand that the origin of Viṣṇu is Kṛṣṇa. As Śrī Kṛṣṇa says in *Bhagavad-gītā* (10.2), *aham ādir hi devānām:* "I am the source of the demigods."

The most important demigods (*devas*) are Brahmā, Śiva and Viṣṇu. In the beginning of the creation there is Lord Viṣṇu, and from Lord Viṣṇu, Brahmā is born. From Lord Brahmā, Lord Śiva is born, and these three gods take charge of the three modes of material nature. Viṣṇu takes charge of *sattva-guṇa* (the mode of goodness), Lord Brahmā takes charge of *rajo-guṇa* (the mode of passion), and Lord Śiva takes charge of *tamo-guṇa* (the mode of ignorance). However, before the creation there was no Brahmā or Śiva. There was only Kṛṣṇa. Kṛṣṇa therefore says, *aham ādir hi devānām.* He is the creator of all demigods and all other living entities. After the cosmic manifestation is created, the living entities are placed in it. Therefore in the *Vedas* it is stated that in the beginning there was neither Brahmā nor Śiva, but only Nārāyaṇa (*eko nārāyaṇa āsīt*). Nārāyaṇa is also another plenary expansion of Kṛṣṇa.

We have to learn from the scriptures that Kṛṣṇa is the origin of all. *Kṛṣṇas tu bhagavān svayam:* all the *viṣṇu-tattvas* and incarnations are but plenary expansions or expansions of the plenary expansions of Kṛṣṇa. There are millions and millions of incarnations. They are as plentiful as waves in the ocean. There are *śaktyāveśa-avatāras, guṇa-avatāras* and *svayam-avatāras,* and these are all described in *Śrīmad-Bhāgavatam.* All these *avatāras,* or incarnations, are *svacchandātmā,* free from care and anxiety. If we organize a business, we have many anxieties. The managing director or proprietor of the business particularly has many anxieties. Although he sits in his office without disturbance, he is not very happy because he is always thinking about how to do this or that, how to manage this affair or that. This is material nature, and therefore it is said that there is always anxiety in the material world. When Hiraṇyakaśipu, the father of Prahlāda Mahārāja, asked his son, "My dear boy, what is the best thing you have learned from your teachers?" Prahlāda Mahārāja immediately replied, *tat sādhu manye 'sura-varya dehināṁ sadā samudvigna-dhiyām asad-grahāt* (*Bhāg.* 7.5.5). "I have learned that materialists have accepted the *asad guṇa.*" *Asat* means "that which is not." We should not remain on this platform, but should go to the platform of *sat* (*oṁ tat sat*). This is the Vedic injunction. The material world is *asad-vastu;* it cannot possibly remain. In the material world, everything will ultimately be vanquished. Whatever exists in the material world exists only for some time. It is temporary. The Māyāvādī philosophers say, *brahma satyaṁ jagan mithyā:* "The Supreme Truth is real, whereas the world is false"—but Vaiṣṇavas do not use the word *mithyā* (false), because God, the Supreme Brahman, is truth, and nothing false can emanate from the truth. If we prepare an earring from gold, the earring is also gold. We cannot say that the earring is false. *Yato imāni bhūtāni jāyante:* the Supreme Absolute Truth is He from whom everything is emanating. If everything is emanating from the Absolute Truth, nothing can actually be false. The Vaiṣṇava philosophers accept the world as temporary, but not false, as the Māyāvādī philosophers do.

The world (*jagat*) has emanated from the Supreme; therefore it is not *mithyā*, but it is temporary. That is also explained in *Bhagavad-gītā* (8.19): *bhūtvā bhūtvā pralīyate.* The material world comes into existence, remains for some time, and is then annihilated. It is not false, for it can be utilized to realize the Supreme Truth. This is Vaiṣṇava philosophy. The world is temporary, but we must use it for spiritual purposes. If something is used for the ultimate truth, the Absolute Truth, it becomes integral with the Absolute Truth. As stated by Śrīla Rūpa Gosvāmī:

anāsaktasya viṣayān
yathārham upayuñjataḥ
nirbandhaḥ kṛṣṇa-sambandhe
yuktaṁ vairāgyam ucyate

prāpañcikatayā buddhyā
hari-sambandhi-vastunaḥ
mumukṣubhiḥ parityāgo
vairāgyaṁ phalgu kathyate
(*Bhakti-rasāmṛta-sindhu* 1.2.255–256)

The word *mumukṣubhiḥ* refers to those who aspire for *mukti*, liberation. When one becomes disgusted with material engagement, one wants to destroy everything that has anything to do with the material world. However, the Vaiṣṇava says, *prāpañcikatayā buddhyā hari-sambandhi-vastunaḥ.* Everything has some relationship with the Supreme Person, the Absolute Truth. For instance, a microphone is made of metal, but what is metal? It is another form of earth. In *Bhagavad-gītā* (7.4) Śrī Kṛṣṇa says:

bhūmir āpo 'nalo vāyuḥ
khaṁ mano buddhir eva ca

ahaṅkāra itīyaṁ me
bhinnā prakṛtir aṣṭadhā

"Earth, water, fire, air, ether, mind, intelligence and false ego—all together these comprise My separated material energies." All of these are Kṛṣṇa's energies, and if Kṛṣṇa is the source of them, how can they be untrue? They are not. A Vaiṣṇava will never say that metal has no connection with Kṛṣṇa. It is a product of one of His energies, just as this material world is a product of the sun. We cannot say that the sunshine is false and that the sun is true. If the sun is true, the sunshine is also true. Similarly, we do not say that the material universe is false. It may be temporary, but it is not false. Therefore the Gosvāmīs and Kṛṣṇa Himself tell us that since everything belongs to Kṛṣṇa, everything should be utilized for His purpose.

This creation emanates from Bhagavān, the Supreme Lord, who is without anxiety. Kṛṣṇa very pleasantly associates with His consort Śrīmatī Rādhārāṇī and enjoys playing His flute. If God is anxious, what kind of God is He? Even Lord Brahmā and other demigods are anxious. Lord Brahmā is engaged in meditation, Lord Śiva dances to annihilate the universe, the goddess Kālī is engaged in killing with her sword, and so forth. The demigods have many activities, but Kṛṣṇa is always peaceful. The Kṛṣṇa who engages in killing demons is Vāsudeva Kṛṣṇa, not the original Kṛṣṇa. The original Kṛṣṇa does not go anywhere; He never takes a step away from Vṛndāvana. The other activities performed by Kṛṣṇa are performed in the Vāsudeva, Saṅkarṣaṇa, Aniruddha or Pradyumna forms. Kṛṣṇa expands as Saṅkarṣaṇa, Nārāyaṇa, Viṣṇu, Mahā-Viṣṇu, Garbhodakaśāyī Viṣṇu and Kṣīrodakaśāyī Viṣṇu. God can expand Himself in many, many forms.

advaitam acyutam anādim ananta-rūpam
ādyaṁ purāṇa-puruṣaṁ nava-yauvanaṁ ca
(*Brahma-saṁhitā* 5.33)

He is the *ādi-puruṣa*, the original soul of all. *Govindam ādi-puruṣaṁ tam ahaṁ bhajāmi:* Lord Brahmā says that he is not *ādi-puruṣa* but that Govinda, Kṛṣṇa, is the *ādi-puruṣa.* This Kṛṣṇa has many expansions (*advaitam acyutam anādim*). He has no beginning, but He is the beginning of everything. He has expanded Himself in many forms. The *viṣṇu-tattva* consists of *bhagavat-tattva-svāṁśa*, the personal expansions. We are also Kṛṣṇa's forms, but we are *vibhinnāṁśa*, separated expansions. We are the expansions of the energies. According to Kṛṣṇa in *Bhagavad-gītā* (7.5):

apareyam itas tv anyāṁ
prakṛtiṁ viddhi me parām
jīva-bhūtāṁ mahā-bāho
yayedaṁ dhāryate jagat

"Besides the inferior nature, O mighty-armed Arjuna, there is a superior energy of Mine, which consists of the living entities who are struggling with material nature and are sustaining the universe."

Thus there are the *jīva-prakṛti*, the *parā prakṛti* expansions, who belong to Kṛṣṇa's superior energy. In any case, Kṛṣṇa is always *svacchandātmā*—without anxiety. Even if He is killing a demon, He experiences no anxiety. That is also confirmed in the *Vedas:*

na tasya kāryaṁ karaṇaṁ ca vidyate
na tat-samaś cābhyadhikaś ca dṛśyate
parāsya śaktir vividhaiva śrūyate
svābhāvikī jñāna-bala-kriyā ca

"The Supreme Lord has nothing to do, for everything is done automatically by His various potencies. No one is seen to be equal to, or greater than, Him." (*Śvetāśvatara Upaniṣad* 6.8)

Śrī Kṛṣṇa has nothing to do personally. It is His energy that acts. When an important man wants to get something done, he simply tells his secretary, who does everything. The important man is quite confident that because he has told his secretary, his desires will be carried out. The secretary is a person, energy (*śakti*). If an ordinary man within this world has many energies in the form of secretaries, then we can hardly imagine the energies possessed by Śrī Kṛṣṇa. Śrī Kṛṣṇa is *jagad-īśvara*, the controller of the entire universe, and thus He is managing the entire universe. Foolish people say that there is no brain behind the universe, but this is due to ignorance. By taking information from the *śāstras*, the scriptures, we can understand who that brain is. According to Śrī Kṛṣṇa in *Bhagavad-gītā* (9.10):

mayādhyakṣeṇa prakṛtiḥ
sūyate sa-carācaram
hetunānena kaunteya
jagad viparivartate

"This material nature is working under My direction, O son of Kuntī, and producing all moving and unmoving beings. By its rule this manifestation is created and annihilated again and again." We see His energies working in this material world all the time. There is thunder and rain, and from rain comes the food we enjoy. This process is outlined in *Bhagavad-gītā* (3.14):

annād bhavanti bhūtāni
parjanyād anna-sambhavaḥ
yajñād bhavati parjanyo
yajñaḥ karma-samudbhavaḥ

"All living beings subsist on food grains, which are produced from rains. Rains are produced by performance of *yajña* [sacrifice], and *yajña* is born of prescribed duties." The origin of everything is the Supreme Personality of Godhead. Through *yajña*, sacrifice, we have to satisfy the Supreme Person, and *yajñas* can be executed when human society is regulated according to the *varṇāśrama-dharma*, the system of four social orders (*varṇas*) and four spiritual orders (*āśramas*). There are four *varṇas* (*brāhmaṇa*, *kṣatriya*, *vaiśya* and *śūdra*) and four *āśramas* (*brahmacarya*, *gṛhastha*, *vānaprastha* and *sannyāsa*). These *varṇas* and *āśramas* have their respective duties, and unless human society is divided according to these eight scientific divisions and everyone acts according to his position, there can be no peace in the world.

varṇāśramācāravatā
puruṣeṇa paraḥ pumān

viṣṇur ārādhyate panthā
nānyat tat-toṣa-kāraṇam

"The Supreme Personality of Godhead, Lord Viṣṇu, is worshiped by the proper execution of prescribed duties in the system of *varṇa* and *āśrama*. There is no other way to satisfy the Supreme Personality of Godhead." (*Viṣṇu Purāṇa* 3.8.9)

The ultimate goal of all activity is the satisfaction of the Supreme Lord, Viṣṇu. *Na te viduḥ svārtha-gatiṁ hi viṣṇum* (*Bhāg.* 7.5.31). Foolish people do not know that their ultimate interest is the satisfaction of Viṣṇu. Therefore, when there are *dharmasya glāniḥ*, discrepancies in *dharma*, Kṛṣṇa or His incarnation personally comes. It is therefore said: *yad yad vidhatte bhagavān*. Although He comes, He has no anxiety. He comes by His internal potency, and He does not take help from anyone. He possesses a variety of energies, all of which work correctly and perfectly (*parāsya śaktir vividhaiva śrūyate svābhāvikī jñāna-bala-kriyā ca*).

Impersonalists cannot understand how everything is being carried out perfectly because they cannot understand the Supreme Personality of Godhead: *mohitaṁ nābhijānāti mām ebhyaḥ param avyayam*. As stated by Kṛṣṇa in *Bhagavad-gītā* (7.14):

daivī hy eṣā guṇamayī
mama māyā duratyayā
mām eva ye prapadyante
māyām etāṁ taranti te

"This divine energy of Mine, consisting of the three modes of material nature, is difficult to overcome. But those who have surrendered unto Me can easily cross beyond it." Being covered by the three modes of material nature, one cannot understand the Supreme Personality of Godhead. However, the Supreme Lord reveals Himself to His devotees.

It is our business to understand Kṛṣṇa in truth; then our lives will be successful. It is not that we can succeed by understanding Kṛṣṇa superficially. It is therefore stated here: *tāni me śraddadhānasya kīrtanyāny anukīrtaya*. The word *anukīrtaya*, as we have initially pointed out, means that we should not manufacture anything. The word *anu* means "to follow." Therefore the *bhagavat-tattva*, or Bhagavān, can be understood only by the *paramparā* system, the system of disciplic succession.

evaṁ paramparā-prāptam
imaṁ rājarṣayo viduḥ
sa kālaneha mahatā
yogo naṣṭaḥ parantapa

"This supreme science was thus received through the chain of disciplic succession, and the saintly kings understood it in that way. But in course of time the succession was broken, and therefore the science as it is appears to be lost." (Bg. 4.2)

Formerly the kings (*rājās*) were great saintly persons. They were not ordinary people engaged in drinking and dancing. They were all *ṛṣis* (sages), up to the time of Mahārāja Parīkṣit. They were trained in such a way that they were not ordinary men but were called *naradeva*. *Naradeva* refers to Bhagavān in the form of a human being. The king was worshiped because he was a *rājarṣi*, both a king and a sage. Śrī Kṛṣṇa says that if the king knows the purpose of life, he can rule well. If he does not, he thinks that eating, sleeping, sex and defense are all in all. In this case, his subjects live like animals. Today no one knows the object of human life; therefore although the foolish people of this age are trying to be happy, their hopes will never be fulfilled. *Na te viduḥ svārtha-gatiṁ hi viṣṇuṁ durāśayāḥ*. People are trying to be happy in this material world by accepting material objects, but their plans will never be fulfilled. Therefore in world history we see that there have been many leaders who have died working hard. They could not adjust things properly, despite all their hard efforts. There were Napoleon, Hitler, Gandhi, Nehru and many others, but they could not ultimately prevail. This is *durāśaya*. The ultimate goal of life is to understand Viṣṇu, yet people are going on blindly trying to satisfy their senses. If one blind man tries to lead another, what is the result? If both the leaders and followers are blind, they will all fall in a ditch, for they are all bound by their nature.

Śravaṇaṁ kīrtanam, hearing and chanting, are the beginning of *bhakti*, devotional service. Therefore it is said: *tāni me śraddadhānasya kīrtanyāny anukīrtaya*. The word *anukīrtaya* means to follow the *paramparā* system. First of all we must receive the information from authorities; then we can speak the truth. One first has to learn how to describe the Absolute Truth, Bhagavān—His actions, His mercy and His compassion upon all living beings. The Supreme Lord is more anxious to give us education and enlightenment than we are to receive them. He gives us His literature, His devotees and the *paramparā* system, but it is up to us to take advantage of these. The Kṛṣṇa consciousness movement is intended to give society the proper understanding of the Absolute Truth. We are not presenting a manufactured, bogus philosophy. Why should we unnecessarily waste our time concocting some philosophy? There is so much to be learned that has already been given by the supreme authority. All we have to do is take this Vedic literature, try to learn it and distribute it. That is Caitanya Mahāprabhu's mission.

bhārata-bhūmite haila manuṣya-janma yāra
janma sārthaka kari' kara para-upakāra
(Cc. *Ādi* 9.41)

It is the duty of everyone, especially one born in the land of Bhāratavarṣa, India, to make his life successful by taking advantage of this Vedic literature. Unfortunately, we are simply trying to learn technology, and that is our misfortune. Real education means solving all life's problems.

Transcendental education means learning how to gain relief from the entanglement of material life. This is made possible by learning about the Lord's transcendental activities.

CHAPTER FOUR

Approaching a Bona Fide Guru

TEXT 4

sūta uvāca
dvaipāyana-sakhas tv evaṁ
maitreyo bhagavāṁs tathā
prāhedaṁ viduraṁ prīta
ānvīkṣikyāṁ pracoditaḥ

TRANSLATION

Śrī Sūta Gosvāmī said: The most powerful sage Maitreya was a friend of Vyāsadeva's. Being encouraged and pleased by Vidura's inquiry about transcendental knowledge, Maitreya spoke as follows.

PURPORT

Questions and answers are very satisfactorily dealt with when the inquirer is bona fide and the speaker is also authorized. Here Maitreya is considered a powerful sage, and therefore he is also described as *bhagavān.* This word can be used not only for the Supreme Personality of Godhead but for anyone who is almost as powerful as the Supreme Lord. Maitreya is addressed as *bhagavān* because he was spiritually far advanced. He was a personal friend of Dvaipāyana Vyāsadeva, a literary incarnation of the Lord. Maitreya was very pleased with the inquiries of Vidura because they were the inquiries of a bona fide, advanced devotee. Thus Maitreya was encouraged to answer. When there are discourses on transcendental topics between devotees of equal mentality, the questions and answers are very fruitful and encouraging.

This is the Vedic process for receiving knowledge. One must approach the proper person, the *guru,* and submissively listen to him expound transcendental knowledge. As Śrī Kṛṣṇa advises in *Bhagavad-gītā* (4.34):

tad viddhi praṇipātena
paripraśnena sevayā

"Just try to learn the truth by approaching a spiritual master. Inquire from him submissively and render service unto him."

Transcendental knowledge is not very difficult, but the process must be known. Sometimes a dictating machine or a typewriter may not work, but if we go to a technician who knows the machine, he can immediately repair it. The process must be known. If one goes to a ditchdigger to repair a dictating machine, he cannot help. He may know how to dig ditches, but not repair a machine. Therefore the *śāstras* enjoin that if one wants transcendental knowledge, one must approach the proper person. The word *tad-vijñāna* refers to transcendental knowledge, not material knowledge. A medical practitioner may have material knowledge of the body, but he has no knowledge of the spirit soul within. He simply studies the mechanical arrangement of the body, which is a machine (*yantra*) made by nature. The body is actually stated in *Bhagavad-gītā* (18.61) to be a machine:

īśvaraḥ sarva-bhūtānāṁ
hṛd-deśe 'rjuna tiṣṭhati
bhrāmayan sarva-bhūtāni
yantrārūḍhāni māyayā

"The Supreme Lord is situated in everyone's heart, O Arjuna, and is directing the wanderings of all living entities, who are seated as on a machine made of the material energy."

For those who are attached to this bodily machine, the *yoga* system is recommended. One who is overly attached to the bodily conception is taught to concentrate the mind by some physical gymnastics. Thus in *haṭha-yoga* one undergoes various physical disciplines, but the real purpose is to understand Viṣṇu, the Supreme. The various *yoga* systems are given for the machine of the body, but the process of *bhakti* is transcendental to mechanical arrangements. It is therefore called *tad-vijñāna*, transcendental to material understanding. If one actually wants to understand spiritual life and spiritual knowledge, one has to approach a *guru*. The word *guru* means "heavy," heavy with knowledge. And what is that knowledge? *Tad-vijñāna.* That heaviness is *brahma-niṣṭhā*—attachment to Brahman and to Parabrahman, Bhagavān. That is the *guru's* qualification. *Brahmaṇy upaśamāśrayam.* According to *Muṇḍaka Upaniṣad* (1.2.12), *tad-vijñānārthaṁ sa gurum evābhigacchet:* "In order to understand that transcendental science, one must approach a bona fide spiritual master." Similarly, as stated in *Śrīmad-Bhāgavatam* (11.3.21):

tasmād guruṁ prapadyeta
jijñāsuḥ śreya uttamam

"Any person who seriously desires to achieve real happiness must seek out a bona fide spiritual master and take shelter of him by initiation."

The *Upaniṣads* inform us that the *guru* is one who has received knowledge by hearing the *Vedas. Śrotriyaṁ brahma-niṣṭham.* The *Vedas* are called *śruti,* and the bona fide *guru* is in the line of hearing from the disciplic succession. As stated in *Bhagavad-gītā* (4.2), *evaṁ paramparā-prāptam.* A bona fide *guru* does not impart some self-styled, concocted knowledge; his knowledge is standard and received from the *paramparā* system. He is also firmly fixed in the service of the Supreme Personality of Godhead (*brahma-niṣṭham*). These are his two qualifications: he must have heard the Vedic knowledge through the disciplic succession, and he must be established in service to the Supreme Lord. He does not have to be a very learned scholar, but he must have heard from the proper authority. God gives us the ears to hear, and simply by hearing we may become great preachers. We don't need Ph.D.'s or academic examinations. One may even remain in his position; no changes are necessary.

For this purpose there is the *varṇāśrama-dharma,* composed of four *varṇas* and four *āśramas.* Unless society is divided into these eight categories, it is simply an animal civilization. There must be some systematized, regulated arrangement. For instance, there are different divisions for the body: the head, the arms, the belly and the legs. Without the four corresponding divisions, no society can be conducted very well. There will simply be chaos. The words *sthāne sthitāḥ* mean "remaining in the *varṇāśrama-dharma.*" Even a *śūdra* can understand what is Brahman, and in that case he becomes a *brāhmaṇa* automatically. It is necessary that one hear attentively. That is all.

It is stated that Vidura heard from Maitreya Ṛṣi, and that Maitreya Ṛṣi was very pleased. Unless one satisfies his *guru*, one cannot receive proper knowledge. That is quite natural. If one receives his *guru* properly and seats him comfortably, and if the *guru* is pleased with one's behavior, the *guru* can speak very frankly and freely, and this will be very beneficial to the student. By going to a spiritual master and asking for his instructions and then not following them, one simply wastes his time. Nor should one approach the spiritual master with a challenging spirit, but should go with the aim of rendering service. The word *nipat* means "to fall down," and *pra* means "without reservation." Transcendental knowledge is based on *praṇipāta*. Therefore Kṛṣṇa says: *sarva-dharmān parityajya mām ekaṁ śaraṇaṁ vraja.* "Just surrender unto Me." Just as we surrender unto Kṛṣṇa, we have to surrender unto His representative, the spiritual master. The *guru* is Kṛṣṇa's external representative, and the internal *guru* is Kṛṣṇa Himself situated in everyone's heart. It is not that Kṛṣṇa is simply in Vaikuṇṭha or Goloka Vṛndāvana. He is everywhere; He is even within the atom. *Goloka eva nivasaty akhilātma-bhūtaḥ* (Bs. 5.37). That is the definition of Paramātma, the Supersoul. I am *ātmā*, a spiritual soul, and you are *ātmā.* We are all situated locally, you within your body and I within mine, but the Paramātmā is situated everywhere. That is the difference between *ātmā* and Paramātmā. Those who are mistaken say that there is no difference between them, but there is a difference. They are one in the sense that both are cognizant and both are living entities (*nityo nityānāṁ cetanaś cetanānām*), but they are different quantitatively. Kṛṣṇa states in *Bhagavad-gītā* (13.3):

kṣetrajñaṁ cāpi māṁ viddhi
sarva-kṣetreṣu bhārata

"O scion of Bharata, you should understand that I am also the knower in all bodies." *Kṣetrajña* is the proprietor of the *kṣetra* (the body). The individual soul is actually not the proprietor but the occupant. In a house, there is a tenant and a landlord. The tenant is the occupant, and the landlord is the proprietor. Similarly, the *ātmā* is simply the occupant of the body; the proprietor is Paramātmā. When the landlord tells the tenant to leave the house, the tenant must do so. Similarly, when the Paramātmā says that we have to leave the body, we have to do so.

To receive this Vedic knowledge, we must approach the proper *guru.* The *guru's* qualification is given in every *śāstra.* In *Śrīmad-Bhāgavatam* (11.3.21) it is said:

tasmād guruṁ prapadyeta
jijñāsuḥ śreya uttamam

One should not accept a *guru* unless one is inquisitive to know the ultimate goal of life. An ordinary man interested in bodily comforts does not need a *guru.* Unfortunately, at the present moment, the word *guru* refers to someone who can give bodily medicine. One approaches a Mahātmājī and says, "I am suffering from this disease. Please help me." And the Mahātmājī says, "Yes, I have a *mantra* that will heal you and give you success. Give me a little money and take it." This is not a real *guru.* One should approach a *guru* to learn about *tattva,* the Absolute Truth. One should not search out a *guru* to cure some material disease; rather, one requires a doctor. Similarly, people think that if a person can make him successful in business, that person is a *guru.* The *śāstras* do not confirm this either. A *guru* is one who knows the *Vedas* and the Vedic conclusion. The Vedic conclusion is the understanding of Kṛṣṇa. *Vedaiś ca sarvair aham eva vedyaḥ:* "By all the *Vedas,* I am to be known." (Bg. 15.15)

It is not that we have to understand Kṛṣṇa fully. That is not possible. We have no capacity to understand the unlimited. *Advaitam acyutam anādim ananta-rūpam* (Bs. 5.33). With our limited knowledge we cannot understand the unlimited; indeed, even Kṛṣṇa does not understand Himself. His attraction is unlimited, and to understand why He is so attractive, He became Lord Caitanya Mahāprabhu and took on the ecstatic emotions of Śrīmatī Rādhārāṇī (*rādhā-bhāva-dyuti*). If Kṛṣṇa cannot comprehend the limit of His own attraction and bliss, it is certainly not possible for us with our limited knowledge. If we can simply understand Kṛṣṇa in part, that is our perfection. Therefore Kṛṣṇa says: *janma karma ca me divyam evaṁ yo vetti tattvataḥ.* If we misunderstand Kṛṣṇa and take Him to be a human being like us, we become *mūḍhas,* fools. Kṛṣṇa's body is not composed of material elements like ours, and if we think this way, we are mistaken. The material nature belongs to Kṛṣṇa, and He is its controller. We are under the control of material nature, and that is the difference.

One who has real knowledge knows that *prakṛti*, material nature, is working under Kṛṣṇa's direction. It is not possible to understand how all this is going on, but we can understand it in summary. *Janmādy asya yato 'nvayād itarataś ca:* everything emanates from the Supreme Absolute Truth, Kṛṣṇa. This much knowledge is sufficient. We can then increase this knowledge to understand just how material nature is working under Kṛṣṇa's direction. Modern scientists mistakenly think that material nature is working independently and that things evolve by some chemical process only. However, life does not merely come from life or some chemical evolution. As Kṛṣṇa states in *Bhagavad-gītā* (10.8):

ahaṁ sarvasya prabhavo
mattaḥ sarvaṁ pravartate

"I am the source of all spiritual and material worlds. Everything emanates from Me." The same conclusion is also given in *Vedānta-sūtra*, wherein it is stated, *janmādy asya yataḥ:* "Brahman is He from whom everything emanates." "Everything" includes living entities and inert matter. Both matter and the living entities come from Kṛṣṇa. Indeed, the whole world is a combination of matter and spirit, *prakṛti* and the living entity.

Material energy is inferior, and spiritual energy is superior. Why? Superior energy (*jīva-bhūta*), the living entity, is controlling material nature. Actually he is not controlling, but is trying to utilize it. For instance, human beings are advanced living entities, and they have created modern civilization by utilizing dull, inert matter. This is our superiority. However, we are also *prakṛti* as well as *parā prakṛti.* In this way, we have to understand *tattva-jñāna.*

Śrīmad-Bhāgavatam is a commentary on *Vedānta-sūtra. Vedānta-sūtra* explains that the Supreme is the source of everything, and the nature of that source is explained in *Śrīmad-Bhāgavatam* (1.1.1): *janmādy asya yato 'nvayād itarataś cārtheṣv abhijñaḥ svarāṭ.* That source is *abhijña*, cognizant. Matter is not cognizant; therefore the theory of modern science that life comes from matter is incorrect. The identity from whom everything emanates is *abhijña*, cognizant, which means He can understand. The *Bhāgavatam* (1.1.1) also states, *tene brahma hṛdā ya ādi-kavaye:* Kṛṣṇa instructed Lord Brahmā in Vedic knowledge. Unless the ultimate source is a living entity, how can He impart knowledge? *Śrīmad-Bhāgavatam* was compiled by Vyāsadeva, who also compiled the *Vedānta-sūtra*. Generally the Māyāvādīs emphasize the commentary made on the *Vedānta-sūtra* by Śaṅkarācarya, the *Śārīraka-bhāṣya*, but that is not the original commentary on *Vedānta-sūtra*. The original commentary is given by the author himself, Vyāsadeva, in the form of *Śrīmad-Bhāgavatam*. To understand the actual meaning of the *Vedānta-sūtra*, we must refer to the commentary made by the author himself. As stated by Śrī Kṛṣṇa Himself in *Bhagavad-gītā* (13.5):

ṛṣibhir bahudhā gītaṁ
chandobhir vividhaiḥ pṛthak
brahma-sūtra-padaiś caiva
hetumadbhir viniścitaiḥ

"The knowledge of the field of activities and of the knower of activities is described by various sages in various Vedic writings—especially in the *Vedānta-sūtra*—and is presented with all reasoning as to cause and effect."

Transcendental knowledge is therefore very logical. According to the Vedic system, the *ācārya* must understand *Vedānta-sūtra* (also called *Brahma-sūtra*) before he can be accepted as an *ācārya*. Both the Māyāvāda-sampradāya and the Vaiṣṇava-sampradāya have explained the *Vedānta-sūtra*. Without understanding *Vedānta-sūtra*, one cannot understand Brahman. It is said that Vidura understood transcendental knowledge from Maitreya, and it is stated that Maitreya is a friend of Vyāsadeva's. This means that both Vidura and Maitreya know what Vyāsadeva knows. We have to approach a spiritual master who is in the disciplic succession from Vyāsadeva. Everyone may claim to be following Vyāsadeva, but one must *actually* follow him. Vyāsadeva accepted Kṛṣṇa as the Supreme Personality of Godhead, and Arjuna also accepted Kṛṣṇa as Parabrahman, the Supreme Person. One may say that because Arjuna was a friend of Kṛṣṇa's, he accepted Him in this way, but this is not the case. Arjuna gave evidence that Vyāsadeva also accepted Kṛṣṇa.

paraṁ brahma paraṁ dhāma
pavitraṁ paramaṁ bhavān
puruṣaṁ śāśvataṁ divyam
ādi-devam ajaṁ vibhum

āhus tvām ṛṣayaḥ sarve
devarṣir nāradas tathā
asito devalo vyāsaḥ
svayaṁ caiva bravīṣi me

"Arjuna said: You are the Supreme Brahman, the ultimate, the supreme abode and purifier, the Absolute Truth and the eternal divine person. You are the primal God, transcendental and original, and You are the unborn and all-pervading beauty. All the great sages such as Nārada, Asita, Devala and Vyāsa proclaim this of You, and now You Yourself are declaring it to me." (Bg. 10.12–13)

Vyāsadeva accepted Kṛṣṇa as *paraṁ brahma*, and Vyāsadeva began his commentary on *Vedānta-sūtra* with the words *oṁ namo bhagavate vāsudevāya.* If we are actually interested in understanding, we must approach a representative of Vyāsadeva like Maitreya. Maitreya is also addressed as *bhagavān*, although of course the Supreme Bhagavān is Kṛṣṇa Himself (*kṛṣṇas tu bhagavān svayam*). But the word *bhagavān* also refers to other powerful persons like Lord Brahmā, Lord Śiva, Vyāsadeva or Maitreya. The actual Bhagavān is Kṛṣṇa Himself, but these great personalities have attained as much knowledge of Kṛṣṇa as possible. It is not possible to have cent per cent knowledge of Kṛṣṇa. Not even Nārāyaṇa Himself is capable of that. Yet those who follow Kṛṣṇa's instructions fully are sometimes called Bhagavān. There are many artificial Bhagavān's, but a real Bhagavān is one who knows what Kṛṣṇa has taught. Vidura was very eager to receive transcendental knowledge, and because of this, Maitreya was very pleased with him. One can please the spiritual master simply by surrendering to him and rendering service, saying, "Sir, I am your most obedient servant. Please accept me and give me instructions." Although Arjuna was a very intimate friend of Kṛṣṇa's, before receiving *Śrīmad Bhagavad-gītā* he surrendered himself, saying, *śiṣyas te 'haṁ śādhi māṁ tvāṁ prapannam:* "Now I am Your disciple and a soul surrendered unto You. Please instruct me." (Bg. 2.7)

This is the proper way to ask for knowledge. One does not approach the spiritual master with a challenging spirit. One should also be inquisitive to understand the spiritual science. It is not that one considers himself superior to the *guru.* One must first find a *guru* to whom one can surrender, and if this is not possible, one shouldn't waste his time. By surrendering to the proper person, one can very quickly come to understand transcendental knowledge.

CHAPTER FIVE

Lord Kapila Takes Charge of His Mother, Devahūti

TEXT 5

maitreya uvāca
pitari prasthite 'raṇyaṁ
mātuḥ priya-cikīrṣayā
tasmin bindusare 'vātsīd
bhagavān kapilaḥ kila

TRANSLATION

Maitreya said: When Kardama left for the forest, Lord Kapila stayed on the strand of the Bindu-sarovara to please His mother, Devahūti.

PURPORT

In the absence of the father it is the duty of the grown son to take charge of his mother and serve her to the best of his ability so that she will not feel separation from her husband. It is also the duty of the husband to leave home as soon as there is a grown son to take charge of his wife and family affairs. That is the Vedic system of household life. One should not remain continually implicated in household affairs up to the time of death. He must leave. Family affairs and the wife may be taken charge of by a grown son.

Being a great *yogī*, Kardama Muni was not very interested in family life. Nonetheless, he decided to marry, and Svāyambhuva Manu brought his daughter Devahūti to him to serve as a wife. Kardama Muni was a *yogī* living in a cottage, and Devahūti was a princess, a king's daughter. Not being used to work, she became very skinny, and Kardama Muni took compassion upon her, thinking, "This girl has come to me, but now she is not in a very comfortable position." Therefore by his yogic powers, Kardama Muni created a large palace with many servants, gardens and other opulences. Not only that, but he also created a great spaceship as large as a small city. Modern airlines have prepared a 747, and although these are very big, Kardama Muni, by his yogic powers, was able to create a spaceship wherein there were lakes, palaces and gardens. This spaceship could also travel all over the universe. Modern scientists labor very hard to make a small spaceship to go to the moon, but Kardama Muni could create a great spaceship that could travel to all planets. This is possible by yogic powers.

There are different *siddhis*, or yogic perfections—*animā*, *lagimā*, *prāpti*, and so on—and whatever *yogīs* choose to do, they can do. That is the real *yoga* system. It is not that one becomes a *yogī* simply by pressing his nose and performing some gymnastics. One must actually attain the yogic *siddhis*. By these *siddhis*, the *yogī* can become very small or very large, very heavy or very light. Whatever he wants, he can immediately produce in his hand, and he can travel wherever he desires. Kardama Muni was such a perfected *siddhi-yogī*. By his wife, Devahūti, he had nine daughters, who were distributed to the Prajāpatis like Dakṣa Mahārāja and many others. The only son of Kardama Muni was Kapiladeva, an incarnation of Kṛṣṇa. This Kapiladeva was one of the *mahājanas*. The word *mahājana* means "authority," and according to the Vedic *śāstras* there are twelve authorities. These are Svayambhū, Nārada, Śambhu, Kumāra, Kapila, Manu, Prahlāda, Janaka, Bhīṣma, Bali, Śukadeva Gosvāmī and Yamarāja. Svayambhū is Brahmā, and Śambhu is Lord Śiva. These authorities should be followed if we want to approach the Supreme Personality of Godhead and understand the purpose of religious life. *Mahājano yena gataḥ sa panthāḥ*. These *mahājanas* follow the principles set forth by the Supreme Personality of Godhead, Kṛṣṇa, in *Bhagavad-gītā*.

We cannot very easily understand the actual truth of religious systems, but if we follow these *mahājanas*, we can understand. Kapila Muni explained the glories of devotional service to His mother, Devahūti. If we follow Him, we may learn the truth of devotional service. According to the system of *varṇāśrama-dharma*, one who is over fifty years of age must leave home, go to the forest and completely devote his life to spiritual realization. This is the actual *varṇāśrama-dharma* system. It is not a Hindu system, for the word "Hindu" is a name given by the Muslims and does not occur in any Vedic literature. However, the *varṇāśrama-dharma* is mentioned. Civilized human beings should strictly follow the *varṇāśrama* institution. If one is born a *brāhmaṇa*, he is trained nicely as a *brahmacārī*, and then he becomes a *gṛhastha*, a householder. When he gives up his home, he is called a *vānaprastha*, and after that he may take *sannyāsa*. Being a *yogī*, Kardama Muni strictly followed these principles; therefore as soon as Kapiladeva was grown, Devahūti was placed in His charge. Kardama Muni then left home. As stated in this verse: *pitari prasthite 'raṇyaṁ mātuḥ priya-cikīrṣayā.*

According to the *Manu-saṁhitā*, a woman should never be given freedom. When she is not under the protection of her husband, she must be under the protection of her sons. Women cannot properly utilize freedom, and it is better for them to remain dependent. A woman cannot be happy if she is independent. That is a fact. In Western countries we have seen many women very unhappy simply for the sake of independence. That independence is not recommended by the Vedic civilization or by the *varṇāśrama-dharma*. Consequently Devahūti was given to her grown son, Kapiladeva, and Kapiladeva was fully aware that He had to take care of His mother. It is the duty of the father to protect his daughter until she attains puberty and is married to a suitable young man. The husband then takes care of the wife. Generally a man should marry at around twenty-five years of age, and a girl should marry no later than sixteen. If this is the case, when the man is fifty years old, his eldest son should be around twenty-five, old enough to take charge of the mother. According to this calculation, Kapiladeva was about twenty-five years old and was quite able to take charge of His mother, Devahūti. He knew that because His father left His mother in His charge, He should take care of her and always please her. *Mātuḥ priya-cikīrṣayā.* Kapiladeva was not irresponsible, but was always ready to please His mother. Kapiladeva was a *brahmacārī*, and His mother took lessons from Him. That is the prerogative of the male. As stated in *Bhagavad-gītā* (9.32):

māṁ hi pārtha vyapāśritya
ye 'pi syuḥ pāpa-yonayaḥ
striyo vaiśyās tathā śūdrās
te 'pi yānti parāṁ gatim

"O son of Pṛthā, those who take shelter in Me, though they be of lower birth—women, *vaiśyas* [merchants] as well as *śūdras* [workers]—can approach the supreme destination." Women are considered on the same platform with *śūdras*, and although a woman may be married to a *brāhmaṇa*, she is not given the sacred thread. It is also said that the *Mahābhārata* was compiled by Vyāsadeva because the direct Vedic knowledge could not be understood by women, *śūdras* and *dvija-bandhus*, those who are born in *brāhmaṇa* families but are not qualified *brāhmaṇas*. *Strī-śūdra-dvijabandhūnāṁ trayī na śruti-gocarā* (*Bhāg.* 1.4.25). Consequently *Mahābhārata* is called the fifth *Veda*. The four preceding *Vedas* are the *Sāma, Yajur, Ṛg* and *Atharva*. The essence of Vedic knowledge, *Bhagavad-gītā*, is given within the *Mahābhārata*. Women are inferior to men, and Vedic civilization is so perfect that men are given full charge of the women. It is therefore said: *mātuḥ priya-cikīrṣayā*. The son is always ready to see that the mother is not unhappy. Kapiladeva was anxious that His mother not feel the absence of His father, and He was ready to take the best care of her and give her knowledge. Because women are supposed to be less intelligent, they should be given knowledge, and they should also follow this knowledge. They should follow their father's instructions, their husband's instructions and the instructions of their grown, scholarly sons like Kapiladeva. In this way, their lives can be perfect. In all cases, women should always remain dependent.

Tasmin bindusare 'vātsīd bhagavān kapilaḥ kila. It is noteworthy that in this verse Kapiladeva is referred to as Bhagavān, which indicates that He possesses all wealth, fame, knowledge, beauty, strength and renunciation. These six opulences are fully represented in Kṛṣṇa; therefore Kṛṣṇa is accepted as the Supreme Personality of Godhead (*kṛṣṇas tu bhagavān svayam*), and others are accepted as His expansions, or incarnations (*viṣṇu-tattva*). In *Bhakti-rasāmṛta-sindhu*, Rūpa Gosvāmī has analyzed the characteristics of Bhagavān. The first Bhagavān is Śrī Kṛṣṇa Himself, but some of His opulences are also bestowed upon Lord Brahmā. Lord Brahmā is a *jīva-tattva*, a living being like us. If we become spiritually powerful, we can also have the post of Lord Brahmā. Superior to Lord Brahmā is Lord Śiva, and superior to Lord Śiva is Viṣṇu, or Lord Nārāyaṇa, and superior to all is Kṛṣṇa. That is the analysis of the Vedic *śāstras* and *Brahma-saṁhitā*. Even Śaṅkarācārya, the Māyāvādī impersonalist philosopher, accepts Kṛṣṇa as the Supreme Personality of Godhead (*sa bhagavān svayaṁ kṛṣṇaḥ*). All the *ācāryas*—Rāmānujācārya, Madhvācārya, Viṣṇusvāmī, Nimbārka and Śrī Caitanya Mahāprabhu—also accept Kṛṣṇa as the Supreme Lord.

Kapiladeva is an incarnation of Kṛṣṇa, and He gave instructions to His mother, Devahūti. We must distinguish between the two Kapilas. One Kapila is this Bhagavān Kapila, and the other Kapila is the atheist Kapila. Bhagavān Kapila is also known as Devahūti-putra Kapila. Both Kapilas expounded Sāṅkhya philosophy, but the atheist Kapila expounded it without understanding, perception or realization of God. On the bank of the Bindu-sarovara Lake, Kapiladeva personally expounded Sāṅkhya philosophy to His mother, Devahūti, just as Kṛṣṇa personally expounded the knowledge of *Bhagavad-gītā* to His friend Arjuna. Like Arjuna, Devahūti was aware that she was before her spiritual master, as indicated in the following verse. Indeed, Lord Brahmā had informed her that her son was a powerful incarnation.

TEXT 6

tam āsīnam akarmāṇaṁ
tattva-mārgāgra-darśanam
sva-sutaṁ devahūty āha
dhātuḥ saṁsmaratī vacaḥ

TRANSLATION

When Kapila, who could show her the ultimate goal of the Absolute Truth, was sitting leisurely before her, Devahūti remembered the words Brahmā had spoken to her, and she therefore began to question Kapila as follows.

PURPORT

The ultimate goal of the Absolute Truth is Kṛṣṇa consciousness, devotional service. The liberated stage is not final. If we simply understand that we are not the body, that we are spirit soul, our knowledge is insufficient. We must also act as Brahman; then our position will be fixed.

brahma-bhūtaḥ prasannātmā
na śocati na kāṅkṣati
samaḥ sarveṣu bhūteṣu
mad-bhaktiṁ labhate parām

"One who is thus transcendentally situated at once realizes the Supreme Brahman and becomes fully joyful. He never laments nor desires to have anything; he is equally disposed to every living entity. In that state he attains pure devotional service unto Me." (Bg. 18.54) *Bhakti* is obtainable for a liberated person; it is not for the conditioned soul. How is this possible? In *Bhagavad-gītā* (14.26) Kṛṣṇa says:

māṁ ca yo 'vyabhicāreṇa
bhakti-yogena sevate
sa guṇān samatītyaitān
brahma-bhūyāya kalpate

"One who engages in full devotional service, who does not fall down in any circumstance, at once transcends the modes of material nature and thus comes to the level of Brahman."

We must engage in the nine processes of devotional service, the first of which is hearing (*śravaṇa*). Then, under the direction of the spiritual master and the *śāstras*, one can immediately become a liberated person. One doesn't have to endeavor separately to become liberated if he immediately engages in devotional service. One must have a firm conviction that he is engaged in Kṛṣṇa's service and is free from all material contamination. This is imperative. The words *tattva-mārga-darśanam* are elucidated elsewhere in *Śrīmad-Bhāgavatam: brahmeti paramātmeti bhagavān iti śabdyate.* The Absolute Truth is understood differently according to the position of the student. Some understand the Absolute Truth as impersonal Brahman, some as localized Paramātmā, and others as the Supreme Personality of Godhead, Kṛṣṇa, or Viṣṇu. Brahman, Paramātmā and Bhagavān, the Supreme Personality of Godhead, are not different. They are simply different aspects of the complete Godhead. Looking at a mountain from a distance, we may see a hazy cloud, and if we come nearer, we may see something green. If we actually climb the mountain, we will find many houses, trees and animals. Our vision is of the same mountain, but due to our different positions we see haze, greenery or variegatedness. In the final stage, there are varieties—trees, animals, men, houses, and so on. The Absolute Truth is not without variety. Just as there is material variety, there is spiritual variety. Because the Māyāvādī philosophers are seeing the Absolute Truth from a distance, they think that the Absolute Truth has no variety. They consider variety to be material, but this is a misunderstanding. The Absolute Truth is described as variegated in *Brahma-saṁhitā* (5.29):

cintāmaṇi-prakara-sadmasu kalpa-vṛkṣa-
lakṣāvṛteṣu surabhīr abhipālayantam
lakṣmī-sahasra-śata-sambhrama-sevyamānaṁ
govindam ādi-puruṣaṁ tam ahaṁ bhajāmi

"I worship Govinda, the primeval Lord, the first progenitor, who is tending the cows, fulfilling all desires, in abodes built with spiritual gems and surrounded by millions of desire trees. He is always served with great reverence and affection by hundreds and thousands of goddesses of fortune."

There are Vaikuṇṭha planets in the spiritual world, and there are devotees who are all liberated. These devotees are *akṣara,* which means they do not fall down into the material world. They remain in the spiritual world of the Vaikuṇṭhas. They are also persons like us, but they are eternal persons, complete with full knowledge and bliss. That is the difference between them and us. That is *tattva-jñāna.* Unless we understand the variegatedness of the Absolute Truth, there is a chance that we will fall down. It is not sufficient simply to stick to the indefinite, impersonal feature of the Absolute Truth:

āruhya kṛcchreṇa paraṁ padaṁ tataḥ
patanty adho 'nādṛta-yuṣmad-aṅghrayaḥ
(*Bhāg.* 10.2.32)

Because the impersonalists are not allowed to enter the Vaikuṇṭha planets, they simply remain in the Brahman effulgence. Thus they fall down again into material variety. We have seen many impersonalist *sannyāsīs* who first of all give up the world as false (*Brahma satyaṁ jagan mithyā*). They consider themselves Brahman (*ahaṁ brahmāsmi*), consider the world false (*jagat* is *mithyā*), and, having nothing more to do with the material world, finally say, "I have become Nārāyaṇa." Then they come to the stage of *daridra-nārāyaṇa* (poor Nārāyaṇa). They become Nārāyaṇa, but for want of anything better to do, for want of variegatedness, they take up material humanitarian activities. Although they consider their wives *mithyā* (false), they return. "You have already left. Why do you come back again?" the wives ask. This means that these so-called *sannyāsīs* have nothing to do. They undergo serious penances and austerities to reach the platform of impersonal Brahman, but because there is no pleasure there, they again descend to enjoy material variety.

We may build a nice spaceship and send it off into space, and the astronauts may go up there and fly in the impersonal sky, but eventually they will become tired and pray to God, "Please let us return to land." We have read that the Russian astronauts were simply missing Moscow while they were traveling in space. This impersonal traveling is actually very agitating; similarly, impersonal realization of the Absolute Truth cannot be permanent because one wants variety. A falldown is inevitable. When one gentleman read my book *Easy Journey to Other Planets*, he became very enthusiastic about going to other planets. "Oh, yes," I said, "we can go with this book." "Yes," the gentleman said, "then I shall come back." "Why return? You should remain there." "No, no," he said. "I don't want to remain. I just want to go and come back." This is the "enjoying" mentality. Without variety, we cannot enjoy. Variety is the mother of enjoyment, and Brahman realization or Paramātmā realization does not give us steady *ānanda*, bliss. We want *ānanda*. *Ānandamayo 'bhyāsāt*. The living entities are Brahman; Kṛṣṇa is Parabrahman. Kṛṣṇa is enjoying perpetual *ānanda*, and, being part and parcel of Kṛṣṇa, we also want *ānanda*. *Ānanda* cannot be impersonal or void; *ānanda* entails variety. No one is simply interested in drinking milk and eating sugar, but with milk and sugar we can make a variety of foods—*perā*, *barfī*, *kṣīra*, *rabarī*, *dahī*, and so on. There are hundreds of preparations. In any case, variety is required for enjoyment.

The last word of *tattva-jñāna* is to understand Kṛṣṇa, who is full of variety. Kapiladeva is *tattva-mārgāgra-darśanam*. He is an incarnation of the Supreme Personality of Godhead, and He will explain to His mother what *tattva* is, how one can approach the *tattva-jñāna*, and how one can actually enjoy *tattva-jñāna*. This is not simply dry speculation. This Kṛṣṇa consciousness philosophy includes spiritual variety. People sometimes misunderstand this variety to be material, and they hanker for *nirviśeṣa, nirākāra*, void. However, our philosophy is not void; it is full of variety and transcendental bliss. This will later be specifically enunciated by Lord Kapiladeva.

CHAPTER SIX

Devahūti Desires Transcendental Knowledge

TEXT 7

devahūtir uvāca
nirviṇṇā nitarāṁ bhūmann
asad-indriya-tarṣaṇāt
yena sambhāvyamānena
prapannāndhaṁ tamaḥ prabho

TRANSLATION

Devahūti said: I am very sick of the disturbance caused by my material senses, for because of this sense disturbance, my Lord, I have fallen into the abyss of ignorance.

PURPORT

Here, at the beginning of Devahūti's questionings, the word *asad-indriya-tarṣaṇāt* is significant. *Asat* means "impermanent," "temporary," *indriya* means "senses," and *tarṣaṇāt* refers to agitation. Thus *asad-indriya-tarṣaṇāt* means "from being agitated by the temporarily manifest senses of the material body." We are evolving through different species of material bodily existence—sometimes in a human body, sometimes in an animal body—and therefore the engagements of our material senses are also changing. Anything which changes is called temporary, or *asat.* We should know that beyond these temporary senses are our permanent senses, which are now covered by the material body. The permanent senses, being contaminated by matter, are not acting properly. Devotional service, therefore, involves freeing the senses from this contamination. When the contamination is completely removed and the senses act in the purity of unalloyed Kṛṣṇa consciousness, we have then attained *sad-indriya,* or eternal sense activities. Eternal sensory activities are called devotional service, whereas temporary sensory activities are called sense gratification. Unless one becomes tired of material sense gratification, there is no opportunity to hear transcendental messages from a person like Kapila. Devahūti expressed that she was tired. Now that her husband had left home, she wanted to get relief by hearing the instructions of Lord Kapila.

The Vedic literatures describe this material world as darkness. Actually it is dark, and therefore we require sunlight, moonlight and electricity. If it were not by nature dark, why would we require so many arrangements for artificial light? The *Vedas* enjoin that we should not remain in darkness: *tamasi mā jyotir gama.* We are instructed to go to the light, and that light is the spiritual world, which is directly lighted by the effulgence, or bodily rays, of Kṛṣṇa. As stated in *Brahma-saṁhitā* (5.40):

yasya prabhā prabhavato jagad-aṇḍa-koṭi-
koṭiṣv aśeṣa-vasudhādi-vibhūti-bhinnam
tad brahma niṣkalam anantam aśeṣa-bhūtaṁ
govindam ādi-puruṣaṁ tam ahaṁ bhajāmi

"I worship Govinda, the primeval Lord, who is endowed with great power. The glowing effulgence of His transcendental form is the impersonal Brahman, which is absolute, complete and unlimited and which displays the varieties of countless planets, with their different opulences, in millions and millions of universes."

Animals have no ability to know that they are in darkness, but human beings can know. Like Devahūti, an intelligent person should become disgusted with the darkness of ignorance. *Na hanyate hanyamāne śarīre.* As stated in *Bhagavad-gītā* (2.20), there is neither birth nor death for the soul. The soul is not destroyed when the body is annihilated. The soul puts bodies on and takes them off like clothes. This simple knowledge is instructed in the beginning of *Bhagavad-gītā,* yet there are many big scholars and leaders who still cannot understand that the body is different from the person. This is because they do not study *Bhagavad-gītā* in the proper way. Consequently no one is fully aware or convinced that the real person is not the body. This is called darkness, and when one is disgusted with this darkness, human life begins.

One who has become disgusted with material existence needs the instructions of a *guru*. *Tasmād guruṁ prapadyeta jijñāsuḥ śreya uttamam.* Being the wife of a great *yogī*, Devahūti understood her constitutional position; therefore she is placing her problem before her son, Kapiladeva, an incarnation of God. Although Kapiladeva is her son, Devahūti does not hesitate to take instructions from Him. She does not say, "Oh, He is my son. What can He tell me? I am His mother, and I shall instruct Him." Instruction has to be taken from one who is in knowledge. It doesn't matter what his position is, whether he is a son, a boy, a *śūdra, brāhmaṇa, sannyāsī* or *gṛhastha.* One should simply learn from one who knows. That is Caitanya Mahāprabhu's instruction. Although Caitanya Mahāprabhu Himself was a *brāhmaṇa* and a *sannyāsī*, He took instructions from Rāmānanda Rāya, who was a *śūdra* and *gṛhastha* but nonetheless, very exalted spiritually. When Caitanya Mahāprabhu saw that Rāmānanda Rāya was hesitant to give instructions, the Lord said, "Why are you hesitating? Although you are a *gṛhastha* and are born in a *śūdra* family, I am prepared to take lessons from you."

kibā viprā, kibā nyāsī, śūdra kene naya
yei kṛṣṇa-tattva-vettā, sei 'guru' haya
(Cc. *Madhya* 8.128)

This is Caitanya Mahāprabhu's teaching. Whoever is qualified in Kṛṣṇa consciousness can become a *guru*. His family or material identity does not matter. He simply must know the science. When we consult an engineer, a doctor or a lawyer, we do not ask whether he is a *brāhmaṇa* or a *śūdra.* If he is qualified, he can help with a particular subject. Similarly, if one knows the science of Kṛṣṇa, he can be a *guru*. Devahūti was taking lessons from her son because He knew the science of Kṛṣṇa. Even if gold is in a filthy place, we should take it. It is also stated in the *Vedas* that if a girl is highly qualified or beautiful, she can be accepted in marriage even though born in a lower family. Thus it is not birth that is important, but qualification. Caitanya Mahāprabhu wanted everyone in India to know the science of Kṛṣṇa and preach Kṛṣṇa consciousness. This is very simple. We need only repeat what Kṛṣṇa has said or what has been said about Kṛṣṇa in the Vedic literatures.

Human society cannot be happy without Kṛṣṇa consciousness. Kṛṣṇa is the supreme enjoyer, and we are His servants. The master is enjoying, and the servants are helping the master enjoy. We living entities are eternal servants of God, and our duty is to help our master enjoy. Śrīmatī Rādhārāṇī is the topmost servant of Kṛṣṇa, and Her business is always to keep Kṛṣṇa pleased. Kṛṣṇa is very fond of Rādhārāṇī because She renders the best service. Her sixty-four qualifications are mentioned in the Vedic literatures. Unfortunately, in the material world we are busy trying to enjoy our material senses. As stated in *Bhagavad-gītā* (3.42):

indriyāṇi parāṇy āhur
indriyebhyaḥ paraṁ manaḥ
manasas tu parā buddhir
yo buddheḥ paratas tu saḥ

"The working senses are superior to dull matter; mind is higher than the senses; intelligence is still higher than the mind; and he (the soul) is even higher than the intelligence." The soul is on the spiritual platform. On the material platform, we are interested in gratifying our senses. In this way we become implicated in the laws of nature. As stated in the *śāstras:*

nūnaṁ pramattaḥ kurute vikarma
yad indriya-prītaya āpṛṇoti
na sādhu manye yata ātmano 'yam
asann api kleśada āsa dehaḥ

"When a person considers sense gratification the aim of life, he certainly becomes mad after materialistic living and engages in all kinds of sinful activity. He does not know that due to his past misdeeds he has already received a body which, although temporary, is the cause of his misery. Actually the living entity should not have taken on a material body, but he has been awarded the material body for sense gratification. Therefore I think it not befitting an intelligent man to involve himself again in the activities of sense gratification by which he perpetually gets material bodies one after another." (*Bhāg.* 5.5.4)

Living entities in this material world are very busy trying to gratify their senses. In the street we see many dogs assembled for sex. This may seem very crude, but human beings are engaged in the same business, perhaps in a more elaborate way. We should know that sense gratification is meant for animals, and that sense control is for human beings. By *tapasya*, penance, we can purify ourselves and regain our eternal life.

Actually our material senses are not our real senses. They are covered, just as the body is covered by clothes. Our real body is within the material body. *Dehino 'smin yathā dehe.* The spiritual body is within the material body. The material body is changing, going through childhood, youth, then old age, and then it vanishes. Although this is not our real body, we are engaged in sense gratification with it. However, for our own ultimate happiness, we should try to purify our senses. There is no question of destroying the senses or becoming desireless. Desire is a material activity, and becoming desireless is not possible. The senses must be purified in order for us to act through them transcendentally. *Bhakti-yoga* does not require us to destroy our senses, but to purify them. When the senses are purified, we can serve Kṛṣṇa:

sarvopādhi-vinirmuktaṁ
tat-paratvena nirmalam
hṛṣīkeṇa hṛṣīkeśa-
sevanaṁ bhaktir ucyate

"*Bhakti,* or devotional service, means engaging all our senses in the service of the Lord, the Supreme Personality of Godhead, the master of all the senses. When the spirit soul renders service unto the Supreme, there are two side effects. One is freed from all material designations, and, simply by being employed in the service of the Lord, one's senses are purified." (*Nārada-pañcarātra*)

We can serve Hṛṣīkeśa, the master of the senses, through the senses. We are part and parcel of Kṛṣṇa, just as the hand is part and parcel of the body. Similarly, our senses are also part and parcel of the spiritual body of Kṛṣṇa. When we purify our senses, we can act in our original constitutional position and serve Kṛṣṇa. When we forget our position and try to satisfy ourselves, we become conditioned materially. When we forget that our duty is to serve Kṛṣṇa, we fall into the material world and become implicated in personal sense gratification. As long as we continue trying to satisfy our own senses, we have to accept another body. Kṛṣṇa is so kind that if we want to become tigers, He will give us a tiger body. If we want to become devotees, He will give us the body of a devotee. This life is a preparation for the next, and if we want to enjoy our transcendental senses, we have to purify ourselves to return home, back to Godhead. For this purpose, Devahūti is submitting to her son just as a disciple submits to his master.

TEXT 8

tasya tvaṁ tamaso 'ndhasya
duṣpārasyādya pāragam
sac-cakṣur janmanām ante
labdhaṁ me tvad-anugrahāt

TRANSLATION

Your Lordship is my only means of getting out of this darkest region of ignorance because You are my transcendental eye, which, by Your mercy only, I have attained after many, many births.

PURPORT

This verse is very instructive, since it indicates the relationship between the spiritual master and the disciple. The disciple or conditioned soul is put into this darkest region of ignorance and therefore is entangled in the material existence of sense gratification. It is very difficult to get out of this entanglement and attain freedom, but if one is fortunate enough to get the association of a spiritual master like Kapila Muni or His representative, then by his grace one can be delivered from the mire of ignorance. The spiritual master is therefore worshiped as one who delivers the disciple from the mire of ignorance with the light of the torch of knowledge. The word *pāragam* is very significant. *Pāragam* refers to one who can take the disciple to the other side. This side is conditioned life; the other side is the life of freedom. The spiritual master takes the disciple to the other side by opening his eyes with knowledge. We are suffering simply because of ignorance. By the instruction of the spiritual master, the darkness of ignorance is removed, and thus the disciple is enabled to go to the side of freedom. It is stated in *Bhagavad-gītā* that after many, many births one surrenders to the Supreme Personality of Godhead. Similarly, if, after many, many births, one is able to find a bona fide spiritual master and surrender to such a bona fide representative of Kṛṣṇa, he can be taken to the side of light.

The bona fide spiritual master is a true Vedāntist, for he actually knows Vedānta and the *Vedas* and understands the Supreme Personality of Godhead, Kṛṣṇa. The word *veda* means "knowledge," and *anta* means "last phase." There are different types of knowledge. We are interested in ordinary knowledge for economic benefit, but that is not actual knowledge. That is the art of livelihood. One may study to be an electrician and earn his livelihood by repairing electric lines. This kind of knowledge is called *śilpa-jñāna.* Real knowledge, however, is Vedic knowledge, knowing oneself, what one is and what God is and understanding one's relationship with God, and one's duty.

One who is searching after knowledge is called *jñānavān.* Knowledge begins with the inquiry *athāto brahma-jijñāsā:* "What is Brahman?" Knowledge also begins by understanding the threefold miseries of the material world—*ādhyātmika, ādhibhautika* and *ādhidaivika.* We are suffering from miseries caused by other living entities and acts of nature as well as from miseries arising from the body and mind themselves. The soul is aloof from the body and mind, but he suffers due to material contamination. We have no control over these threefold miseries. They are controlled by Kṛṣṇa's maidservant, goddess Durgā, who is material nature. She is not independent of Kṛṣṇa. However, she is so powerful that she can create and maintain. *Prakṛti,* nature, can be very unkind. Mother Durgā is often portrayed as chastising demons by piercing them with a trident.

Those who are learned and intelligent look to the mercy of the Supreme Personality of Godhead for relief from the threefold miseries of material existence. Although this material world is nothing but darkness, people are very proud of their eyes. They are always saying, "Can you show me God?" The answer to that is: "Have you the eyes to see God?" Why is the emphasis placed on seeing? Certainly, God can be seen, as stated in *Brahma-saṁhitā* (5.38), *premāñjana-cchurita-bhakti-vilocanena:* "Govinda [Kṛṣṇa] is always seen by the devotee whose eyes are anointed by the pulp of love."

If we are devotees, lovers of God, the ointment of love will clear our eyes. In order to see God, we have to cleanse our eyes by wiping away the cataracts of material contamination. Although we may be eager to see God, we cannot see Him with these material eyes. Not only can we not see Him, but we cannot understand Him, although His name is there. Understanding God means first of all understanding His name. Therefore from the beginning we should chant the Hare Kṛṣṇa *mahā-mantra.* God is not different from His name. Kṛṣṇa's name and Kṛṣṇa's person are the same. "Absolute" means that Kṛṣṇa's name, form, place, dress, pastimes and everything are nondifferent from Him. Kṛṣṇa is present in His name, but because we have no love for Him, we cannot see Him.

Sanātana Gosvāmī was a great learned scholar, and he was called a *paṇḍita,* which indicates that he was a learned *brāhmaṇa.* When Sanātana Gosvāmī approached Śrī Caitanya Mahāprabhu, he said, "The people in my neighborhood are calling me a *paṇḍita,* and I am very unhappy because of this." Caitanya Mahāprabhu asked, "Why are you dissatisfied?" Sanātana Gosvāmī replied, "I am such a poor *paṇḍita* that I do not even know the goal of life. I do not even know what is beneficial for me. I am simply being carried away by sense gratification." In this way, Sanātana Gosvāmī approached Śrī Caitanya Mahāprabhu. He did not approach Him to get some gold or some medicine. He went to find out his real self-interest. This is the real purpose for approaching a *guru.*

Devahūti approached Lord Kapiladeva in the same way. She said, "My dear Kapila, You have come as my son, but You are my *guru* because You can inform me how I can cross the ocean of nescience, which is the material world." Thus one who feels the need to cross the dark ocean of nescience, which is material existence, requires a *guru.* It is not the *guru's* task to supply gold and medicine. Now it has become a fashion to keep a *guru* as if he were a dog or a cat. This is of no use. We must inquire about that portion of God's creation which is beyond this darkness. The *Upaniṣads* and *Bhagavad-gītā* describe another world, beyond this material nature. According to Kṛṣṇa in *Bhagavad-gītā* (15.6):

na tad bhāsayate sūryo
na śaśāṅko na pāvakaḥ
yad gatvā na nivartante
tad dhāma paramaṁ mama

"That abode of Mine is not illumined by the sun or moon, nor by electricity. One who reaches it never returns to this material world."

It is not possible for us to go to that *paravyoma* by material means. It is impossible to penetrate the material universe unless one understands Kṛṣṇa. One can be enlightened by the mercy of God because Kṛṣṇa Himself comes to give us information. If He does not come personally, He sends His devotee, or He leaves behind Him *Bhagavad-gītā.* However, we are so foolish that we do not take advantage of them. We do not take advantage of His devotee, who hankers to give this knowledge, sacrificing everything. Therefore Śrī Caitanya Mahāprabhu said:

brahmāṇḍa bhramite kona bhāgyavān jīva
guru-kṛṣṇa-prasāde pāya bhakti-latā-bīja

"The fallen, conditioned living entity, trapped by the external energy, loiters in the material world, but if by good fortune he meets a bona fide representative of the Lord, and if he takes advantage of such a *guru,* he receives the seed of devotional service." (Cc. *Madhya* 19.151)

The seed of devotional service is received by a most fortunate person. Those who are cultivating *bhakti* in the International Society for Krishna Consciousness are the most fortunate people in the world. By Kṛṣṇa's mercy one can receive the *bhakti-latā-bīja,* the seed of devotional service. Unless one is free from the reactions of sin, one cannot understand *bhakti* or Bhagavān. Therefore we must act piously by giving up illicit sex, intoxication, meat-eating and gambling. If we lead a pious life, we can understand God. This Kṛṣṇa consciousness movement is engaged in training people to this end so that their lives will be successful.

TEXT 9

ya ādyo bhagavān puṁsām
īśvaro vai bhavān kila
lokasya tamasāndhasya
cakṣuḥ sūrya ivoditaḥ

TRANSLATION

You are the Supreme Personality of Godhead, the origin and Supreme Lord of all living entities. You have arisen to disseminate

the rays of the sun in order to dissipate the darkness of the ignorance of the universe.

PURPORT

Kapila Muni is accepted as an incarnation of the Supreme Personality of Godhead, Kṛṣṇa. Here the word *ādya* means "the origin of all living entities," and *puṁsām īśvaraḥ* means "the Lord (*īśvara*) of the living entities" (*īśvaraḥ paramaḥ kṛṣṇaḥ*). Kapila Muni is the direct expansion of Kṛṣṇa, who is the sun of spiritual knowledge. The sun dissipates the darkness of the universe, and when the light of the Supreme Personality of Godhead comes down, it at once similarly dissipates the darkness of *māyā*. We have our eyes, but without the light of the sun, our eyes are of no value. Similarly, without the light of the Supreme Lord, or without the divine grace of the spiritual master, one cannot see things as they are.

In this verse, Devahūti also addresses her son as Bhagavān. Bhagavān is the Supreme Person. If we could just use a little common sense we could understand that an organization requires a leader. Without a leader, we cannot organize anything. Foolish philosophers say that the universe automatically came into being by nature. They say that in the beginning there was a chunk, and this cosmic manifestation came out of that chunk of matter. But where did this chunk come from? The fact is that there must be a brain, a leader, behind anything organized. We have information of this leader from the *Vedas: nityo nityānāṁ cetanaś cetanānām.* The Supreme Lord is eternal, and we are also eternal. But the Supreme Lord is one, and we are many. The Supreme Lord is very great, and we are very small. He is all-pervading and infinite, and we are finite and infinitesimal. Even if we analyze the creation, we will find that not everyone is on the same level. One person is more intelligent or opulent than another. If we analyze things in this way, we will come to the demigods, and among them we will find that the most important demigod is Lord Brahmā. He is the original creature within this universe, yet he is not the most intelligent being. It is said that in the beginning, Brahmā received knowledge from the Supreme Personality of Godhead.

Recently newspapers are reporting that faith in a personal God is diminishing. This means that people are becoming more and more foolish. This is natural in Kali-yuga, for as the age of Kali progresses, bodily strength, memory and mercy diminish. We actually see that the present generation is not as strong as the previous. People also have short memories. We also understand that sometimes people are killed while other people pass by, not caring. Thus mercy is also diminishing. Because everything is diminishing, God consciousness is diminishing also; therefore it is natural to receive news that faith in a personal God is diminishing. In *Bhagavad-gītā* (7.15), one who does not accept a personal God is described as a *mūḍha*, a fool.

na māṁ duṣkṛtino mūḍhāḥ
prapadyante narādhamāḥ
māyayāpahṛta-jñānā
āsuraṁ bhāvam āśritāḥ

"Those miscreants who are grossly foolish, lowest among mankind, whose knowledge is stolen by illusion, and who partake of the atheistic nature of demons, do not surrender unto Me."

Actually, people today do not even know the meaning of God, so there is no question of surrender. There are also those who are scholarly and well educated, but their knowledge is taken away by *māyā*, illusion. Although they may superficially hold degrees, they have no real knowledge. They are also *asuras*, demons who simply defy God, saying, "I am God, you are God. Why are you searching for God? There are many Gods loitering in the street. Take care of them." Therefore it is not surprising that newspapers report that faith in a personal God is decreasing. Nonetheless, God is a person. *Ya ādyo bhagavān.* Lord Brahmā also worships Kṛṣṇa by saying, *govindam ādi-puruṣaṁ tam ahaṁ bhajāmi.* He says, "I worship that original person, Govinda." *Ādi-puruṣam*, Kṛṣṇa, has no one preceding Him; therefore He is called original. It is said that Kṛṣṇa was born of Vasudeva, but this simply means that Kṛṣṇa accepted Vasudeva as His father. Śrī Kṛṣṇa deals with His devotees in different relationships, or *rasas—śānta, dāsya, sakhya, vātsalya* and *mādhurya.*

We all have some relationship with Kṛṣṇa, but presently that is covered. Therefore we have to revive it. Simple appreciation of the Supreme is called *śānta-rasa.* When one appreciates the Supreme fully, he wishes to render some service, and that is called *dāsya.* When one becomes more intimate, he becomes a friend of Kṛṣṇa's, and that is called *sakhya.* When one is more advanced, he wants to render service to Kṛṣṇa as a father or a mother, and this is *vātsalya.* Being a father or a mother means serving the son. The Christian conception of God as the Supreme Father is not very perfect because if we conceive of God as a father, our position will be to take things from Him. Everyone wants to take something from the father. One is always saying, "Father, give me this. Father, give me that." However, accepting the Supreme Lord as one's son means rendering service. Yaśodāmayī got Kṛṣṇa as her son, and she was always anxious that He not be in danger. Thus she was always protecting Him. Actually Kṛṣṇa protects the entire universe, but Yaśodā was giving protection to Kṛṣṇa. This is Vaiṣṇava philosophy. Yaśodā became mad when she saw Kṛṣṇa taken away by the Tṛṇāvarta demon. However, Kṛṣṇa became so heavy that the demon could not fly in the sky, and thus the demon fell to the earth and died. Yaśodā immediately said, "God has saved my Kṛṣṇa!" She then began to thank some other God, some *devatā.* She did not know that Kṛṣṇa is the Supreme Personality of Godhead. If she had thought of Kṛṣṇa as the Supreme Personality of Godhead, the relationship between mother and son would have been destroyed. Therefore Kṛṣṇa was playing just like an ordinary child, and mother Yaśodā was treating Him as her son. Kṛṣṇa's friends, the cowherd boys, did not consider Him the Supreme Lord either. The *gopīs* even used to chastise Kṛṣṇa. If a devotee can have such a relationship with Kṛṣṇa, why should he want to become one with God? It is better to be God's father, God's controller. This is *bhakti-mārga,* the path of devotional service. A devotee does not want to be equal to God or one with God. He simply wants to render service.

In order to understand the Absolute Truth, we have to understand the meaning of Bhagavān. Devahūti was not an ordinary woman. She was the wife of Kardama Muni, a great *yogī.* She had obviously learned something from her husband, for had she not been very exalted, how could Bhagavān Kapiladeva have become her son? Everyone should know what is Bhagavān and take lessons from Bhagavān. Lord Kapila is Bhagavān, and He personally instructed His mother in Sāṅkhya philosophy. By this knowledge we can develop or awaken our dormant love for God. Then we can see God when our eyes are anointed with love for Him. Indeed, we can see God everywhere and at all times. We will see God and nothing but God. We will see God not only within our hearts. If we go to the ocean, we will see God. If one is a little thoughtful, he will see that the great ocean stays in its place. The ocean has received its orders not to go beyond such and such a limit. Any intelligent man can see God while walking down the beach. However, this requires a little intelligence. People who are asses, *mūḍhas, duskṛtīs,* cannot see God, but those who are intelligent can see God everywhere because God is omnipresent. He is within the universe and within our heart, and He is even within the atom. Why are we saying that we cannot see Him? God says, "Try to see Me in this way, but if you are too dull, then try to see Me another way."

What is the easy way? Kṛṣṇa says in *Bhagavad-gītā,* "I am the taste of water." Is there anyone who has not tasted water? He also says, "I am the light of the sun." Is there anyone who has not seen sunshine? Then why are people saying, "I have not seen God"? First of all we have to *try* to see God. It is as easy as ABCD. When we see God everywhere, we will see the personal God. Then we will understand.

Bhagavān puṁsām īśvaraḥ. Bhagavān is *īśvara,* the controller. We are not independent. No one can actually say, "I am independent." We are bound tightly by the modes of material nature, and yet we are thinking that we are independent. This is simply foolishness. Therefore it is said that all the people in the material world are blinded by the darkness of ignorance. When people are blind, out of their ignorance they say, "There is no God. I cannot see God." Then God comes as Kṛṣṇa or Kapiladeva and says, "Here I am. See My features. I am a person. I play the flute and enjoy Myself in Vṛndāvana. Why can't you see Me?" Thus God comes, explains Himself and leaves behind His instruction, *Bhagavad-gītā.* Still, people are so foolish that they claim not to understand God. If we try to see God through the instructions given to Devahūti by Lord Kapila, our lives will be successful.

TEXT 10

atha me deva sammoham
apākraṣṭuṁ tvam arhasi
yo 'vagraho 'haṁ mametīty
etasmin yojitas tvayā

TRANSLATION

Now be pleased, my Lord, to dispel my great delusion. Due to my feeling of false ego, I have been engaged by Your māyā and have identified myself with the body and consequent bodily relations.

PURPORT

Māyā is the false ego of identifying one's body with one's self and of claiming things possessed in relationship with the body. In *Bhagavad-gītā*, Fifteenth Chapter, the Lord says, "I am sitting in everyone's heart, and from Me comes everyone's remembrance and forgetfulness." Devahūti has stated that false identification of the body with the self and attachment for bodily possessions are also under the direction of the Lord. Does this mean that the Lord discriminates by engaging one in His devotional service and another in sense gratification? If that were true, it would be an incongruity on the part of the Supreme Lord, but that is not the actual fact. As soon as the living entity forgets his real constitutional position of eternal servitorship to the Lord and wants instead to enjoy himself by sense gratification, he is captured by *māyā*. This capture leads to the consciousness of false identification with the body and attachment for the possessions of the body. These are the activities of *māyā*, and since *māyā* is also an agent of the Lord, it is indirectly the action of the Lord. The Lord is merciful; if anyone wants to forget Him and enjoy this material world, He gives him full facility, not directly but through the agency of His material potency. Therefore, since the material potency is the Lord's energy, indirectly it is the Lord who gives the facility to forget Him. Devahūti therefore said, "My engagement in sense gratification was also due to You. Now kindly get me free from this entanglement."

By the grace of the Lord one is allowed to enjoy this material world, but when one is disgusted with material enjoyment and is frustrated, and when one sincerely surrenders unto the lotus feet of the Lord, then the Lord is so kind that He frees one from entanglement. Kṛṣṇa says, therefore, in *Bhagavad-gītā*, "First of all surrender, and then I will take charge of you and free you from all reactions of sinful activities." Sinful activities are those activities performed in forgetfulness of our relationship with the Lord. In this material world, activities for material enjoyment that are considered pious are also sinful. For example, one sometimes gives money in charity to a needy person with a view to get back the money four times increased. Giving with the purpose of gaining something is called charity in the mode of passion. Everything done here is done in the modes of material nature, and therefore all activities but service to the Lord are sinful. Because of sinful activities we become attracted by the illusion of material attachment, and we think, "I am this body." I think of the body as myself and of bodily possessions as "mine." Devahūti requested Lord Kapila to free her from that entanglement of false identification and false possession.

In asking this, Devahūti is accepting her son, Kapila, as her *guru.* He consequently tells her how to solve all material problems. Material life is nothing but sex attraction. *Puṁsaḥ striyā mithunī-bhāvam etam* (*Bhāg.* 5.5.8). Material life means that men are after women and women are after men. We find this not only in human society but in bird, dog, cat and demigod society. As soon as people join to satisfy their sex desire, the attraction becomes greater and greater. An apartment is needed for privacy, and then one has to earn a livelihood and acquire some land. Without children, married life is frustrated, and of course the children have to be educated. Thus one becomes entangled in material life by creating so many situations, but at the time of death Kṛṣṇa comes and takes away everything—house, land, wife, children, friends, reputation and whatever. Then we have to begin another life. It is not that we simply die and finish everything. We are living eternally; the body is finished, but we have to accept another body out of the 8,400,000 forms. In this way, our life is going on, but we are thinking in terms of wife, children, and so forth. This is all illusion.

In any case, we will not be allowed to stay here, and although we are attached to all this, everything will be taken away at death. Whatever post we are occupying—be it president or Lord Brahmā—we are occupying temporarily. We may be here five years, ten years, one hundred years or five million years. Whatever, our position is limited. Our position in the material world is not eternal, but *we* are eternal. Why, then, should we be illusioned by the noneternal? By nature we are part and parcel of Kṛṣṇa, and Kṛṣṇa is *sac-cid-ānanda-vigraha.* In order to transcend the darkness of material life and go to the world of light, we need to approach a *guru.* It is for this reason that Devahūti is approaching Lord Kapiladeva.

In the morning, when the sun arises, the darkness of night immediately goes away. Similarly, when God or His incarnation comes, the darkness of material life is dissipated. When Kṛṣṇa, the Supreme Personality of Godhead, came, Arjuna's illusion was dispelled. He was thinking, "Why should I fight with my relatives?" Actually the whole world is going on under this conception of "my" and "mine." There are fights between nations, societies, communities and families. People are thinking, "Why are you interfering with my business?" Then there is a fight. Because of illusion, we do not consider these situations temporary. On a train, people may argue and fight over a seat, but one who knows that he will only be on the train for two or three hours thinks, "Why should I fight? I shall only be here for a short while." One person thinks in this way, and the other person is ready to fight, thinking that his seat is permanent. No one will be allowed to stay within this material world; everyone will have to change his body and position, and as long as one remains here, he will have to fight and struggle for existence. This is the way of material life. We may temporarily make some compromises, but ultimately the material world is full of misery.

We are very much attached to this material world, but according to the Vedic system, renunciation is compulsory, for when one reaches the age of fifty, he renounces his family life. Nature gives warning, "You are now past fifty. That's all right. You have fought in this material world. Now stop this business." Children play on the beach and make houses out of sand, but after a while the father comes and says, "Now, my dear children, time is up. Stop this business and come home." This is the business of the *guru*—to teach his disciples detachment. The world is not our place; our place is Vaikuṇṭhaloka. Kṛṣṇa also comes to remind us of this. The *dharma*, or order, of the Supreme Person is to become His devotee and always think of Him. Kṛṣṇa says:

man-manā bhava mad-bhakto
mad-yājī māṁ namaskuru

"Engage your mind always in thinking of Me, offer obeisances and worship Me." (Bg. 9.34)

In this way, Kṛṣṇa opens the door, but we unfortunately do not accept Him. Kṛṣṇa tells Arjuna, "Because you are My friend, I am revealing to you the most confidential *dharma.*" What is that? "Simply surrender unto Me." This is the *dharma* taught by the Supreme Personality of Godhead, and Kṛṣṇa's incarnation and His devotee will teach the same *dharma.*

We are all after happiness, but we do not know how to enjoy happiness. We want to enjoy our senses, but it is not possible with these covered false senses. The senses must be opened, and that is the process of purification. We are thinking of ourselves according to so many false material identifications, but we should take Śrī Caitanya Mahāprabhu's advice: *jīvera 'svarūpa' haya——kṛṣṇera 'nitya-dāsa.'* We must come to understand, "I am the eternal servant of Kṛṣṇa." After all, our senses are employed for the satisfaction of somebody—either for ourselves or for someone else. That is *kāma, krodha, lobha* and *matsara*—illusion. If we are not serving our own lusty desires (*kāma*), we are serving anger (*krodha*). If I am the master of anger, I can control my anger, and if I am the master of my desires, I can control my desires. In any case, I am a servant, and my service should be transferred to Kṛṣṇa. That is the perfection of life.

If we are situated in the transcendental position (*bhakti*), we can understand Kṛṣṇa. Kṛṣṇa cannot be understood by mental speculation; otherwise He would have said that He could be understood by *jñāna, karma* or *yoga.* However, He clearly says, *bhaktyā mām abhijānāti:* "Only by devotional service can I be understood." If we want to know Kṛṣṇa as He is, we have to accept the process of *bhakti.* It is this *bhakti* process that Kapiladeva will reveal to Devahūti.

TEXT 11

taṁ tvā gatāhaṁ śaraṇaṁ śaraṇyaṁ
sva-bhṛtya-saṁsāra-taroḥ kuṭhāram
jijñāsayāhaṁ prakṛteḥ pūruṣasya
namāmi sad-dharma-vidāṁ variṣṭham

TRANSLATION

Devahūti continued: I have taken shelter of Your lotus feet because You are the only person of whom to take shelter. You are the

ax which can cut the tree of material existence. I therefore offer my obeisances unto You, who are the greatest of all transcendentalists, and I inquire from You as to the relationship between man and woman and between spirit and matter.

PURPORT

Sāṅkhya philosophy, as is well known, deals with *prakṛti* and *puruṣa*. *Puruṣa* is the Supreme Personality of Godhead or anyone who imitates the Supreme Personality of Godhead as an enjoyer, and *prakṛti* is nature. In this material world, material nature is being exploited by the *puruṣas*, or the living entities. The intricacies in the material world of the relationship of the *prakṛti* and *puruṣa*, or the enjoyed and the enjoyer, give rise to *saṁsāra*, or material entanglement. Devahūti wanted to cut the tree of material entanglement, and she found the suitable weapon in Kapila Muni. The tree of material existence is explained in the Fifteenth Chapter of *Bhagavad-gītā* as an *aśvattha* tree whose root is upward and whose branches are downward. It is recommended there that one has to cut the root of this material existential tree with the ax of detachment. What is the attachment? The attachment involves *prakṛti* and *puruṣa*. The living entities are trying to lord it over material nature. Since the conditioned soul takes material nature to be the object of his enjoyment, and he takes the position of the enjoyer, he is therefore called *puruṣa*.

Devahūti questioned Kapila Muni, for she knew that only He could cut her attachment to this material world. The living entities, in the guises of men and women, are trying to enjoy the material energy; therefore in one sense everyone is *puruṣa* because *puruṣa* means "enjoyer," and *prakṛti* means "enjoyed." In this material world both so-called men and women are imitating the real *puruṣa;* the Supreme Personality of Godhead is actually the enjoyer in the transcendental sense, whereas all others are *prakṛti*.

In *Bhagavad-gītā*, matter is analyzed as *aparā*, or inferior nature, whereas beyond this inferior nature there is another, superior nature—the living entities. Living entities are also *prakṛti*, or enjoyed, but under the spell of *māyā*, the living entities are falsely trying to take the position of enjoyers. That is the cause of *saṁsāra-bandha*, or conditional life. Devahūti wanted to get out of conditional life and place herself in full surrender. The Lord is *śaraṇya*, which means "the only worthy personality to whom one can fully surrender," because He is full of all opulences. If anyone actually wants relief, the best course is to surrender unto the Supreme Personality of Godhead. The Lord is also described here as *sad-dharma-vidāṁ variṣṭham.* This indicates that of all transcendental occupations, the best is eternal loving service unto the Supreme Personality of Godhead. *Dharma* is sometimes translated as "religion," but that is not exactly the meaning. *Dharma* actually means "that which one cannot give up," "that which is inseparable from oneself." The warmth of fire is inseparable from fire; therefore warmth is called the *dharma,* or nature, of fire. Similarly, *sad-dharma* means "eternal occupation." That eternal occupation is engagement in the transcendental loving service of the Lord. The purpose of Kapiladeva's Sāṅkhya philosophy is to propagate pure, uncontaminated devotional service, and therefore He is addressed here as the most important personality among those who know the transcendental occupation of the living entity.

As pointed out before, Bhagavān, the Supreme Personality of Godhead, is everyone's real shelter (*śaraṇaṁ śaraṇyam*). Everyone is seeking shelter because we are all constitutionally servants. Originally we are servants of God; therefore it is our nature to take His shelter. Some seek an occupation or the service of a great man; others seek the service of the government or whatever. In any case, the ultimate shelter is Kṛṣṇa, the Supreme Personality of Godhead. Being Kṛṣṇa's incarnation, Kapiladeva is also a shelter. Kṛṣṇa has unlimited forms and unlimited incarnations. It is said in *Śrīmad-Bhāgavatam* that His incarnations are expanding continuously, like waves in the ocean. Indeed, we cannot even count them. In *Brahma-saṁhitā* it is said: *Advaitam acyutam anādim ananta-rūpam.* In India there are many thousands of temples, and within these temples there are *arcā-vigrahas,* Deities. All these Kṛṣṇas are non-different; they are one. Kṛṣṇa resides in Vaikuṇṭha and also in the temple. The Kṛṣṇas are not different, although they are *ananta,* unlimited. Kṛṣṇa is also the witness within everyone's heart, and He is seeing all of our activities. We cannot hide anything from Him, and we receive the results of our *karma* because the witness is Kṛṣṇa Himself within the heart. How, then, can we avoid Him? Without Kṛṣṇa's permission, we cannot do anything. Why does Kṛṣṇa give us permission to do something wrong? He does so because we persist. Actually He does not tell us to do anything other than surrender unto Him. We want to do something, and Kṛṣṇa may sanction it, but we go ahead and do it at our own risk. Kṛṣṇa is not responsible. However, we should know that without the sanction of Kṛṣṇa, we cannot do anything. That is a fact. Actually we are constitutionally servants of Kṛṣṇa. Even though we may declare ourselves independent, we are not. Rather, we are servants falsely declaring that we are independent. Self-realization is understanding that we are dependent on the Supreme Personality of Godhead. As Caitanya Mahāprabhu says:

ayi nanda-tanuja kiṅkaraṁ
patitaṁ māṁ viṣame bhavāmbudhau
kṛpayā tava pāda-paṅkaja-
sthita-dhūlī-sadṛśaṁ vicintaya

"My dear Lord Kṛṣṇa, son of Mahārāja Nanda, I am Your eternal servant, but somehow or other I have fallen into this ocean of nescience. Please pick Me up from this ocean of death and place Me as one of the atoms at Your lotus feet." (*Śikṣāṣṭaka* 5) Because we are under illusion, Devahūti says: *sva-bhṛtya-saṁsāra-taroḥ kuṭhāram.* In *Bhagavad-gītā* (15.1–4), material existence is likened unto a banyan tree with its roots upward and its branches below. The roots of this banyan tree are very strong, but they can be cut with an ax (*kuṭhāram*). By taking shelter of Kṛṣṇa's lotus feet, we can cut the strong root of material existence. Because we have given up Kṛṣṇa's service, we have become servants of so many things. We are obliged to serve our parents, wife, children, country and so forth. We are indebted to many people and to the demigods who give heat and light. Although we are not paying the bill, we are taking advantage of the sunlight and the sun's heat. If we take advantage of electricity, we have to pay the bill, but we don't pay the sun bill. This means that we are actually indebted to the sun-god, Vivasvān. Similarly, the King of heaven, Indra, is supplying water in the form of rain. Rascals say that all this comes about by nature, but they do not know that nature is controlled. If we don't pay our debts by performing sacrifices, there will certainly be a scarcity. All of these things are coming from the Supreme Father, the Supreme Personality of Godhead, but we are thinking that they are coming from nature, and we are utilizing them without caring whether we pay the bill or not. It is all right to use our father's property, but at the present moment we are not acting as our Father's sons; we are *māyā's* sons. We do not care for our Father; however, nature is nonetheless working under His direction. If we do not care for Him, nature will reduce her supply, for nature will not allow demons to flourish. As stated in *Bhagavad-gītā* (16.19):

tān ahaṁ dviṣataḥ krūrān
saṁsāreṣu narādhamān
kṣipāmy ajasram aśubhān
āsurīṣv eva yoniṣu

"Those who are envious and mischievous, who are the lowest among men, are cast by Me into the ocean of material existence, into various demoniac species of life."

Demons are always subject to be punished, and great demons like Rāvaṇa and Hiraṇyakaśipu are personally punished by the Lord. Otherwise, ordinary demons are punished by the laws of material nature. Kṛṣṇa does not need to come to punish the petty demons, but when there are great demons like Rāvaṇa, Hiraṇyakaśipu and Kaṁsa, the Lord comes as Lord Rāmacandra, Lord Nṛsiṁhadeva or Śrī Kṛṣṇa to punish them. If we do not want to be punished, we have to follow the rules and regulations (*sad-dharma*). *Dharma* means "the laws given by God." *Dharmaṁ tu sākṣād bhagavat-praṇītam.* The laws are given by Bhagavān and are written in books like *Manu-saṁhitā* and other Vedic literatures. According to the law, we have to obey the government, and according to *dharma*, we have to obey Kṛṣṇa, God. We cannot manufacture our laws at home, and we cannot manufacture *dharma*. If one tries, he is simply cheating the public. Such false *dharmas* are kicked out of *Śrīmad-Bhāgavatam* (1.1.2): *dharmaḥ projjhita.* The real *dharma* is set forth by Śrī Kṛṣṇa when He says: *sarva-dharmān parityajya mām ekaṁ śaraṇaṁ vraja* (Bg. 18.66). All other *dharmas* are simply forms of cheating. We must accept the principles of *Bhagavad-gītā*, which constitute the ABC's of *dharma.* Actually, we only have to accept the principle of surrender unto Kṛṣṇa, but this acceptance comes after many, many births. It is not very easy, for only after many births of struggle does one come to his real perfection and surrender unto Kṛṣṇa. At this time he understands perfectly that Vāsudeva, Kṛṣṇa, is everything. This is the greatest lesson of *Bhagavad-gītā.* Everything is Kṛṣṇa's energy, and whatever we see is but an exhibition of two types of energy. Everyone knows that the sun has two types of energy—heat and light. Similarly, Kṛṣṇa has an external energy and an internal energy, and He also has a marginal energy, which is a mixture of the other two. The external energy is this material world, the internal energy is the spiritual world, and the marginal energy is the living entity. The living entity is marginal because he can remain in the material world or the spiritual world. *Bhagavad-gītā* describes two types of living entities, *kṣara* and *akṣara,* those living in the material world and those in the spiritual world. Those who have fallen into the material world are attracted by the tree of *saṁsāra,* the banyan tree of material existence described in *Bhagavad-gītā* (Fifteenth Chapter).

It is essential that we disassociate ourselves from this tree by detachment. Cutting down this tree is very difficult, but it is possible with the weapon of detachment. There is a Bengali proverb that states: "I'll catch the fish, but I will not touch the water." That type of intelligence is required. In America we see many old men on the beach who have retired from their business to waste their time trying to catch fish. They are not very cautious, and they touch the water. However, we have to live in this material world in such a way that we do everything for Kṛṣṇa but do not touch the water of the material world. In this way, we will have no attachment to things of this material world. We may have many great temples, but we should not be attached to them. It is for Kṛṣṇa's sake that we construct temples, but we must understand that the temples are Kṛṣṇa's property. Our mission is to teach people that everything belongs to Kṛṣṇa. Only a thief will occupy something belonging to another and claim it to be his.

The Kṛṣṇa consciousness movement preaches that everything belongs to Kṛṣṇa and that everything should be utilized for Kṛṣṇa's benefit. He is the beneficiary of everything, and it is to our benefit that we come to this knowledge. *Īśāvāsyam idaṁ sarvam.* If one realizes that everything belongs to Kṛṣṇa, one becomes the greatest *mahātmā.* Being a *mahātmā* does not mean that one wears a big beard and a particular type of dress. No, this awareness must be there. Whatever we have should be offered to Kṛṣṇa. If we have first-class food, we should offer it to Him. If we have nothing, we can offer Him a leaf, a flower, a little water or fruit. This can be collected by anyone anywhere without having to pay money. As Śrī Kṛṣṇa states in *Bhagavad-gītā* (9.26):

patraṁ puṣpaṁ phalaṁ toyaṁ
yo me bhaktyā prayacchati
tad ahaṁ bhakty-upahṛtam
aśnāmi prayatātmanaḥ

"If one offers Me with love and devotion a leaf, a flower, fruit or water, I will accept it."

The point is that we should offer something to Kṛṣṇa with devotion. It is not that Kṛṣṇa is hungry and is asking for food. No, He is feeding everyone, supplying everyone with all the necessities: *eko bahūnāṁ yo vidadhāti kāmān* (*Kaṭha Upaniṣad* 2.2.13). What, then, is He requesting? He is asking for *bhakti*, devotion, because He wants us to love Him. We are suffering in this material world, entangled in the tree of material existence, moving from one branch to another, and because of this we are suffering. Kṛṣṇa does not want us to suffer, jumping like monkeys from branch to branch. We must come to Him and surrender to Him. When we come to this knowledge, we become perfect in knowledge. When we take shelter at the lotus feet of Kṛṣṇa, we are no longer debtors to anyone. *Na kiṅkaro nāyam ṛṇi* (*Bhāg.* 11.5.41). Kṛṣṇa assures us, *ahaṁ tvāṁ sarva-pāpebhyo mokṣayiṣyāmi:* "I'll give you all relief." (Bg. 18.66) This is what we actually want. Therefore Devahūti herein takes shelter of Kapiladeva and tells Him, "You are the ax capable of making me detached." When our attachment to the material world is severed, we become free. *Bhakti* is the means by which we can develop this detachment. *Vairāgya-vidyā-nija-bhakti-yoga. Bhakti-yoga* is the science of detachment. This verse was composed by Sārvabhauma Bhaṭṭācārya when he understood that Lord Śrī Caitanya Mahāprabhu was the Supreme Personality of Godhead. Sārvabhauma Bhaṭṭācārya was a great logician, and he composed a hundred verses to Caitanya Mahāprabhu, wherein he tells the Lord:

vairāgya-vidyā-nija-bhakti-yoga-
śikṣārtham ekaḥ puruṣaḥ purāṇaḥ

śrī-kṛṣṇa-caitanya-śarīra-dhārī
kṛpāmbudhir yas tam ahaṁ prapadye

"Let me take shelter of the Supreme Personality of Godhead, Śrī Kṛṣṇa, who has descended in the form of Lord Caitanya Mahāprabhu to teach us real knowledge, His devotional service, and detachment from whatever does not foster Kṛṣṇa consciousness. He has descended because He is an ocean of transcendental mercy. Let me surrender unto His lotus feet." (Cc. *Madhya* 6.254)

When a person advances in *bhakti-yoga,* he will automatically become detached from material attractions. There are many American and European boys and girls in this Kṛṣṇa consciousness movement who have been born in countries where they can enjoy a good deal of material affluence, but they consider this material happiness and affluence like garbage in the street. Because they are devotees of Vāsudeva, they are no longer attached to these material things. This is the result of *bhakti-yoga,* which enables one to be detached from material enjoyment. That detachment is the sign that one is advancing in *bhakti-yoga. Bhaktiḥ pareśānubhavo viraktir anyatra ca* (*Bhāg.* 11.2.42). That is the test of advancing in *bhakti.* If we are advanced, we are no longer attached to material enjoyment. It is not that we think ourselves great devotees and then go ahead and enjoy material things. As stated in *Bhagavad-gītā* (5.22):

ye hi saṁsparśajā bhogā
duḥkha-yonaya eva te
ādy-antavantaḥ kaunteya
na teṣu ramate budhaḥ

"An intelligent person does not take part in the sources of misery, which are due to contact with the material senses. O son of Kuntī, such pleasures have a beginning and an end, and so the wise man does not delight in them." When one sees something superior, he immediately rejects that which is inferior. Actually we cannot bring all this about by our own endeavor; therefore we have to take shelter of Kṛṣṇa, and He will help. Since our only business is to take shelter of Kṛṣṇa, Devahūti says, "I am taking shelter of You so that You can cut my attachment to this material life. Why should You do this? Because I am Your eternal servant."

Bhaktivinoda Ṭhākura says, *anādi karama-phale, paḍi' bhavārṇava-jale, taribāre nā dekhi upāya.* If we are thrown into the ocean, there is a great struggle, even if we may be very great swimmers. There is no peace in this material world, however expert we may be in dealing with it. There is nothing but struggle. We cannot live here peacefully. It is not possible. Even if we are nonviolent and hurt no one, there will be trouble. However, if somehow or other we manage to reach the shore, we will find peace. There is peace even if we are an inch out of the water. *Tava pāda-paṅkaja-sthita-dhūlī sadṛśaṁ vicintaya* (*Śikṣāṣṭaka* 5). If somehow or other we become one of the particles of dust at Kṛṣṇa's lotus feet, we will be liberated.

We may be a Hindu or a Muslim or a Christian for fifty or sixty years, or at the utmost one hundred, but again we have to take birth and be something else. We are thinking in terms of these religious designations, which are called *asad-dharma,* meaning that they may change at any moment. But what is our real *dharma?* Real *dharma* is *sad-dharma,* that which will not change, and this *sad-dharma* necessitates surrendering unto Kṛṣṇa. This *dharma* will continue eternally. There are many propounders of *sad-dharma,* but actually the Supreme Personality of Godhead is the best propounder because He knows the reality. It is therefore said of the Gosvāmīs: *nānā-śāstra-vicāraṇaika-nipuṇau sad-dharma-saṁsthāpakau.* Śrī Caitanya Mahāprabhu's direct disciples, the Gosvāmīs, tried to establish *sad-dharma,* and we are trying to follow in their footsteps by establishing real *dharma* throughout the world with this Kṛṣṇa consciousness movement.

CHAPTER SEVEN

Lord Kapila Begins to Explain Self-realization

TEXT 12

maitreya uvāca
iti sva-mātur niravadyam īpsitaṁ
niśamya puṁsām apavarga-vardhanam
dhiyābhinandyātmavatāṁ satāṁ gatir
babhāṣa īṣat-smita-śobhitānanaḥ

TRANSLATION

After hearing of His mother's uncontaminated desire for transcendental realization, the Lord thanked her within Himself for her questions, and thus, His face smiling, He explained the path of the transcendentalists, who are interested in self-realization.

PURPORT

Devahūti has surrendered her confession of material entanglement and her desire to gain release. Her questions to Lord Kapila are very interesting for persons who are actually trying to get liberation from material entanglement and attain perfection. Unless one is interested in understanding his spiritual life, or his constitutional position, and unless he also feels inconvenience in material existence, his human form of life is spoiled. Only a foolish man does not care for the transcendental necessities of life and simply engages like an animal in eating, sleeping, defending and mating. Lord Kapila was very much satisfied by His mother's questions because the answers stimulate one's desire for liberation from the conditional life of material existence. Such questions are called *apavarga-vardhanam.* Those who are actually spiritually interested are called *sat,* or devotees. *Satāṁ prasaṅgāt. Sat* means "that which eternally exists," and *asat* means "that which is not eternal." Unless one is situated on the spiritual platform, he is not *sat;* he is *asat.* The *asat* stands on a platform which will not exist, but anyone who stands on the spiritual platform will exist eternally. As spirit soul, everyone exists eternally, but the *asat* has accepted the material world as his shelter, and therefore he is full of anxiety. *Asad-grāhān,* the desire to enjoy matter, is the cause of the soul's being *asat.* Actually, the spirit soul is not *asat.* As soon as one is conscious of this fact and takes to Kṛṣṇa consciousness, he becomes *sat. Satāṁ gatiḥ,* the path of the eternal, is very interesting to persons who are after liberation, and His Lordship Kapila began to speak about that path.

Those who are *sat* are thus transcendentalists advanced in spiritual life, and when they hear questions from those who want to understand spiritual life, they become very happy. Transcendentalists are not interested in worldly talks. Indeed, worldly talks are very disgusting to them, and they avoid the company of those who talk about nonsensical worldly affairs. Śrī Caitanya Mahāprabhu advised His disciples: *grāmya-kathā nā śunibe.* The word *grāmya* refers to that pertaining to one's village, society or neighborhood. People are interested in talking about *grāmya-kathā.* Newspapers, for instance, are filled with *grāmya-kathā.* There is no spiritual understanding in them. In the United States there are many newspapers, and simply to publish the *New York Times* many trees have to be killed. Now there is a paper scarcity. Why are they uselessly killing trees just for *grāmya-kathā?* They are only interested in making a profit.

There is, however, another kind of *kathā—kṛṣṇa-kathā.* There are literatures which may be nicely presented from the literary point of view, but if there is no glorification of the Supreme Lord, they are useless.

na yad vacaś citra-padaṁ harer yaśo
jagat-pavitraṁ pragṛṇīta karhicit
tad vāyasaṁ tīrtham uśanti mānasā
na yatra haṁsā niramanty uśikkṣayāḥ

"Those words which do not describe the glories of the Lord, who alone can sanctify the atmosphere of the whole universe, are considered by saintly persons to be like unto a pilgrimage for crows. Since the all-perfect persons are inhabitants of the transcendental abode, they do not derive any pleasure there." (*Bhāg.* 1.5.10)

Worldly literatures are like places where crows take pleasure. In the bird society, there are crows and swans, and crows are interested in places where filthy things are thrown. However, swans prefer nice clear water with lotus flowers, and it is in such places that they take their pleasure. Similarly, there are men who are like crows and men like swans. That is a natural division. According to an old English proverb, Birds of a feather flock together. Crows mix with crows, and swans mix with swans. Since devotees are like swans (*haṁsas*), a most advanced devotee is called *paramahaṁsa.* The *paramahaṁsas* are not interested in subjects fit for crows. A person who is interested in inquiring about transcendental subjects, *kṛṣṇa-kathā,* makes a *paramahaṁsa* very glad. Therefore Kapiladeva was very glad to hear that His mother was eager to receive information on how to be delivered from material bondage:

atha me deva sammoham
apākraṣṭuṁ tvam arhasi
yo 'vagraho 'haṁ mametīty
etasmin yojitas tvayā

"Now be pleased, my Lord, to dispel my great delusion. Due to my feeling of false ego, I have been engaged by Your *māyā* and have identified myself with the body and consequent bodily relations." (*Bhāg.* 3.25.10)

Caitanya Mahāprabhu advised His disciples never to eat palatable food, never to talk about village topics and never to read ordinary novels, poems and newspapers. One may ask, "How is it that in the modern age these Europeans and Americans of the Kṛṣṇa consciousness movement do not take interest in newspapers?" Newspapers are very popular in the West. Each day the papers are published in three or four editions, and they are all selling. However, these American boys and girls who have come to Kṛṣṇa consciousness have stopped reading newspapers. They do not know what is happening from day to day, and it does not matter. All of this is a waste of time. It is better that they read literatures like *Śrīmad-Bhāgavatam* and *Bhagavad-gītā.* Why waste one's valuable time?

Kapiladeva was very glad that His mother was interested only in spiritual advancement. This material world is called *pavarga*, and to nullify it is called *apavarga*. In this material world, people are laboring very hard simply to earn some money. This creates a hellish situation, and this is the way of material life. People have become so dull that they do not understand the meaning of liberation. They have become just like animals. If an animal is informed that there is such a thing as liberation, how will he understand it? It is not possible. Similarly, at the present moment, human beings have become exactly like animals. They do not know the meaning of *apavarga*, liberation. Yet there was a time when people understood that human life was meant for *apavarga*. The questions are raised by Devahūti, and the answers are given by Kapiladeva. That is *apavarga-vardhanam*. As far as material maintenance is concerned, the *śāstras* never stress it. Rather, they say that one's maintenance will come automatically. God gives food to animals, birds and aquatics. Why should He not give it to one who is interested in *apavarga?* Unfortunately people have no faith, and therefore good association is required.

People should not waste their time associating with crows; they should associate with swans. When garbage is thrown out, crows and dogs come to see what is there, but no sane man will go. Those who are interested in trying to get pleasure out of this material world are actually chewing the chewed. *Punaḥ punaś carvita-carvaṇānām* (*Bhāg.* 7.5.30). If one picks up a piece of sugarcane which has already been chewed, he is a fool. We must know that the juice has already been taken out of that sugarcane. What will one get by chewing it? However, there are animals who are simply interested in chewing the chewed. Material life means chewing the chewed. A father educates his son to earn a livelihood, get married and settle down, but he himself already knows that by doing this he has not become satisfied. Why, then, is he engaging his son in this same business? A real father is one who does not allow his son to chew the chewed. *Pitā na sa syāj jananī na sā syāt . . . na mocayed yaḥ samupeta-mṛtyum:* one should not become a father or a mother unless one is able to save his children from the impending clutches of death. (*Bhāg.* 5.5.18) That is the duty of the father and mother. How can this be done? A father and mother should educate their son in Kṛṣṇa consciousness. Then he can be saved. They should educate the son in such a way that there is no *pavarga.* If we do not go forward to liberation, we promote a civilization of cats and dogs. Eating, sleeping, mating, defending, fearing and dying are all experienced by cats and dogs, but human life is meant for another purpose. Of course we have to maintain the body; it is not that we should neglect it. But we should not unnecessarily engage in the maintenance of the body.

yasyātma-buddhiḥ kuṇape tri-dhātuke
sva-dhīḥ kalatrādiṣu bhauma ijya-dhīḥ
yat tīrtha-buddhiḥ salile na karhicij
janeṣv abhijñeṣu sa eva go-kharaḥ

"A human being who identifies this body made of three elements as the self, who considers the by-products of the body to be his kinsmen, who considers the land of his birth as worshipable, and who goes to a place of pilgrimage simply to take a bath rather than meet men of transcendental knowledge there, is to be considered like a cow or an ass." (*Bhāg.* 10.84.13)

From the *Vedas* we can receive education of all kinds. On a mango tree, there are ripened mangoes and green mangoes. The *Śrīmad-Bhāgavatam* is the ripened mango of the desire tree of Vedic knowledge: *nigama-kalpa-taror galitaṁ phalam.* If the mango is tasted by the parrot, it becomes doubly tasty. The word *śuka* means parrot, and Śukadeva Gosvāmī spoke *Śrīmad-Bhāgavatam.* It is therefore more relishable from his lips.

nigama-kalpa-taror galitaṁ phalaṁ
śuka-mukhād amṛta-drava-saṁyutam
pibata bhāgavataṁ rasam ālayaṁ
muhur aho rasikā bhuvi bhāvukāḥ

"O expert and thoughtful men, relish *Śrīmad-Bhāgavatam,* the mature fruit of the desire tree of Vedic literatures. It emanated from the lips of Śrī Śukadeva Gosvāmī. Therefore this fruit has become even more tasteful, although its nectarean juice was already relishable for all, including liberated souls." (*Bhāg.* 1.1.3) It is regrettable that in India, where these literatures are available, people are not interested. They are interested in Marxist literature but not *Śrīmad-Bhāgavatam,* and this is India's misfortune.

When a student hears spiritual subjects attentively, the spiritual master becomes very happy. Kapiladeva was very happy to see His mother eager to understand spiritual subject matters. He therefore thanked His mother for her inquiry.

Generally people are interested in things that give immediate pleasure. We want to taste something tasty to the tongue, regardless of whether it is edible or not. Hogs very readily eat stool, and they do so without discrimination. They have no idea of *tapasya*, penance. When one engages in spiritual realization, one has to undergo *tapasya*. However, this has been made very easy by Caitanya Mahāprabhu. *Ceto-darpaṇa-mārjanaṁ bhava-mahā-dāvāgni-nirvāpaṇam.* All we have to do is spare a little time and chant Hare Kṛṣṇa, but we are not even ready for this much *tapasya*. Kṛṣṇa is more interested in leading us down the path of liberation than we are in going. He has given us a very simple method: *harer nāma harer nāma harer nāmaiva kevalam.* We need only chant Hare Kṛṣṇa. To perfect this chanting of Hare Kṛṣṇa, there is no hard-and-fast rule. Simply by chanting, we will attain perfection. Being contaminated by Kali-yuga, however, we are unfortunate and therefore we have no attraction to the holy names of Kṛṣṇa. Thus when Kapiladeva or His representative sees someone a little interested, he becomes very glad and thanks him. When Kapiladeva saw His mother interested, He thanked her from within, not openly.

Kapiladeva was very glad, and He began to speak. Kapiladeva was an incarnation of God and was a young boy; therefore His face was very beautiful. When He answered this question, He became even more beautiful, and He smiled because He was pleased at His mother's question. Kṛṣṇa is also very beautiful, but when a devotee serves Him and comes to Him, He becomes even more beautiful. When a devotee with all his heart and soul serves Kṛṣṇa, dresses Him in nice garments and gives Him a flower, Kṛṣṇa smiles. If you can get Kṛṣṇa to smile upon you just once, your life's goal is fulfilled.

Thus smiling, Kapiladeva began to enlighten His mother.

TEXT 13

śrī-bhagavān uvāca
yoga ādhyātmikaḥ puṁsāṁ

mato niḥśreyasāya me
atyantoparatir yatra
duḥkhasya ca sukhasya ca

TRANSLATION

The Personality of Godhead answered: That yoga system which relates to the Lord and the individual soul, which is meant for the ultimate benefit of the living entity, and which causes detachment from all happiness and distress in the material world, is the highest yoga system.

PURPORT

In the material world, everyone is striving for some material happiness, but as soon as we get some material happiness, there is also material distress. In the material world one cannot have unadulterated happiness. Any kind of happiness one has is contaminated by distress also. For example, if we want to drink milk, we have to bother to maintain a cow and keep her fit to supply milk. Drinking milk is very nice; it is also pleasure. But for the sake of drinking milk one has to accept so much trouble. The *yoga* system, as here stated by the Lord, is meant to end all material happiness and material distress. The best *yoga*, as taught in *Bhagavad-gītā* by Kṛṣṇa, is *bhakti-yoga*. It is also mentioned in the *Gītā* that one should try to be tolerant and not be disturbed by material happiness or distress. Of course, one may say that he is not disturbed by material happiness, but he does not know that just after one enjoys so-called material happiness, material distress will follow. This is the law of the material world. Lord Kapila states that the *yoga* system is the science of the spirit. One practices *yoga* in order to attain perfection on the spiritual platform. There is no question of material happiness or distress. It is transcendental. Lord Kapila will eventually explain how it is transcendental, but the preliminary introduction is given here.

The attempt in this material world to maximize happiness and minimize distress is called the struggle for existence. Generally *yoga* is practiced to acquire some material profit. There are eight kinds of yogic perfection (*siddhis*): *aṇimā, laghimā, prāpti, īśitva, vaśitva, mahimā, prākāmya* and *kāmāvasāyitā.* A real *yogī* can become smaller than the smallest, lighter than the lightest and bigger than the biggest. Whatever he wants he can produce immediately in his hand. He can even create a planet. These are some of the *yoga-siddhis*, but here it is stated that the supreme *yoga* system does not aim at material happiness or relief from distresses caused by material inconvenience. Everyone is trying to get out of material distress and gain some happiness. In any case, when something is material, there is only so-called happiness and so-called distress. For instance, there may be fireworks going on, and this may be happiness for someone but distress for us. Some people are thinking that these fireworks are very enjoyable, and we are thinking that they are very inconvenient. That is the material world. On one side there is happiness, and on the other side there is distress. Both happiness and distress are actually illusions. In summer, water is happiness, but in winter it is distress. The water is the same, but at one time it brings happiness and at another time it brings distress. When a son is born, he brings happiness, but when he dies, he brings distress. In either case, the son is the same.

This material world is the world of duality, and we cannot understand happiness without distress or distress without happiness. This is therefore called the relative world. Spiritual happiness is above these dualities, and that spiritual happiness is the perfection of *yoga*. *Yoga ādhyātmikaḥ*. *Yoga* is the happiness of the soul, and the individual soul can be happy when it is with the Supersoul, the Supreme Soul. *Nityo nityānāṁ cetanaś cetanānām*. There is the Supreme Soul, or the supreme living being, and there are many individual souls, individual beings. We are many, but the principal living being is one, Kṛṣṇa. He is the fire, and we are the sparks from that fire. The sparks are illuminated when they are with the original fire, but if the sparks no longer associate with the original fire, they are extinguished. Similarly, our real happiness is in enjoying with the Supreme Being. Happiness is being in His company. Kṛṣṇa is not alone, but is always with His friends, either the *gopīs* or the cowherd boys, or with His mother and father. We never find Kṛṣṇa alone. He may be with Rādhārāṇī or with His devotees. He is like a king or president. When one says that the king or president is coming, it is understood that he is not coming alone. He comes with His secretaries, ministers and many others.

The word *yoga* means "connection," and *ātmā* means "soul" and sometimes "mind" or "body." The material body has nothing to do with the Supreme Being because the Supreme Being is completely spiritual. He has no material covering. One who thinks that Kṛṣṇa, the Supreme Being, has a material covering is himself covered by *māyā.* Kṛṣṇa does not say that He comes as an ordinary living being. Rather, His advent is totally transcendental. *Janma karma ca me divyam evaṁ yo vetti tattvataḥ* (Bg. 4.4). We therefore have to learn how Kṛṣṇa takes His birth, which is not ordinary. If it were ordinary, why should we observe the Janmāṣṭamī ceremony? His birth is *divyam,* divine. Everything about Kṛṣṇa is divine, and if we think that Kṛṣṇa is like us, we immediately become *mūḍhas,* fools. In the words of *Bhagavad-gītā* (9.11):

avajānanti māṁ mūḍhā
mānuṣīṁ tanum āśritam
paraṁ bhāvam ajānanto
mama bhūta-maheśvaram

"Fools deride Me when I descend in the human form. They do not know My transcendental nature and My supreme dominion over all that be."

Actually Kṛṣṇa is the original Supreme Being, the original spirit soul. We are simply minute parts and parcels of Kṛṣṇa. If we connect with Kṛṣṇa, we are illuminated just as Kṛṣṇa is illuminated. If we fall down from Kṛṣṇa, our spiritual power and illumination are extinguished. The word *yoga* means connecting or linking with that original source. *Yoga* is the Sanskrit word meaning "connection," and *viyoga* means "disconnection."

Kapiladeva is referred to as Bhagavān, the Supreme Personality of Godhead. Bhagavān makes no mistakes. *Nārāyaṇaḥ paro 'vyaktāt:* even Śaṅkarācārya says that "Bhagavān, Nārāyaṇa, does not belong to this material world." When we speak of Bhagavān, or when the *śāstras* refer to Bhagavān, we refer to Him who is above material understanding. As stated here, *śrī-bhagavān uvāca.* It does not say *vyāsadeva uvāca* or *kapiladeva uvāca.* Similarly, in *Bhagavad-gītā,* Vyāsadeva says, *śrī-bhagavān uvāca. Bhagavān* refers to Him who is above the defects of this material world. Bhagavān is not subject to the four deficiencies of the living entities. Being imperfect, living entities are illusioned and subject to commit mistakes. They also have the tendency to cheat others. When one who has no knowledge tries to become a teacher or preacher, he is actually cheating others. Since we ourselves do not possess perfect knowledge, we simply try to teach what Śrī Bhagavān says. We do not manufacture our own teachings. So-called scholars and learned men manufacture their own teachings and give their opinions. In the West especially, we find much philosophical speculation and mental gymnastics, but such philosophy can never be perfect. We have to take our ideas from Bhagavān; then they will be perfect. We read *Bhagavad-gītā* because it is perfect. There is no mistake in it; there is no illusion in it; there is no cheating in it. Nor is it delivered by one whose senses are imperfect. Kṛṣṇa says in *Bhagavad-gītā* (7.26):

vedāhaṁ samatītāni
vartamānāni cārjuna
bhaviṣyāṇi ca bhūtāni
māṁ tu veda na kaścana

"O Arjuna, as the Supreme Personality of Godhead, I know everything that has happened in the past, all that is happening in the present, and all things that are yet to come. I also know all living entities; but Me no one knows."

God knows everything, but we do not know what is God. That is our position. Our position is not knowing. *Īśvaraḥ sarva-bhūtānāṁ hṛd-deśe 'rjuna tiṣṭhati* (Bg. 18.61). *Īśvara*, God, Kṛṣṇa, is situated in everyone's heart. *Sarvasya cāhaṁ hṛdi sanniviṣṭaḥ:* "I have entered into everyone's heart." (Bg. 15.15) The Supreme Lord refers not only to the hearts of human beings but to those of animals and everything else.

aṇḍāntara-stha-paramāṇu-cayāntara-sthaṁ
govindam ādi-puruṣaṁ tam ahaṁ bhajāmi
(*Brahma-saṁhitā* 5.35)

The Supreme Lord is within the atom as Paramātmā, and therefore He is also within the individual soul. Being within everything, He knows everything. Since He knows everything, we have to take lessons from Him. If we take what Bhagavān says as perfect knowledge, we receive perfect knowledge. For receiving this knowledge, there is a disciplic succession (*paramparā*), which is described in *Bhagavad-gītā* (4.2):

evaṁ paramparā-prāptam
imaṁ rājarṣayo viduḥ

"This supreme science was thus received through the chain of disciplic succession, and the saintly kings understood it in that way." This Kṛṣṇa consciousness philosophy is very easy because we do not manufacture ideas. We take the ideas and the words delivered by the Supreme Person, Kṛṣṇa, or His incarnation or representative. His representative does not say anything which Kṛṣṇa Himself does not say. It is very easy to be a representative, but one cannot be a representative of Kṛṣṇa if one tries to interpret Kṛṣṇa's words in a whimsical way.

There is no authority superior to Śrī Kṛṣṇa, and if we stick to this principle, we can become *gurus.* We don't need to change our position to become a *guru.* All we have to do is follow in the disciplic succession stemming from Śrī Kṛṣṇa. Caitanya Mahāprabhu has advised: *āmāra ājñāya guru hañā tāra' ei deśa* (Cc. *Madhya* 7.128). Caitanya Mahāprabhu instructed people to learn from Him and then go teach people within their own villages. One may think, "I am illiterate and have no education. I was not born in a very high family. How can I become a *guru?*" Caitanya Mahāprabhu says that it is not very difficult. *Yāre dekha, tāre kaha 'kṛṣṇa'-upadeśa:* "Simply speak whatever Kṛṣṇa speaks. Then you become a *guru.*" Whoever speaks what Kṛṣṇa has not spoken is not a *guru* but a rascal. A *guru* only speaks what Kṛṣṇa has spoken. This is the śāstric injunction.

ṣaṭ-karma-nipuṇo vipro
mantra-tantra-viśāradaḥ
avaiṣṇavo gurur na syād
vaiṣṇavaḥ śva-paco guruḥ

"A scholarly *brāhmaṇa* expert in all subjects of Vedic knowledge is unfit to become a spiritual master without being a Vaiṣṇava, but a person born in a family of a lower class can become a spiritual master if he is a Vaiṣṇava." (*Padma Purāṇa*)

People are in darkness, and they have to be enlightened. We have finally come from the animal kingdom to the human form, and now this human form gives us the opportunity to get out of the cycle of birth and death. The mission of this Kṛṣṇa consciousness society is to awaken people to their original consciousness. *Jīva jāga, jīva jāga, gorācānda bale.* The word *gorācānda* refers to Caitanya Mahāprabhu, who tells the living entity, "Get up! Get up! How long will you continue to sleep?" *Kata nidrā yāo māyā-piśācīra kole.* The same is stated here. It is the prime business of human beings to connect again with the Supreme Soul. The purpose of *yoga* is to awaken to Kṛṣṇa consciousness and connect oneself again with Kṛṣṇa. That is *ādhyātmika-yoga. Yoga* does not mean showing some mystic magic. The supreme *yogī* is described by Śrī Kṛṣṇa Himself in *Bhagavad-gītā* (6.47):

yoginām api sarveṣāṁ
mad-gatenāntarātmanā
śraddhāvān bhajate yo māṁ
sa me yuktatamo mataḥ

"And of all *yogīs*, he who always abides in Me with great faith, worshiping Me in transcendental loving service, is most intimately united with Me in *yoga* and is the highest of all."

There are many *yogīs* and many different types of *yoga* systems, and all of these are discussed in *Bhagavad-gītā*. There is *haṭha-yoga, karma-yoga, jñāna-yoga* and *rāja-yoga;* however, the real *yoga* system is meant for reviving our connection with Kṛṣṇa. Here it is said: *yoga ādhyātmikaḥ puṁsām. Ādhyātmikaḥ:* we are living entities, souls. It is not that we are disconnected from Kṛṣṇa, but we have simply forgotten Him. It is not possible to be disconnected, but it is possible to be covered. In the words of Kṛṣṇa in *Bhagavad-gītā* (7.25):

nāhaṁ prakāśaḥ sarvasya
yogamāyā-samāvṛtaḥ
mūḍho 'yaṁ nābhijānāti
loko mām ajam avyayam

"I am never manifest to the foolish and unintelligent. For them I am covered by My eternal creative potency [*yogamāyā*]; and so the deluded world knows Me not, who am unborn and infallible."

There is *yoga*, and there is *yogamāyā*. *Yogamāyā* means forgetfulness. First of all we have to understand what is the soul. At the present moment, people are in such darkness that they do not even understand the soul. Therefore *Bhagavad-gītā* (2.13) first of all teaches what the soul is:

dehino 'smin yathā dehe
kaumāraṁ yauvanaṁ jarā
tathā dehāntara-prāptir
dhīras tatra na muhyati

"As the embodied soul continually passes in this body from boyhood to youth to old age, the soul similarly passes into another body at death. The self-realized soul is not bewildered by such a change." The word *dehī* means "the proprietor of the body." We are thinking, "I am this body," but actually this is not so. We are the proprietors of the body, and that is the real understanding of the self. We do not say, "I am this finger" or "I am this hand." Rather, we say, "This is my finger, this is my head, this is my leg, etc." Similarly, the same can be said about the entire body. "This is *my* body." This means that I am the proprietor of this body. The body has been given by *māyā*, the material energy.

prakṛteḥ kriyamāṇāni
guṇaiḥ karmāṇi sarvaśaḥ
ahaṅkāra-vimūḍhātmā
kartāham iti manyate

"The bewildered spirit soul, under the influence of the three modes of material nature, thinks himself to be the doer of activities that are in actuality carried out by nature." (Bg. 3.27)

The living entity receives different types of bodies according to *karma*. One living entity may receive a cat body, another a dog body, and so forth. Why are there so many different bodies? Why not one kind of body? The answer to this is also given in *Bhagavad-gītā* (13.22):

kāraṇaṁ guṇa-saṅgo 'sya
sad-asad-yoni-janmasu

"It is due to his association with the modes of material nature. Thus he meets with good and evil among various species."

Because the soul within the body associates with the three modes of material nature (goodness, passion and ignorance), he receives different types of bodies. One doesn't have to aspire for his next body; one need only rest assured that it will be a different body. On the other hand, Kṛṣṇa does not say what kind of body one will be awarded. That depends on qualification. If one associates with the mode of goodness, he is elevated to the higher planetary systems. If he associates with the mode of passion, he remains here. And if one associates with the mode of ignorance and darkness, he goes down to lower life forms—animals, trees and plants. This is the proclamation of Śrī Kṛṣṇa in *Bhagavad-gītā* (14.18):

ūrdhvaṁ gacchanti sattva-sthā
madhye tiṣṭhanti rājasāḥ
jaghanya-guṇa-vṛtti-sthā
adho gacchanti tāmasāḥ

"Those situated in the mode of goodness gradually go upward to the higher planets; those in the mode of passion live on the earthly planets; and those in the mode of ignorance go down to the hellish worlds."

There are 8,400,000 species of life, and all of these arise from one's association with the modes of nature (*kāraṇaṁ guṇa-saṅgo 'sya*). And, according to the body, one undergoes distress and happiness. One cannot expect a dog to enjoy the same happiness that a king or rich man enjoys. Whether one enjoys this or that happiness or suffers this or that distress, both distress and happiness are due to the material body. *Yoga* means transcending the distress or happiness of the material body. If we connect ourselves with Kṛṣṇa through the supreme *yoga*, we can get rid of material happiness and distress arising from the body. Reconnecting with Kṛṣṇa is called *bhakti-yoga*, and Kṛṣṇa comes to instruct us in this supreme *yoga*. In essence, He says, "Just revive your connection with Me, you rascal. Give up all these manufactured *yogas* and religions and just surrender unto Me." That is Kṛṣṇa's instruction, and Kṛṣṇa's representative, the incarnation or the *guru*, says the same thing. Although Kapiladeva is an incarnation of Kṛṣṇa, He acts as the representative of

Kṛṣṇa, the *guru.* If we just accept the principle of surrender unto Kṛṣṇa, we will become actually transcendental to so-called material happiness. We should not be captivated by material happiness or aggrieved by material distress. These are causes for bondage. Material happiness is not actual happiness. It is actually distress. We try to be happy by obtaining money, but money is not very easily obtained, and we have to undergo a great deal of distress to get it. However, we accept this distress with the hope of getting some false happiness. If we purify our senses, on the other hand, we can come to the spiritual platform. Real happiness lies in engaging our senses to satisfy the senses of Kṛṣṇa. In this way our senses are spiritualized, and this is called *ādhyātmika-yoga* or *bhakti-yoga.* This is the *yoga* that Lord Kapiladeva is herein expounding.

CHAPTER EIGHT

Bhakti-yoga: The Supreme Yoga System

TEXT 14

tam imaṁ te pravakṣyāmi
yam avocaṁ purānaghe
ṛṣīṇāṁ śrotu-kāmānāṁ
yogaṁ sarvāṅga-naipuṇam

TRANSLATION

O most pious mother, I shall now explain unto you the ancient yoga system, which I explained formerly to the great sages. It is serviceable and practical in every way.

PURPORT

The Lord does not manufacture a new system of *yoga*. Sometimes it is claimed that someone has become an incarnation of God and is expounding a new theological aspect of the Absolute Truth. But here we find that although Kapila Muni is the Lord Himself and is capable of manufacturing a new doctrine for His mother, He nevertheless says, "I shall just explain the ancient system that I once explained to the great sages because they were also anxious to hear about it." When we have a superexcellent process already present in Vedic scriptures, there is no need to concoct a new system, to mislead the innocent public. At present it has become a fashion to reject the standard system and present something bogus in the name of a newly invented process of *yoga*.

The supreme ancient system of *yoga* pertains to the soul. Presently, in America especially, *haṭha-yoga* is very popular. It appeals to fat ladies who go to the classes to reduce and keep their digestive systems regular.

Many people are interested in this kind of gymnastic *yoga*, but real *yoga* is *ādhyātmika*. *Ādhyātmika* means to awaken the soul to his proper position. The soul is *puruṣa*, spirit, and his business is to reconnect his lost relationship with Kṛṣṇa.

Herein Kapiladeva says that He previously delivered this *yoga* system to the great *ṛṣis*, the great sages. This is the process of *śravaṇa*, hearing. One must be very eager to hear, for spiritual life begins with hearing.

ataḥ śrī-kṛṣṇa-nāmādi
na bhaved grāhyam indriyaiḥ
sevonmukhe hi jihvādau
svayam eva sphuraty adaḥ
(*Bhakti-rasāmṛta-sindu* 1.2.234)

It is thus stated in the *śāstras* that it is not possible to appreciate or understand Kṛṣṇa with our blunt material senses. Kṛṣṇa's name, form, qualities, pastimes, paraphernalia and abode are all part and parcel of Kṛṣṇa. However, understanding Kṛṣṇa begins with hearing and chanting His name. Then there is His form. Generally, for the neophyte, these items are essential—to hear His name and qualities and see and worship His form. That is Kṛṣṇa's personal instruction:

man-manā bhava mad-bhakto
mad-yājī māṁ namaskuru

"Engage your mind always in thinking of Me, offer obeisances and worship Me." (Bg. 9.34)

Bhagavān Śrī Kṛṣṇa is present in the temple Deity, and even if a child comes to offer his respects, he is counted as a devotee. A small child may not know anything, but simply by seeing the Deity, chanting and dancing, he is benefited. Temples are meant to give everyone a chance to advance in Kṛṣṇa consciousness one step at a time.

svalpam apy asya dharmasya
trāyate mahato bhayāt

"A little advancement on this path can protect one from the most dangerous type of fear." (Bg. 2.40) Even if we do a little on the path of *bhakti*, it goes to our account. For instance, if we deposit only two dollars in a savings bank, it is kept in our account, and it will increase with interest. Similarly, if one performs even a little devotional service, it is not lost. One may come and join this Kṛṣṇa consciousness movement, render some service and after a while fall down. However, whatever service has been rendered is to one's permanent credit. That will never be lost. When one begins again, he begins at the point where he has left off. This is the instruction of *Bhagavad-gītā* (6.41):

śucīnāṁ śrīmatāṁ gehe
yoga-bhraṣṭo 'bhijāyate

"The unsuccessful *yogī* is born into a family of righteous people or into a family of rich aristocracy." Thus if one fails to perfect his *bhakti-yoga*, he is given another chance in the next life. According to a Bengali poem:

śuci haya muci haya yadi kṛṣṇa tyāje
muci haya śuci haya yadi kṛṣṇa-bhaje

If one takes to Kṛṣṇa consciousness, even if he is born in a family of a cobbler (*muci*), he becomes greater than a *brāhmaṇa* (*śuci*). However, if one is born in a *brāhmaṇa* family and gives up Kṛṣṇa consciousness, he becomes a *muci*, a cobbler. Thus the door of devotion is open to everyone, whoever he may be. Kṛṣṇa Himself says that regardless of one's position, if one takes shelter of Him, one can approach the supreme destination.

māṁ hi pārtha vyapāśritya
ye 'pi syuḥ pāpa-yonayaḥ
striyo vaiśyās tathā śūdrās
te 'pi yānti parāṁ gatiṁ

"O son of Pṛthā, those who take shelter in Me, though they be of lower birth—women, *vaiśyas* [merchants], as well as *śūdras* [workers]—can approach the supreme destination." (Bg. 9.32) And Śukadeva Gosvāmī says:

kirāta-hūṇāndhra-pulinda-pulkaśā
ābhīra-śumbhā yavanāḥ khasādayaḥ
ye 'nye ca pāpā yad-apāśrayāśrayāḥ
śudhyanti tasmai prabhaviṣṇave namaḥ

"Kirāta, Hūṇa, Āndhra, Pulinda, Pulkaśa, Ābhīra, Śumbha, Yavana and the Khasa races and even others who are addicted to sinful acts can be purified by taking shelter of the devotees of the Lord, due to His being the supreme power. I beg to offer my respectful obeisances unto Him." (*Bhāg.* 2.4.18) Kṛṣṇa consciousness is so complete that it is all-embracing. Everyone has an occupational duty as a *brāhmaṇa, kṣatriya, vaiśya* or *śūdra*, but one does not have to give up his occupational duty to take to Kṛṣṇa consciousness. And if one takes to Kṛṣṇa consciousness but does not succeed, what has he lost? Even if he falls down, there is no loss. On the other hand, if a man perfectly performs his own duties (*sva-dharma*) but is not Kṛṣṇa conscious, what does he gain? There is actually no gain. Kapiladeva explains that once one takes to the path of *bhakti-yoga*, one never actually falls down. Once begun, *bhakti-yoga* continues, even if one temporarily falls down. One is given another chance by taking birth in a good family, either in a wealthy family, a learned family or a *brāhmaṇa* family. If one executes his duties as a *brāhmaṇa*, Viṣṇu will be very pleased, and if one executes his duties perfectly as a *kṣatriya* or *śūdra*, Viṣṇu will also be very pleased. One does not have to change one's position. In *Bhagavad-gītā* (18.46) Śrī Kṛṣṇa says that every man can become perfect by following his qualities of work:

yataḥ pravṛttir bhūtānāṁ
yena sarvam idaṁ tatam
sva-karmaṇā tam abhyarcya
siddhiṁ vindati mānavaḥ

"By worship of the Lord, who is the source of all beings and who is all-pervading, man can, in the performance of his own duty, attain perfection." Thus if one executes his duties as a perfect *kṣatriya, vaiśya, śūdra* or whatever, Viṣṇu will be pleased. The purpose of work is to please

Viṣṇu. Unfortunately, people have forgotten this. *Varṇāśrama-dharma*, the Vedic system of society, is therefore very important in that it is meant to give human beings a chance to perfect their lives by pleasing Kṛṣṇa. Unfortunately, the *varṇāśrama-dharma* has been lost in this age. Therefore Caitanya Mahāprabhu, just to give relief to the rotting, conditioned souls of this age of Kali-yuga, has given us the *mahā-mantra.*

harer nāma harer nāma
harer nāmaiva kevalam
kalau nāsty eva nāsty eva
nāsty eva gatir anyathā

"In this age of quarrel and hypocrisy, the only means of deliverance is chanting of the holy name of the Lord. There is no other way. There is no other way. There is no other way." (*Bṛhan-nāradīya Purāṇa*) Although we may try to revive the perfect *varṇāśrama* system, it is not possible in this age. People are fallen, distúrbed and unfortunate:

prāyeṇālpāyuṣaḥ sabhya
kalāv asmin yuge janāḥ
mandāḥ sumanda-matayo
manda-bhāgyā hy upadrutāḥ

"O learned one, in this iron age of Kali men have but short lives. They are quarrelsome, lazy, misguided, unlucky and, above all, always disturbed." (*Bhāg.* 1.1.10) In this age, there will be insufficient rainfall and food, and the government will plunder one's income by heavy taxation. All of these characteristics of Kali-yuga are described in *Śrīmad-Bhāgavatam.* People will become so disgusted that they will suddenly leave their wife and children and go to the forest. How can the peaceful *varṇāśrama-dharma* be revived when people are so harassed in this age? It is virtually impossible. Therefore the system of *bhakti-yoga*, the chanting of the Hare Kṛṣṇa *mahā-mantra*, should be adopted. The whole aim of *bhakti-yoga* is to satisfy Viṣṇu. *Yajñaiḥ saṅkīrtana-prāyaiḥ:* Viṣṇu, Kṛṣṇa, came Himself as Caitanya Mahāprabhu to teach us the way of *saṅkīrtana.* Presently it has become fashionable to manufacture a new system of religion, but Kapiladeva, like Kṛṣṇa, does not manufacture anything new. This system is not new, but very old (*purā*). Kṛṣṇa also says the same in *Bhagavad-gītā* (4.2), *evaṁ paramparā-prāptam imaṁ rājarṣayo viduḥ:* "This supreme science was thus received through the chain of disciplic succession, and the saintly kings understood it in that way." Thus Kṛṣṇa and Kapiladeva are not teaching anything new. They are simply repeating the same message because, in the course of time, the knowledge has been lost. Arjuna asks, "Why are you telling me? Why not another?" Śrī Kṛṣṇa answers, *bhakto 'si me sakhā ceti:* "Because you are My devotee as well as My friend." (Bg. 4.3)

Thus without being a *bhakta*, a devotee of Kṛṣṇa's, one cannot actually understand the science of *bhakti-yoga.* Understanding *Bhagavad-gītā* means understanding Kṛṣṇa. All this information is explained only in the *bhakti-sampradāya*, not in any other school. Therefore Kṛṣṇa says at the conclusion of *Bhagavad-gītā* (18.55), *bhaktyā mām abhijānāti:* if one actually wants to understand Kṛṣṇa and one's relationship with Him, one must take to this process of *bhakti-yoga. Bhakti-yoga* as explained by Lord Kapiladeva is *sāṅkhya-yoga.*

Lord Kapiladeva states here:

tam imaṁ te pravakṣyāmi
yam avocaṁ purānaghe

The word *anaghe* refers to one without sin. The word *agha* refers to past sins, and *an* means "without." Therefore one cannot understand Kṛṣṇa consciousness unless he is free from sin. *Yeṣāṁ tv anta-gataṁ pāpam:* one can stick to Kṛṣṇa consciousness only when one is completely free from all sinful reactions. One may say, "That will take some time. I cannot get free from sinful reactions overnight." However, Kṛṣṇa says, "No, no. This can be done immediately. Simply surrender unto Me, and I will absolve you from all sin." Thus by simply surrendering unto Kṛṣṇa, our spiritual life begins.

We have to understand that we receive different bodies due to our sinful actions. Now we are given a chance to execute our duty in the human form. *Bahūnāṁ janmanām ante.* We have received this body through the evolutionary processes, and this human form is a great opportunity. Narottama dāsa Ṭhākura sings: *hari hari viphale janama goṅāinu:* "My dear Lord Kṛṣṇa, I have simply wasted my time." Why?

manuṣya-janama pāiyā, rādhā-kṛṣṇa nā bhajiyā,
jāniyā śuniyā viṣa khāinu

"Because I have received the human form of life, which is meant for understanding Kṛṣṇa, yet I have simply wasted my time by not taking advantage of this opportunity. I have done everything but worship Rādhā-Kṛṣṇa. Therefore I have taken poison knowingly." When one takes poison knowingly, he commits suicide, and not taking advantage of the human form is something like that. If we do not understand Kṛṣṇa in this life, we are knowingly taking poison. This material life is just like a blazing forest fire. Eating, sleeping, enjoying sex and defending are the main material activities. When we are engaged simply in these things, our hearts are always burning as if we had taken poison. How can we be cured?

golokera prema-dhana, hari-nāma-saṅkīrtana,
rati nā janmila kene tāya

"My dear Lord, You have given us the medicine of *hari-nāma-saṅkīrtana*, the chanting of Hare Kṛṣṇa. Unfortunately, I have no attraction for Your holy names." It is also stated:

vrajendra-nandana yei, śacī-suta haila sei,
balarāma haila nitāi

"Kṛṣṇa has now come as Śrī Caitanya Mahāprabhu, the son of mother Śacī. And Balarāma has come as Lord Nityānanda." What is Their business? They are delivering all kinds of sinful men simply by chanting Hare Kṛṣṇa. And what is the evidence of this? The evidence is that Śrī Caitanya Mahāprabhu and Nityānanda Prabhu delivered the sinful Jagāi and Mādhāi. At the present moment everyone is like Jagāi and Mādhāi, for everyone is intoxicated and mad after sex. Now, by the grace of Caitanya Mahāprabhu, thousands of Jagāis and Mādhāis are being delivered. It is this active medicine, this Hare Kṛṣṇa *mahā-mantra*, that is doing it. It is the perfect *yoga* system. This process is not manufactured, and we have not concocted anything. Our business is simply to accept the words of Kṛṣṇa as they are. Śrī Kṛṣṇa Himself characterizes His devotee in this way:

satataṁ kīrtayanto māṁ
yatantaś ca dṛḍha-vratāḥ
namasyantaś ca māṁ bhaktyā
nitya-yuktā upāsate

"Always chanting My glories, endeavoring with great determination, bowing down before Me, these great souls perpetually worship Me with devotion." (Bg. 9.14)

We do not need to be very learned. Our only requirement is that we receive the blessings of the Lord. The Lord's blessings will enable us to become learned and follow His instructions. We only need to stick to this Kṛṣṇa consciousness movement on the basis of *Bhagavad-gītā.* When we are a little further advanced, we can read *Śrīmad-Bhāgavatam.* Caitanya Mahāprabhu Himself has opened the way with this *saṅkīrtana* movement. The entire world is in darkness without Kṛṣṇa consciousness, and in this age people are so dull that they do not even know the difference between *mukti* (liberation) and *bandha* (bondage). If a human being does not know this difference, he is no better than an animal.

Presently we are under the sway of the three *guṇas,* the modes of material nature—*sattva-guṇa, rajo-guṇa* and *tamo-guṇa.* Out of these three *guṇas, sattva-guṇa,* the mode of goodness, is the best. A *brāhmaṇa,* characterized by the mode of goodness, is truthful and self-controlled. He controls his mind and senses, and he is very tolerant and simple. He has full knowledge, and he knows how to apply knowledge in life. He has full faith in the authority of the *Vedas,* a quality called *āstikyam.* Caitanya Mahāprabhu has explained the difference between *nāstikyam* and *āstikyam.* According to Vedic understanding, one who does not believe in the *Vedas* is called *nāstika.* Caitanya Mahāprabhu says: *veda nā māniyā bauddha haya ta' nāstika* (Cc. *Madhya* 6.168). Lord Buddha defied Vedic authority, but His mission was to stop animal killing. In the *Vedas* there are recommendations for animal sacrifice, and therefore to prevent the killing of animals, Lord Buddha rejected the *Vedas.* Such sacrifice is not possible in this age because there is no *brāhmaṇa* qualified to carry it out. Those who are intelligent know that such a sacrifice cannot be successful in this age because no one knows the proper *mantras* capable of giving an old animal the body of a new animal. When an animal sacrifice is properly conducted, an old animal is sacrificed, and it emerges from the fire in a new body. This is not possible in this age, but what *is* possible is *saṅkīrtana-yajña*, the chanting of the Hare Kṛṣṇa *mahā-mantra.* This is the *yajña,* or sacrifice, especially intended for this age. We need only chant Hare Kṛṣṇa, Hare Kṛṣṇa, Kṛṣṇa Kṛṣṇa, Hare Hare/ Hare Rāma, Hare Rāma, Rāma Rāma, Hare Hare. By performing this *yajña,* the results will be *ceto-darpaṇa-mārjanam*—the mirror of the mind will be cleansed. When the mirror of the mind is cleansed, one is automatically liberated.

Consciousness is the main principle, either for conditional life or for liberated life. We are therefore proposing Kṛṣṇa consciousness, which means liberation from the repetition of birth and death. Unfortunately, people are so dull in this age that they have no idea how birth and death can be stopped. They think that birth and death cannot be stopped; even famous scientists admit this. However, in *Bhagavad-gītā* Śrī Kṛṣṇa says that we should always keep in mind the four miserable conditions. These are birth, old age, disease and death. When we are able to put an end to these, we are liberated. This simply requires that we clear our consciousness by thinking of Kṛṣṇa. The purpose of this Kṛṣṇa consciousness movement is to keep our minds constantly on Kṛṣṇa. Kṛṣṇa is the Supreme Personality of Godhead, and He is a person. When He was realized by Arjuna, He was addressed as *puruṣam.* God is *puruṣa,* male, not female. *Puruṣa* means "the enjoyer," and *prakṛti* means "the enjoyed." Everything is enjoyed by the supreme *puruṣa.* It is also stated that we are actually *prakṛti,* not *puruṣa.* The human dress is simply *māyā,* illusion. We are thinking that we are *puruṣa,* the enjoyer, but actually we are the enjoyed. A man, thinking of enjoying himself, tries to imitate *puruṣa,* but actually he is *prakṛti.* As a consequence, he is cast into this material world. Because the living entity wants to enjoy the material world and is attached to the three *guṇas,* he receives different types of bodies. One who is in the mode of goodness receives the body of a learned *brāhmaṇa.* This is somewhat elevated, for he can gradually understand what is God. In the modes of passion and ignorance, no one can understand God. Also, from the material point of view, if one is situated in the mode of goodness, he can be elevated to higher planetary systems. Nonetheless, even if one goes to Brahmaloka, the highest planet in the material atmosphere, one is not actually perfectly situated. There is really no benefit because even on Brahmaloka the four miseries of material existence are found: birth, old age, disease and death. Lord Brahmā also dies and takes birth. From Vedic literatures we understand that Lord Brahmā took birth from the lotus flower generated from the navel of Viṣṇu. Thus he had his birth, and when Lord Brahmā dies, the entire material cosmic manifestation will be finished. Just as Lord Brahmā undergoes birth, old age, disease and death, so also a small ant or insect undergoes the same process. The point is that the living entity has to be free from this bondage because he is by nature eternal. According to *Bhagavad-gītā*, the living entity never actually takes birth, and he never actually dies. *Na jāyate mriyate vā kadācit:* "For the soul there is never birth nor death." (Bg. 2.20)

It is the body that is destined to die, whether the body be that of Lord Brahmā or of a small ant. One should not think that one is liberated because one can live millions and millions of years. The life of Lord Brahmā covers millions of earth years, yet he is also subjected to birth and death. That is the way of conditional life. We should take advantage of the perfect knowledge given by Vedic literatures, by the great *ṛṣis* and Bhagavān Kapiladeva, as well as by Bhagavān Śrī Kṛṣṇa, in order to attain liberation from the cycle of birth and death.

Receiving Kṛṣṇa consciousness means receiving light. People are exhausted with the materialistic way of life, especially in the West. Now the Kṛṣṇa consciousness movement is giving new life to Western society. By nature, we living entities are liberated. There is actually no question of birth, death, old age and disease. Since we are part and parcel of Kṛṣṇa, the Supreme Lord, how can there be a question of these things? Kṛṣṇa is *sac-cid-ānanda-vigraha*, and being part and parcel of Kṛṣṇa, we are also of the same nature. We are equal in quality, although not in quantity. Why, then, should we suffer the pangs of death? Therefore in the previous verse Kapiladeva instructed: *yoga ādhyātmikaḥ puṁsāṁ mato niḥśreyasāya.* The soul is entrapped in the body, and the process of perfect *yoga* is the process of saving the soul from bodily confinement and the four miseries that plague the body. How can this perfect *yoga* be attained? That is explained by Lord Kapila in the next verse: *rataṁ vā puṁsi muktaye.* If our consciousness is simply attached to Kṛṣṇa, we will be liberated.

The great souls are always chanting about Kṛṣṇa. Hare Kṛṣṇa, Hare Kṛṣṇa, Kṛṣṇa Kṛṣṇa, Hare Hare/ Hare Rāma, Hare Rāma, Rāma Rāma,

Hare Hare. They are also endeavoring with great determination in their devotional service. For instance, in the Kṛṣṇa consciousness temples the devotees rise early in the morning, at 4:00 A.M., and they immediately bathe. Then they go to *maṅgala-ārati* at 4:30, and after *maṅgala-ārati* they study the Vedic literatures. These are the processes by which we can awaken our dormant love for Kṛṣṇa. Because we are part and parcel of Kṛṣṇa—just as a son is part and parcel of his father—there is a natural love between us. However, somehow or other the son leaves home and forgets his father. The father, of course, never forgets his son. He thinks, "Oh, my son has left. If he would only come back!" Kṛṣṇa thinks in this way. We are all sons of Kṛṣṇa, and Kṛṣṇa is more anxious to get us back home, back to Godhead, than we are to go. Therefore Kṛṣṇa comes and says, "You rascal! Give up all this nonsensical material engagement. You have manufactured so many religions and *dharmas*. Just give them all up and simply surrender unto Me." Kṛṣṇa comes Himself and leaves behind His words. His words are also Himself because His words are absolute. Presently we do not see Kṛṣṇa, but if we actually advance, we will see Him. When we see the Deity in the temple, we think, "Oh, this is an idol. It is not Kṛṣṇa." If we think in this way, we have not seen Kṛṣṇa. Kṛṣṇa is also present in His words, in *Bhagavad-gītā*. That is *kṛṣṇa-vāṇī*, the message of Kṛṣṇa. The stage of awareness of Kṛṣṇa can be attained when one is advanced in Kṛṣṇa consciousness. Then one can understand that Kṛṣṇa is present in the Deity, in *Bhagavad-gītā*, in the taste of water, in the sunshine, in the moonshine and in all sound. Kṛṣṇa is present everywhere, but one has to acquire knowledge in order to know how to see Kṛṣṇa. That is *mukti*, liberation. That is Kṛṣṇa consciousness. That is also the process of *bhakti-yoga—śravaṇaṁ kīrtanaṁ viṣṇoḥ smaraṇam. . . .* Deity worship is *arcanam*, chanting is *vandanam*, and *dāsyam* is working for Kṛṣṇa and spreading this Kṛṣṇa consciousness movement.

Generally we experience that people are primarily interested in seeing Kṛṣṇa, but why is the emphasis on seeing? Let us hear about Him. We must come with a little faith, and as we hear, that faith will increase. One should come to the temple, listen to talks about Kṛṣṇa, and then, after some time, officially take initiation into the service of the Lord. That is called *bhajana-kriyā*. At that time one has to abandon illicit sex, intoxication, meat-eating and gambling. If one is still attached to all these habits, he should know that he is not making progress. When one is actually advanced in *bhajana-kriyā*, all these *anarthas* (unwanted things) will be finished. *Paraṁ dṛṣṭvā nivartate.* When one appreciates something better, he rejects all kinds of nonsense. Once one gets a taste of Kṛṣṇa consciousness, he cannot remain without it. A drunkard cannot remain without a drink, but a devotee is drunk with Kṛṣṇa consciousness. The immunization against all material diseases is this Kṛṣṇa consciousness. To be immuned to the infection of the *guṇas*, we have to engage in *bhakti-yoga.* Once we attain the perfectional stage, we attain ecstatic love of Godhead. In that state we cannot remain without Kṛṣṇa for a moment. That is called *bhāva*, and that *bhāva* may increase to *mahā-bhāva.* This is not possible for ordinary human beings, but it was possible for the *gopīs* and Rādhārāṇī. Indeed, they could not live without Kṛṣṇa. This is the highest stage of liberation.

CHAPTER NINE

Purifying the Mind for Self-realization

TEXT 15

cetaḥ khalv asya bandhāya
muktaye cātmano matam
guṇeṣu saktaṁ bandhāya
rataṁ vā puṁsi muktaye

TRANSLATION

The stage in which the consciousness of the living entity is attracted by the three modes of material nature is called conditional life. But when that same consciousness is attached to the Supreme Personality of Godhead, one is situated in the consciousness of liberation.

PURPORT

There is a distinction here between Kṛṣṇa consciousness and *māyā* consciousness. *Guṇeṣu,* or *māyā* consciousness, involves attachment to the three material modes of nature, under which one works sometimes in goodness and knowledge, sometimes in passion and sometimes in ignorance. These different qualitative activities, with the central attachment for material enjoyment, are the cause of one's conditional life. When the same *cetaḥ,* or consciousness, is transferred to the Supreme Personality of Godhead, Kṛṣṇa, or when one becomes Kṛṣṇa conscious, he is on the path of liberation.

TEXT 16

ahaṁ-mamābhimānotthaiḥ
kāma-lobhādibhir malaiḥ

vītaṁ yadā manaḥ śuddham
aduḥkham asukhaṁ samam

TRANSLATION

When one is completely cleansed of the impurities of lust and greed produced from the false identification of the body as "I" and bodily possessions as "mine," one's mind becomes purified. In that pure state he transcends the stage of material happiness and distress.

PURPORT

Kāma and *lobha* are the symptoms of material existence. Everyone always desires to possess something. It is said here that desire and greed are the products of false identification of oneself with the body. When one becomes free from this contamination, his mind and consciousness also become freed and attain their original state. Mind, consciousness and the living entity exist. Whenever we speak of the living entity, this includes the mind and consciousness. The difference between conditional life and liberated life occurs when we purify the mind and the consciousness. When they are purified, one becomes transcendental to material happiness and distress.

In the beginning Lord Kapila has said that perfect *yoga* enables one to transcend the platform of material distress and happiness. How this can be done is explained here: one has to purify his mind and consciousness. This can be done by the *bhakti-yoga* system. As explained in the *Nārada-pañcarātra*, one's mind and senses should be purified (*tat-paratvena nirmalam*). One's senses must be engaged in devotional service of the Lord. That is the process. The mind must have some engagement. One cannot make the mind vacant. Of course there are some foolish attempts to try to make the mind vacant or void, but that is not possible. The only process that will purify the mind is to engage it in Kṛṣṇa. The mind must be engaged. If we engage our mind in Kṛṣṇa, naturally the consciousness becomes fully purified, and there is no chance that material desire and greed will enter.

Our mind is our friend, and our mind is our enemy. If it is cleansed, it is a friend, and if it is dirty, we contact material diseases. If we keep ourselves clean, pure, we will not be contaminated. According to Vedic civilization, one has to cleanse himself externally three times daily—once in the morning, again at noon, and again in the evening. Those who strictly follow the brahminical rules and regulations follow this process. Cleanliness is next to godliness. Conditional life means that the mind is covered with dirty things, and this is our disease. When we are in the lower modes of *tamo-guṇa* and *rajo-guṇa*, these dirty things are very prominent. One has to raise himself to the mode of *sattva* (goodness) by the process of *saṅkīrtana* and *śravaṇa.* One has to hear *kṛṣṇa-kathā.* Kṛṣṇa is within everyone's heart. The individual soul is part and parcel of Kṛṣṇa, and Kṛṣṇa wants the individual soul to turn to Him. Unfortunately the conditioned soul is attached to material enjoyment, and this is the cause of his bondage to birth, death, old age and disease. He is so foolish that he does not take into consideration that these miseries are repeated. He is like an ass that belongs to a washerman who loads him down with heavy clothes. For a few morsels of grass, the ass has to carry heavy loads all day, although not a single piece of clothing belongs to him. This is the way of the *karmīs.* They may become big multimillionaires, but they are just like asses, working hard day and night. Regardless of how much money they may have, their stomachs can only hold so much. And they require only six feet of space to sleep. Nonetheless, these big *karmīs* are thinking themselves very important. They think, "Without me, all the members of my nation will die. Let me work day and night to the point of death." People are thinking, "I belong to this family, this nation, this community. I have this duty or that duty," and so on. People do not know that these are all false designations.

Śrī Caitanya Mahāprabhu therefore enjoins, *jīvera 'svarūpa' haya— kṛṣṇera 'nitya-dāsa':* our actual position is that of eternal servants of Kṛṣṇa. We are mistakenly thinking that we are servants of a family or nation, but this is due to ignorance, *tamo-guṇa.* However, we can attain the platform of *sattva-guṇa* by following the instructions given in *Bhagavad-gītā.* Hearing *kṛṣṇa-kathā,* topics about Kṛṣṇa, clears all the dirty things from the mind. Also, if we chant and dance, these dirty things will be wiped away. The mind is the cause of bondage, and the mind is the cause of liberation. When it is dirty, it brings about bondage. In conditional life, we take birth, remain for some time, and enjoy or suffer. But really there is no question of enjoyment. There is only suffering. When we die, we have to give up the body and then take on another body. We immediately enter the womb of another mother, stay for nine months or so, and then come out. Then a new chapter of life begins. This is conditioned life, and it goes on again and again and again. In this way we undergo the tribulations of birth, old age, disease and death. The dogs and cats cannot understand this process, but we can understand it in human life through the Vedic literatures. If we don't take advantage of these literatures, all our education is for nothing.

People actually waste their time talking politics, sociology, anthropology, and so on. They read many literatures that do not glorify the Supreme Lord Hari, and thus they waste their time. This Kṛṣṇa consciousness movement is giving everyone a chance to become pious. *Puṇya-śravaṇa-kīrtanaḥ.* It is not necessary to give money or bathe in the Ganges. There are many pious activities and many processes recommended in the *śāstras* for becoming pious. However, in Kali-yuga people have lost all their stamina. They are so sinful that there is no question of becoming pious through all these prescribed methods. The only means is hearing about Kṛṣṇa and chanting His names. Kṛṣṇa has given us ears to hear and a tongue to speak. We can hear from a realized soul and thus perfect our lives. In this way we are given a chance to purify ourselves. Unless we are purified, we cannot become devotees. Human life is meant for purification. Unfortunately in this age people are not interested in Kṛṣṇa, and they suffer through material existence one life after another after another. In one life they may be very opulent. Then they don't care about the next life. They think, "Let me eat, drink and be merry." This is going on all over the world, but the *śāstras* say that people are making mistakes in this way. *Nūnaṁ pramattaḥ kurute vikarmaḥ* (*Bhāg.* 5.5.4): people have become mad with sense gratification, and therefore they engage in all sorts of forbidden things. *Karma* means regulated work, and *vikarma* means just the opposite—unlawful, forbidden activities. The word *akarma* means that one is not affected by the results of work. As stated in *Bhagavad-gītā* (3.9):

yajñārthāt karmaṇo 'nyatra
loko 'yaṁ karma-bandhanaḥ
tad-arthaṁ karma kaunteya
mukta-saṅgaḥ samācara

"Work done as a sacrifice for Viṣṇu has to be performed, otherwise work binds one to this material world. Therefore, O son of Kuntī, perform your prescribed duties for His satisfaction, and in that way you will always remain unattached and free from bondage."

When people are in the modes of passion and ignorance, they perform *vikarma*. They do not care for their future lives, and they are habituated to eating anything and everything, just like hogs. They do not care for the sastric injunctions, and they are totally irresponsible. They are just like street boys who have no education and do not care for anything. Such urchins do whatever they like, for their fathers and mothers do not care for them. Life in ignorance, *tamo-guṇa*, is such a careless life. People simply act unlawfully, not considering the results of their actions. They act for sense gratification, and actually they take pleasure in committing sins. In Calcutta I have seen people taking pleasure in cutting the throats of chickens and laughing when the chicken jumps and flaps about. Sometimes in Western countries students are taken to slaughterhouses just to see how the cows are butchered. In this age, people take pleasure in committing all kinds of sins. They have no brains to see that this body is temporary and full of suffering. They are completely in the mode of darkness, just like the animals they slaughter. There may be many animals in a pasture, and if one takes an animal aside and cuts its throat, the other animals will simply stand, look, and continue eating grass. They do not realize that the next time they may be slaughtered. The people in Kali-yuga are in the same situation, but the Kṛṣṇa consciousness movement is trying to give these rascals a little sense. We are saying, "Don't remain animals. Become human beings." In the words of Caitanya Mahāprabhu:

kṛṣṇa bhuli' sei jīva anādi-bahirmukha
ataeva māyā tāre deya saṁsāra-duḥkha

"Forgetting Kṛṣṇa, the living entity has been attracted by the external feature from time immemorial. Therefore the illusory energy (*māyā*) gives him all kinds of misery in his material existence. (Cc. *Madhya* 20.117) When one forgets his relationship with Kṛṣṇa, he acts in a very foolish way, and *māyā* gives him one misery after another. It is also stated:

māyā-mugdha jīvera nāhi svataḥ kṛṣṇa-jñāna
jīvere kṛpāya kailā kṛṣṇa veda-purāṇa

"The conditioned soul cannot revive his Kṛṣṇa consciousness by his own effort. But out of causeless mercy, Lord Kṛṣṇa compiled the Vedic literature and its supplements, the *Purāṇas.*" (Cc. *Madhya* 20.122)

The Vedic literatures—the *Vedānta, Upaniṣads, Rāmāyaṇa, Mahābhārata* and many others—should be utilized if we wish to become free from the contamination of *tamo-guṇa* and *rajo-guṇa.* The whole world is revolving due to *kāma* and *lobha. Kāma* means "lusty desire," and *lobha* means "greed." People cannot have enough sex or money, and because of this, their hearts are filled with contaminations, which have to be cleansed by hearing, repeating and chanting. Human life is meant to get rid of *anarthas,* unwanted things, but where is the university or college where this science of purification is taught? The only institution is this Kṛṣṇa consciousness society. Kṛṣṇa is within the heart, and the contaminations are also there, but Kṛṣṇa will help us cleanse them. *Naṣṭa-prāyeṣv abhadreṣu nityaṁ bhāgavata-sevayā* (*Bhāg.* 1.2.18). We must regularly hear *Śrīmad-Bhāgavatam* and chant Hare Kṛṣṇa; these are the two processes recommended by Caitanya Mahāprabhu. Haridāsa Ṭhākura was chanting three hundred thousand holy names a day, but we have fixed the number at sixteen rounds. Nonetheless, we are so unfortunate and fallen that we cannot even perform them. We should not waste our time reading and talking nonsense, but should engage in the study of *Śrīmad-Bhāgavatam.* Our time is very valuable, and we should not waste it. Cāṇakya Paṇḍita has said: *āyuṣaḥ kṣaṇa eko 'pi na labhyaḥ svarṇa-koṭibhiḥ.* We may live for a hundred years, but not one moment of these hundred years can be returned, not even if we are prepared to pay millions of dollars. We cannot add a moment, nor can we get a moment back. If time is money, we should just consider how much money we have lost. However, time is even more precious because it cannot be regained. Therefore not a single moment should be lost. Human life should be utilized only for chanting and reading Vedic literatures. The International Society for Krishna Consciousness is publishing many books so that people can utilize their time properly by reading them and make their lives successful. Not only should we read *Śrīmad-Bhāgavatam,* but we should also serve the person *bhāgavata,* one whose life is nothing but *Śrīmad-Bhāgavatam. Nityaṁ bhāgavata-sevayā.* By this process we can attain the stage of *bhagavad-bhakti,* but first we must get rid of all these *anarthas,* unwanted things. Presently we are wasting our time thinking, "This is my country. This is my nation. This is my body and my family," and so on. *Nityaṁ bhāgavata-sevayā.* We can vanquish all these false conceptions when we come to the platform of *sattva-guṇa.* Then we will not be disturbed by *tamo-guṇa* or *rajo-guṇa,* nor by *kāma* or *lobha* (lust and greed). This is the *vasudeva* platform. *Oṁ namo bhagavate vāsudevāya.*

Lord Kapiladeva, in the next verse, points out the results that follow the successful completion of this purificatory process.

TEXT 17

tadā puruṣa ātmānaṁ
kevalaṁ prakṛteḥ param
nirantaraṁ svayaṁ-jyotir
aṇimānam akhaṇḍitam

TRANSLATION

At that time the soul can see himself to be transcendental to material existence and always self-effulgent, never fragmented, although very minute in size.

PURPORT

In the state of pure consciousness, or Kṛṣṇa consciousness, one can see himself as a minute particle nondifferent from the Supreme Lord. As stated in *Bhagavad-gītā,* the *jīva,* or the individual soul, is eternally part and parcel of the Supreme Lord. Just as the sun's rays are minute particles of the brilliant sun, so a living entity is a minute particle of the Supreme Spirit. The individual soul and the Supreme Lord are not separated as in material differentiation. The individual soul is a particle from the very beginning. One should not think that because the individual soul is a particle, it is fragmented from the whole spirit. Māyāvāda philosophy enunciates that the whole spirit exists, but a part of it, which is called the *jīva*, is entrapped by illusion. This philosophy, however, is unacceptable because spirit cannot be divided like a fragment of matter. That part, the *jīva*, is eternally a part. As long as the Supreme Spirit exists, His part and parcel also exists. As long as the sun exists, the molecules of the sun's rays also exist.

The *jīva* particle is estimated in the Vedic literature to be one ten-thousandth the size of the upper portion of a hair. He is therefore infinitesimal. The Supreme Spirit is infinite, but the living entity, or individual soul, is infinitesimal, although he is not different in quality from the Supreme Spirit.

Two words in this verse are to be particularly noted. One is *nirantaram*, which means "nondifferent" or "of the same quality." The individual soul is also expressed here as *aṇimānam*. *Aṇimānam* means "infinitesimal." The Supreme Spirit is all-pervading, but the very small spirit is the individual soul. *Akhaṇḍitam* means not exactly "fragmented" but "constitutionally always infinitesimal." No one can separate the molecular parts of the sunshine from the sun, but at the same time the molecular part of the sunshine is not as expansive as the sun itself. Similarly, the living entity, by his constitutional position, is qualitatively the same as the Supreme Spirit, but he is infinitesimal.

Self-realization means seeing one's proper identity as the infinitesimal *jīva*. At the present moment, we are seeing the body, but this is not our proper identity. We have no vision of the real person occupying the body. The first lesson we receive from *Bhagavad-gītā* (2.13) informs us that the body and the owner of the body are different. When we can understand that we are not the body, that is the beginning of self-realization, and that is called the *brahma-bhūta* stage. *Ahaṁ brahmāsmi*. I am not this material body, but spirit soul. And what are the characteristics of the *jīva*, the soul? First of all, he is *aṇimānam*, very minute, infinitesimal. We are also *jyoti*, effulgent, like God, but God is *brahma-jyoti*, all-pervading and infinite. According to the Māyāvāda theory, we are the same as that *brahmajyoti*. Māyāvādīs give the example of a pot and the sky. Outside the pot there is sky, and within the pot there is sky. The separation is only due to the wall of the pot. When the pot is broken, the inside and outside become one. However, this example does not properly apply to the soul, as it is described in *Bhagavad-gītā* (2.24):

acchedyo 'yam adāhyo 'yam
akledyo 'śoṣya eva ca
nityaḥ sarva-gataḥ sthāṇur
acalo 'yaṁ sanātanaḥ

"This individual soul is unbreakable and insoluble, and can be neither burned nor dried. He is everlasting, all-pervading, unchangeable, immovable and eternally the same." The Soul cannot be cut in pieces or segmented. This means that the soul is eternally, perpetually minute. We are the eternal parts and parcels of Śrī Kṛṣṇa. As Śrī Kṛṣṇa Himself states in *Bhagavad-gītā* (15.7):

mamaivāṁśo jīva-loke
jīva-bhūtaḥ sanātanaḥ

"The living entities in the conditioned world are My eternal, fragmental parts." The word *sanātana* means "eternal," and the word *aṁśa* means "particles." God, Kṛṣṇa, is very great. No one is equal to Him or greater than Him. It is said that God is great, but we do not actually realize how great God is. He is so great that millions of universes are emanating from the pores of His body.

yasyaika-niśvasita-kālam athāvalambya
jīvanti loma-vilajā jagad-aṇḍa-nāthāḥ
viṣṇur mahān sa iha yasya kalā-viśeṣo
govindam ādi-puruṣaṁ tam ahaṁ bhajāmi

"The Brahmās and other lords of the mundane worlds appear from the pores of the Mahā-Viṣṇu and remain alive for the duration of His one exhalation. I adore the primeval Lord, Govinda, for Mahā-Viṣṇu is a portion of His plenary portion." (*Brahma-saṁhitā* 5.48)

Millions of universes emanate from the breathing of the Mahā-Viṣṇu. In the Tenth Chapter of *Bhagavad-gītā*, Kṛṣṇa gives Arjuna some indication of His infinite glory, and He concludes His descriptions with the following statement (Bg. 10.42):

athavā bahunaitena
kiṁ jñātena tavārjuna
viṣṭabhyāham idaṁ kṛtsnam
ekāṁśena sthito jagat

"But what need is there, Arjuna, for all this detailed knowledge? With a single fragment of Myself I pervade and support this entire universe."

This universe (*jagat*) is situated on the strength of one part of Kṛṣṇa's yogic powers. In this way we must understand the greatness of God and our own identity as minute particles. It is stated in the *Purāṇas* that the individual soul is one ten-thousandth part of the tip of a hair. If we could somehow divide the tip of a hair into ten thousand parts, we might begin to understand how the soul is invisible. Self-realization means knowing our identity as small particles. The small particle of spirit soul is within every one of us, but it is not possible to see with material eyes. There is no instrument existing in the material universe by which one can actually *see* the soul. Because of our inability to perceive the soul, we say it is *nirākāra*, formless. We cannot even calculate its dimension (*ākāra*). Although we cannot calculate it, it is there nonetheless. The living entity has full form. There are small microbes and insects we can barely see, but they have an anatomy consisting of many working parts. Within a small insect there is also the spirit soul, and that spirit soul also exists within the elephant and other big animals.

When we actually realize our identity as Brahman, our life becomes successful. Presently we are identifying with the body, but as long as we do so, we are no better than cats and dogs, although we may have a considerable amount of scientific knowledge. Conditioned souls consider the body to be the self, and because of this the *jīvas* identify themselves as American, Indian, *brāhmaṇa*, *kṣatriya*, man, woman, elephant and so forth. Thinking in these bodily terms, people consider their wives and children to be theirs and the land of their birth to be worshipable. Thinking thus, people are willing to fight and die for their country. Presently everyone is laboring under this delusion, but in order to understand our spiritual identity, we must find the proper *guru*.

Realizing our identity means realizing that we are Kṛṣṇa's eternal parts and parcels, that we are very minute, infinitesimal, and that we have a perpetual and eternal relationship with Kṛṣṇa, just as a part has its relationship to the whole. At no time can we be as great as Kṛṣṇa, although we are the same qualitatively. No one is equal to God, and no one is greater than Him. If someone claims to be God, he has to prove that no one is equal to him and that no one is greater. If he can do this, he is God. This is a very simple definition. *Brahma-saṁhitā* (5.1) also verifies this statement: *īśvaraḥ paramaḥ kṛṣṇaḥ*. The word *īśvara* means "controller," and the word *parama* means "supreme." We small living entities are controllers to a degree. We can control, at times, our family members, wives, children and so forth. Or we can control our office, factory, country or whatever. There are small controllers and larger controllers. If we go to Brahmā, we see that he is controlling the entire universe, but he is not the supreme controller. It is stated in the *śāstras* that Brahmā, the greatest living being within this universe, is also meditating in order to learn how to control. *Tene brahma hṛdā ya ādi-kavaye* (*Bhāg.* 1.1.1).

First of all, Brahmā learned to control the universe; then he became qualified as Brahmā. Although he was born Brahmā, he still had to be educated. If he was the first living being in the universe, who educated him? Kṛṣṇa. Śrī Kṛṣṇa says in *Bhagavad-gītā* (10.2), *aham ādir hi devānām:* "I am the source of the demigods."

The original demigods are Brahmā, Viṣṇu and Śiva. Lord Kṛṣṇa is Viṣṇu, but He is the instructor of Brahmā and Śiva. Therefore it is said that Lord Kṛṣṇa is the source of all the demigods.

We should not foolishly claim that we are as great as the Supreme God. We should understand that we are like sparks of the original fire. The spark is also fire, but if it falls from the original flame, it will go out. One should not think that because he is qualitatively one with God, he is God. One may be an *īśvara*, a controller, but one cannot be *īśvaraḥ paramaḥ*, the supreme controller. It is very fashionable nowadays to claim to have become Nārāyaṇa, God. The Māyāvādīs address one another as Nārāyaṇa, and thus everyone supposedly becomes Nārāyaṇa. In this way we are overcrowded with Nārāyaṇas here and there. But how can everyone become Nārāyaṇa? Nārāyaṇa is one, and the *śāstras* warn:

yas tu nārāyaṇaṁ devaṁ
brahma-rudrādi-devataiḥ

samatvenaiva vīkṣeta
sa pāṣaṇḍī bhaved dhruvam

"Whoever thinks Lord Viṣṇu and the demigods are on the same level is to be immediately considered a rogue as far as spiritual understanding is concerned." If one compares Nārāyaṇa to the demigods, he simply reveals his lack of intelligence. It is also fashionable to speak of *daridra-nārāyaṇa*, poor Nārāyaṇa, claiming that the poor man in the street is Nārāyaṇa. But what is this nonsense? Nārāyaṇa is the exalted Supreme Personality of Godhead. Even Śaṅkārācarya says: *nārāyaṇaḥ paro 'vyaktāt.* Nārāyaṇa is beyond this universe. *Avyaktād aṇḍa-sambhavaḥ:* the entire universe is a product of this *avyakta.* We should not compare Nārāyaṇa to anyone, what to speak of the poor man in the street (*daridra*). This is all foolishness. Nārāyaṇa is Lakṣmīpati, the husband and controller of the goddess of fortune. How, then, can He be *daridra?* This is all due to misunderstanding. Therefore the *śāstras* warn that if one thinks that the demigods are equal to Nārāyaṇa, one is a *pāṣaṇḍī,* an atheist. We should not think that because we have become liberated, we have attained the position of Nārāyaṇa. By severe austerity and penance one may elevate himself to the position of Brahman, but this is not the position of Parabrahman. *Āruhya kṛcchreṇa paraṁ padaṁ tataḥ* (*Bhāg.* 10.2.32). Although one rises to the platform of Brahman, one again falls down to the material position if he neglects to worship the lotus feet of Kṛṣṇa. One may rise to the Brahma effulgence, but because there is no shelter there one will return to the material atmosphere. One may go to Brahmaloka, the highest planet in the material sky, but one's position there is temporary. However, in the *paravyoma,* the spiritual sky, there are many spiritual planets, called Vaikuṇṭhalokas. There are millions of these gigantic planets, and unless we take shelter of one of them, we will fall down again into the material atmosphere.

It is not sufficient to rise to the platform of Brahman. Brahman is *sat* (being), and a partial realization of the Absolute Truth. We are actually after *ānanda. Sac-cid-ānanda: cit* means "knowledge," and that is also partial. We must add *ānanda* (bliss) in order to have complete realization. If we simply fly in the sky, we can't have *ānanda.* We have to descend to an airport at some time or another. If we simply rise to the Brahman effulgence, we do not experience *ānanda. Ānanda* is experienced when we enter the spiritual planets, where Nārāyaṇa, Kṛṣṇa, is present. *Paras tasmāt tu bhāvo 'nyo 'vyakto 'vyaktāt sanātanaḥ* (Bg. 8.20). We have to enter the eternal planets and associate with the Supreme Personality of Godhead in order to be happy. If we do not attain this position, we will return to the material world. And how can this position be attained? We simply have to try to understand Kṛṣṇa. Why does He come? What is His business? What is His form?

The purpose of this Kṛṣṇa consciousness movement is to teach people how to understand Kṛṣṇa. If one is fortunate in understanding Him, one's life is successful. As long as we have lusty desires and greed, we cannot come to this understanding. The *bhakti-yoga* process is the process of purification whereby we can become free from *kāma* and *lobha,* lust and greed, and the influence of the lower *guṇas, tamo-guṇa* and *rajo-guṇa,* ignorance and passion. As soon as we engage in devotional service, we immediately become freed from the influence of the *guṇas.* Because we are not expert in approaching the Supreme Lord, we have to follow the principles of *bhakti-yoga* enunciated by the *ācāryas.* When a boy goes to school, he has to follow the rules and regulations, but after a while he becomes accustomed to them and does not have to be taught. In other words, he learns automatically to come to school at a certain time, take his seat and study nicely. Similarly, in this Kṛṣṇa consciousness movement, we have certain rules and regulations. We must rise early in the morning for *maṅgala-ārati,* chant sixteen rounds of Hare Kṛṣṇa daily, and execute all the functions of *bhakti-yoga.* In this way, we become attached to rendering service to Kṛṣṇa, and we become practiced in this science. When we attain this stage, we immediately become self-realized.

CHAPTER TEN

Spiritual Attachment and Material Detachment

TEXT 18

jñāna-vairāgya-yuktena
bhakti-yuktena cātmanā
paripaśyaty udāsīnaṁ
prakṛtiṁ ca hataujasam

TRANSLATION

In that position of self-realization, by practice of knowledge and renunciation in devotional service, one sees everything in the right perspective; he becomes indifferent to material existence, and the material influence acts less powerfully upon him.

PURPORT

As the contamination of the germs of a particular disease can influence a weaker person, similarly the influence of material nature, or illusory energy, can act on the weaker, or conditioned, soul but not on the liberated soul. Self-realization is the position of the liberated state. One understands his constitutional position by knowledge and *vairāgya*, renunciation. Without knowledge, one cannot have realization. The realization that one is the infinitesimal part and parcel of the Supreme Spirit makes one unattached to material, conditional life. That is the beginning of devotional service. Unless one is liberated from material contamination, one cannot engage in the devotional service of the Lord. In this verse, therefore, it is stated, *jñāna-vairāgya-yuktena:* when one is in full knowledge of one's constitutional position and is in the renounced order of life, detached from material attraction, then, by pure devotional service, *bhakti-yuktena*, he can engage himself as a loving servant of the Lord. *Paripaśyati* means that he can see everything in its right perspective. Then the influence of material nature becomes almost nil. This is also confirmed in *Bhagavad-gītā*. *Brahma-bhūtaḥ prasannātmā:* when one is self-realized he becomes happy and free from the influence of material nature, and at that time he is freed from lamentation and hankering. The Lord states that position as *mad-bhaktiṁ labhate parām*, the real beginning of devotional service. Similarly, it is confirmed in the *Nārada-pañcarātra* that when the senses are purified, they can then be engaged in the devotional service of the Lord. One who is attached to material contamination cannot be a devotee.

In the conditional state, we are influenced by material nature. We have already discussed how we are conditioned by the three modes of material nature—ignorance, passion and goodness. Goodness is superior to ignorance and passion because from the platform of goodness we can come to understand Kṛṣṇa and thereby transcend the modes altogether. In this age, people are generally influenced by the lower modes, the modes of ignorance and passion. In these modes, we are not able to serve Kṛṣṇa. It is our constitutional position to serve someone, but when we do not serve Kṛṣṇa, we serve *māyā*. In any case, we cannot become master. Who can say that he is a master, that he is not serving anyone? We may serve our family, society, country, business, automobile or whatever. If one cannot find anything to serve, he goes and buys a cat or dog and serves it. Why is this? It is because service is our nature. We are simply lacking the knowledge of where to direct the service. Service is meant to be rendered to Kṛṣṇa. In the material world we are serving our lusty desires, not Kṛṣṇa, and we are deriving no pleasure from this. We are also serving in an office or in some employment in order to get some money. In this case, we are serving money, not the person. Thus in the material world we serve the senses and money. In any case, service is there. We must serve.

Actually the only master is Kṛṣṇa. *Ekale īśvara kṛṣṇa, āra saba bhṛtya* (Cc. *Ādi* 5.142). All the demigods, human beings, animals, trees and everything else are servants. Self-realization is realizing that one is the eternal servant of Kṛṣṇa and that one's duty is to serve Him. Self-realization is not thinking *ahaṁ brahmāsmi*, "I have become Brahman, Bhagavān." How can we become Bhagavān? If we are Bhagavān, we are actually the supreme powerful one. If this is the case, why are we in a miserable condition? Why are we under the influence of *māyā?* Does Bhagavān come under the influence of *māyā?* No. Kṛṣṇa says specifically in *Bhagavad-gītā* that *prakṛti, māyā,* is working under His directions. *Māyā* is the maidservant of Kṛṣṇa, and if we are the servants of *māyā,* how can we be Kṛṣṇa, Bhagavān? When we come to our spiritual senses, we can understand that we are erroneously engaged in *māyā's* service and that our duty is to engage in Kṛṣṇa's service. That is self-realization. As stated here: *jñāna-vairāgya-yuktena.* Real understanding is knowing oneself to be the servant of Kṛṣṇa, no one else. Because we are under illusion, we are serving *kāma, lobha, moha, mātsarya*—lust and greed—without benefit and without pleasure. *Kāmādīnāṁ kati na katidhā pālitā durnideśā:* "There is no limit to the unwanted orders of lusty desires." (*Bhakti-rasāmṛta-sindhu* 3.2.25) When we come to the understanding that our pleasure lies in serving Kṛṣṇa only, we have attained *jñāna-vairāgya.* Therefore in *Śrīmad-Bhāgavatam* (1.2.7) it is stated:

vāsudeve bhagavati
bhakti-yogaḥ prayojitaḥ
janayaty āśu vairāgyaṁ
jñānaṁ ca yad ahaitukam

"By rendering devotional service unto the Supreme Personality of Godhead, Śrī Kṛṣṇa, one immediately acquires causeless knowledge and detachment from the world." If one engages in the service of Vāsudeva, Kṛṣṇa, this knowledge comes, and one becomes a *mahātmā.* A *mahātmā* is one who realizes that Kṛṣṇa is everything. He does not defy Kṛṣṇa or try to become Kṛṣṇa. One who does so is not a *mahātmā* but a *durātmā,* a rascal. What is the position and knowledge of a *mahātmā?* Kṛṣṇa states:

mahātmānas tu māṁ pārtha
daivīṁ prakṛtim āśritāḥ
bhajanty ananya-manaso
jñātvā bhūtādim avyayam

"O son of Pṛthā, those who are not deluded, the great souls, are under the protection of the divine nature. They are fully engaged in devotional service because they know Me as the Supreme Personality of Godhead, original and inexhaustible." (Bg. 9.13)

A *mahātmā* cannot be manufactured. He is under the *daivī prakṛti*, the divine nature. There are two kinds of *prakṛti—parā prakṛti* and *aparā prakṛti. Aparā prakṛti* is the material world, and *daivī prakṛti* is the spiritual world. As soon as one understands that he is uselessly serving *māyā* in the material world in the form of society, friends, country and so forth, one reaches the stage called *jñāna*, knowledge. As soon as one attains this knowledge, he reaches the *brahma-bhūta* stage, Brahman realization, and he becomes *prasannātmā*, happy. One may ask, "Why should I serve Kṛṣṇa?" We have already explained that being a part means serving the whole. The whole is Kṛṣṇa, and the individuals are meant for Kṛṣṇa's satisfaction. *Īśāvāsyam idaṁ sarvam.*

There are many *īśvaras*, controllers, but the supreme *īśvara* is Kṛṣṇa. As soon as one attains this realization, he has attained perfect knowledge, and he renders service in *bhakti-yoga*. Foolish people say that *bhakti* is meant for *ajñānīs*, unintelligent people, but this is not the case. In *Bhagavad-gītā* Kṛṣṇa indicates that after many births, the *jñānī*, the man in knowledge, surrenders unto Him.

As long as we do not understand Kṛṣṇa, Vāsudeva, we should understand that we are still fools. We may advertise ourselves as very great *jñānīs*, learned personalities, but we are actually fools. That is the śāstric conclusion. If we are actually *jñānīs*, we should surrender unto Kṛṣṇa.

There are many *dharmas*, or activities. Some are pious and some impious, but Kṛṣṇa tells us to give up both. Arjuna was thinking that it was impious to fight with his relatives, but Kṛṣṇa was insisting that he fight. How could Arjuna act impiously? He could not, because Kṛṣṇa's service is transcendental to pious and impious activity. At midnight, when the *gopīs* heard the sound of Kṛṣṇa's flute, they ran to the forest to join Him. According to the *śāstras*, it is immoral for young girls to go see a young boy in a forest in the dead of night. But this was not an impious activity because the *gopīs* did this for Kṛṣṇa. Caitanya Mahāprabhu, who was so strict that no woman could even come near Him to offer respects, actually said: *ramyā kacid upāsanā vraja-vadhū-vargeṇa yā kalpitā.* "What could be more wonderful than that worship conceived by the *gopīs?*" Although it actually appeared immoral for the *gopīs* to dance with Kṛṣṇa, Caitanya Mahāprabhu states that their relation with Kṛṣṇa is the highest form of worship. This is actually transcendental knowledge. One becomes transcendental to all pious and impious activities when one serves Kṛṣṇa. After all, piety and impiety are within the material modes. Kṛṣṇa's service is transcendental to good and bad, pious and impious. *Bhakti-yoga* begins when *jñāna* and *vairāgya* are complete. *Jñāna* is knowledge, and *vairāgya* is detachment from matter and engagement of the mind in spirit. Both of these are automatically attained when we engage in devotional service to Kṛṣṇa.

TEXT 19

na yujyamānayā bhaktyā
bhagavaty akhilātmani
sadṛśo 'sti śivaḥ panthā
yogināṁ brahma-siddhaye

TRANSLATION

Perfection in self-realization cannot be attained by any kind of yogī unless he engages in devotional service to the Supreme Personality of Godhead, for that is the only auspicious path.

PURPORT

That knowledge and renunciation are never perfect unless joined by devotional service is explicitly explained here. *Na yujyamānayā* means "without being dovetailed." When there is devotional service, the question arises where to offer that service. Devotional service is to be offered to the Supreme Personality of Godhead, who is the Supersoul of everything, for that is the only reliable path of self-realization, or Brahman realization. The word *brahma-siddhaye* means to understand oneself to be different from matter, to understand oneself to be Brahman. The Vedic words are *ahaṁ brahmāsmi. Brahma-siddhi* means that one should know that he is not matter; he is pure soul. There are different kinds of *yogīs*, but every *yogī* is supposed to have attained self-realization, or Brahman realization. It is clearly stated here that unless one is fully engaged in the devotional service of the Supreme Personality of Godhead, one cannot easily approach the path of *brahma-siddhi.*

In the beginning of the Second Chapter of *Śrīmad-Bhāgavatam* it is stated that when one engages in the devotional service of Vāsudeva, spiritual knowledge and renunciation of the material world are automatically manifest. Thus a devotee does not have to strive separately for renunciation or knowledge. Devotional service itself is so powerful that by one's service, everything is revealed. It is stated here, *śivaḥ panthā:* this is the only auspicious path for self-realization. The path of devotional service is the most confidential means for attaining Brahman realization. That perfection in Brahman realization is attained through the auspicious path of devotional service indicates that the so-called Brahman realization, or realization of the *brahmajyoti* effulgence, is not *brahma-siddhi.* Beyond that *brahmajyoti* there is the Supreme Personality of Godhead. In the *Upaniṣads* a devotee prays to the Lord to kindly put aside the effulgence, *brahmajyoti,* so that the devotee may see within the *brahmajyoti* the actual eternal form of the Lord. Unless one attains realization of the transcendental form of the Lord, there is no question of *bhakti. Bhakti* necessitates the existence of the recipient of devotional service and the devotee who renders devotional service. *Brahma-siddhi* through devotional service is realization of the Supreme Personality of Godhead. The understanding of the effulgent rays of the body of the Supreme Godhead is not the perfect stage of *brahma-siddhi,* or Brahman realization. Nor is the realization of the Paramātmā feature of the Supreme Person perfect because Bhagavān, the Supreme Personality of Godhead, is *akhilātmā*—He is the Supersoul. One who realizes the Supreme Personality realizes the other features, namely the Paramātmā feature and the Brahman feature, and that total realization is *brahma-siddhi.*

As stated before, the word *yoga* means "to connect." *Brahma-siddhaye* means "self-realization," and *ahaṁ brahmāsmi* means "I am spirit soul." Actually, realizing oneself to be spirit is not sufficient. One has to progress further. One's fever may be cured, but one must also regain his strength and appetite in order to be totally cured. Then one can have a normal, healthy life, free of disease. Similarly, simply realizing that one is spirit soul is not sufficient. One has to engage in spiritual activity, and that spiritual activity is *bhakti.* Māyāvādī philosophers think that it is sufficient to stop all material activity, and the Buddhist philosophers advocate *nirvāṇa,* cessation of material life. Neither give more information. Actually we are suffering due to this material combination, and that is a fact. This body is composed of earth, water, fire, air, ether, mind, intelligence and ego. The Buddhists and Māyāvādīs advocate the annihilation of the components. They say, "Let the earth go to earth, let the water go to water, let the fire go to fire and become zero." If we dismantle the house of the material body and become zero, we attain *nirvāṇa*. *Nirvāṇa* means the cessation of pleasure and pain. The Māyāvādīs and Buddhists claim that if we fill an empty pitcher, the water will make some sound as long as the pitcher is not completely filled. When the pitcher is filled, there will no longer be any sound. Thus they claim that all the Vedic *mantras* and hymns stop when one is completely Brahman-realized. In other words, the Buddhists and Māyāvādīs claim that the material world is false, *mithyā*, and that we should somehow or other make it zero. However, simply realizing Brahman, realizing one's identity as spirit soul, is insufficient. We must realize that Bhagavān is everywhere:

eko 'py asau racayituṁ jagad-aṇḍa-koṭiṁ
yac-chaktir asti jagad-aṇḍa-cayā yad-antaḥ
aṇḍāntara-stha-paramāṇu-cayāntara-sthaṁ
govindam ādi-puruṣaṁ tam ahaṁ bhajāmi

"I worship the Personality of Godhead, Govinda, who, by one of His plenary portions, enters the existence of every universe and every atomic particle and thus unlimitedly manifests His infinite energy all over the material creation." (*Brahma-saṁhitā* 5.35)

Śrī Bhagavān is not alone. He is not only localized, but is everywhere. Although Kṛṣṇa has a particular place, He is everywhere. It is not that because Kṛṣṇa is in one place, He cannot be in others. Since we are conditioned, when we sit in our office we cannot be at home. Kṛṣṇa is not like this. *Goloka eva nivasaty akhilātma-bhūtaḥ*. Kṛṣṇa is always in Goloka Vṛndāvana, yet He is *aṇḍāntara-stha-parāmaṇu-cayāntara-stham*. He is within every atom of this universe. This universe is existing due to the Garbhodakaśāyī Viṣṇu. There is not only one universe, but there are many millions, and they are all working very nicely because the Garbhodakaśāyī Viṣṇu is present. We should not think that all these planets are floating in space without any arrangement having been made. There is definitely an arrangement.

In order to be completely free of the material modes, one has to come not only to the platform of *jñāna* and *vairāgya*, but to *bhakti* also. When we mention *bhakti*, some people say, "I render *bhakti* to my wife. I love her very much and take care of her. If I do not see her, I become mad." Thus people have *bhakti* for their family, country, goddess Durgā, other demigods and so on. However, that kind of *bhakti* will not do. Therefore it is said, *bhaktir bhagavati. Bhakti* must be rendered unto the Supreme. It is not that one should render *bhakti* unto an imitation Bhagavān. If one says that he is Bhagavān, we should ask, "Are you present in everyone's heart? Can you tell me what I am thinking now?" If one is Bhagavān, he must be *akhilātmā*. If one is *īśvara*, he must be present in everyone's heart. Kṛṣṇa is present in everyone's heart (*sarvasya cāhaṁ hṛdi sanniviṣṭaḥ*). All this should be scrutinizingly studied. It is not that one should accept this rascal or that rascal as Bhagavān. Nor should one render *bhakti* to this demigod or that demigod, to one's family, country, society, wife, cat, dog or whatever. All this is not really *bhakti* but imitation *bhakti*. It is actually lustful desire. If we can develop *bhakti* for Kṛṣṇa, Kṛṣṇa consciousness, our lives will be successful. Actually there is no alternative. As stated in this verse, *sādṛśo 'sti śivaḥ panthā*. Parabrahman is Kṛṣṇa, and *brahma-siddhaye* means understanding our relationship with Kṛṣṇa. It is all right for one to understand oneself as Brahman (*ahaṁ brahmāsmi*), but what is our relationship with the Parabrahman? There are always two: Brahman and Parabrahman, *ātmā* and Paramātmā, *īśvara* and Parameśvara, the individual living being and the supreme living being, *nitya* and *nityānām*, *cetanaś* and *cetanānām*. There are always two present, and two means a relationship. We should therefore understand our relationship with the Supreme, with Parabrahman. Understanding that relationship is *brahma-siddhaye*.

We are qualitatively one with Parabrahman, but Parabrahman is very great whereas we are very small. Parabrahman is one (*kaivalya*). There is no alternative and no duplicate. There is no one equal to Him or greater than Him. That is the meaning of *kaivalya*. Human life is meant for inquiring about Parabrahman and one's relationship with Him. Unfortunately, people are not asking questions about Parabrahman. Everyone is asking about the news and the morning paper, and everyone is concerned with going to the market and purchasing so many goods for cheaper prices. All this is going on in human society and in cat and dog society also.

This world is full of darkness and ignorance, but Kṛṣṇa consciousness is transcendental to this material world. In Kṛṣṇa consciousness, there is no darkness but simply light. If we try to find things at night, it becomes very difficult; however, in the daytime, there is no difficulty. The *śāstras* enjoin that we leave this darkness and come to light. This light is given by the *guru.*

om ajñāna timirāndhasya
jñānāñjana-śalākayā
cakṣur unmīlitaṁ yena
tasmai śrī-gurave namaḥ

"I was born in the darkest ignorance, and my spiritual master opened my eyes with the torch of knowledge. I offer my respectful obeisances unto him."

It is the *guru's* business to give light by knowledge. The *guru* has completely assimilated the Vedic essence of life. *Śruti,* knowledge, is received by hearing. It is not experimental. We cannot understand that which is beyond our sense perception by experiment. We cannot understand who our father is by experimental knowledge. One cannot say, "Let me find out who my father is by experiment." Our father was existing before we were existing, and it is not possible to understand by experimental knowledge that this or that man is my father. The real authority is the mother; therefore Vedic knowledge has been likened to the mother and the *Purāṇas* to the sisters. We should understand from the *Vedas* what ultimate knowledge really is. The ultimate knowable objective is Kṛṣṇa, and simply by understanding Kṛṣṇa, we can understand everything. We do not have to understand things separately. Kṛṣṇa is within our hearts. He is not far away; rather, He is everywhere. If Kṛṣṇa sees that we are attached to Him, He becomes our friend. He is a friend to everyone, but He is especially a friend to His devotees. As Kṛṣṇa Himself says in *Bhagavad-gītā* (10.11):

teṣām evānukampārtham
aham ajñānajaṁ tamaḥ

nāśayāmy ātma-bhāva-stho
jñāna-dīpena bhāsvatā

"Out of compassion for them, I, dwelling in their hearts, destroy with the shining lamp of knowledge the darkness born of ignorance."

Jñāna is there, it is simply covered with the curtain of ignorance. Light is there, and darkness is there, but when we are in darkness we cannot see things as they are. Kṛṣṇa says that as one devotes himself to rendering service, He Himself dispels the darkness of ignorance. If we actually want to become perfect in this life, we only need to engage in devotional service to the Supreme Personality of Godhead, Bhagavān. It is not that Bhagavān is difficult to find. Bhagavān is within the heart. *Īśvaraḥ sarva bhūtānāṁ hṛd-deśe 'rjuna tiṣṭhati* (Bg. 18.61). That is the real Bhagavān, within the hearts of all. That Bhagavān is always active. He instructed Brahmā, the lord of the universe, and Brahmā, having received Kṛṣṇa's instructions, created the entire universe. Kṛṣṇa will also give instructions to us if we simply take to devotional service.

TEXT 20

prasaṅgam ajaraṁ pāśam
ātmanaḥ kavayo viduḥ
sa eva sādhuṣu kṛto
mokṣa-dvāram apāvṛtam

TRANSLATION

Every learned man knows very well that attachment for the material is the greatest entanglement of the spirit soul. But that same attachment, when applied to self-realized devotees, opens the door of liberation.

PURPORT

Here it is clearly stated that attachment for one thing is the cause of bondage in conditioned life, and the same attachment, when applied to something else, opens the door of liberation. Attachment cannot be killed; it has simply to be transferred. Attachment for material things is called material consciousness, and attachment for Kṛṣṇa or His devotee is called Kṛṣṇa consciousness. Consciousness, therefore, is the platform of attachment. It is clearly stated here that when we simply purify the consciousness from material consciousness to Kṛṣṇa consciousness, we attain liberation. Despite the statement that one should give up attachment, desirelessness is not possible for a living entity. A living entity, by constitution, has the propensity to be attached to something. We see that if someone has no object of attachment, if he has no children, he transfers his attachment to cats and dogs. This indicates that the propensity for attachment cannot be stopped; rather, it must be utilized for the best purpose. Our attachment for material things perpetuates our conditional state, but the same attachment, when transferred to the Supreme Personality of Godhead or His devotee, is the source of liberation.

Here it is recommended that attachment should be transferred to the self-realized devotees, the *sādhus*. And who is a *sādhu?* A *sādhu* is not just an ordinary man with a saffron robe or long beard. A *sādhu* is described in *Bhagavad-gītā* as one who unflinchingly engages in devotional service. Even though one is found not to be following the strict rules and regulations of devotional service, if one simply has unflinching faith in Kṛṣṇa, the Supreme Person, he is understood to be a *sādhu. Sādhur eva sa mantavyaḥ.* A *sādhu* is a strict follower of devotional service. It is recommended here that if one at all wants to realize Brahman, or spiritual perfection, his attachment should be transferred to the *sādhu,* or devotee. Lord Caitanya also confirmed this. *Lava-mātra sādhu-saṅge sarva-siddhi haya:* simply by a moment's association with a *sādhu,* one can attain perfection.

Mahātmā is a synonym of *sādhu.* It is said that service to a *mahātmā,* or elevated devotee of the Lord, is *dvāram āhur vimukteḥ,* the royal road of liberation. *Mahat-sevāṁ dvāram āhur vimuktes tamo-dvāraṁ yoṣitāṁ saṅgi-saṅgam* (*Bhāg.* 5.5.2). Rendering service to the materialists has the opposite effect. If anyone offers service to a gross materialist, or a person engaged only in sense enjoyment, then by association with such a person the door to hell is opened. The same principle is confirmed here. Attachment to a devotee is attachment to the service of the Lord because if one associates with a *sādhu,* the *sādhu* will teach one how to become a devotee, a worshiper and a sincere servitor of the Lord. These are the gifts of a *sādhu.* If we want to associate with a *sādhu,* we cannot expect him to give us instructions on how to improve our material condition, but he will instruct us how to cut the knot of the contamination of material attraction and how to elevate ourselves in devotional service. That is the result of associating with a *sādhu.* Kapila Muni first of all instructs that the path of liberation begins with such association.

According to Śrī Caitanya Mahāprabhu:

'sādhu-saṅga', 'sādhu-saṅga'—sarva-śāstre kaya
lava-mātra sādhu-saṅge sarva-siddhi haya

"The verdict of all revealed scriptures is that by even a moment's association with a pure devotee, one can attain all success." (Cc. *Madhya* 22.54)

It is said that man is a social animal, and, according to our association, we can mold our character. Businessmen associate with one another to develop their business capabilities. There are many different types of association, and association brings about bondage to a particular thing. If one associates with materialistic people, one's bondage to sense gratification tightens. Woman is the symbol of sense gratification; therefore anything dealing with sense gratification is called *yoṣit-saṅga.* This material world is filled with *yoṣit-saṅga* because everyone is interested in sense gratification. As stated in *Bhagavad-gītā* (2.44):

bhogaiśvarya-prasaktānāṁ
tayāpahṛta-cetasām
vyavasāyātmikā buddhiḥ
samādhau na vidhīyate

"In the minds of those who are too attached to sense enjoyment and material opulence, and who are bewildered by such things, the resolute determination of devotional service to the Supreme Lord does not take place." The word *bhoga* means "sense gratification." *Bhogaiśvarya:* Those who are overly attached to opulence and sense gratification cannot understand spiritual life, and they are very slow to take to it. At the present moment people are *manda,* very slow. They do not take this Kṛṣṇa consciousness movement very seriously because they have been taught by modern civilization simply to enjoy life for sense gratification. In the Western countries, especially, there are many implements for sense gratification. There are even machines for shaving, although formerly an ordinary razor would do. Now, thanks to the machine, one does not even have to move his hand. So this is considered progress. However, we learn from the *śāstras* that human life is not meant for sense enjoyment but for *tapasya*. That is Vedic civilization. First of all, one must be trained in the *brahmacārī* system and learn how to deny the senses. A *brahmacārī* should be trained in *tapasya*, not in enjoyment. Formerly, *brahmacārīs* would have to go from door to door to beg alms for the *āśrama*, and they were trained from the very beginning to address every woman as mother.

Presently, people are in such a miserable condition that they are saying, "Let us die. Let us die." However, Kṛṣṇa in *Bhagavad-gītā* says, "Why should you die?" People want to die in order to put an end to the threefold miseries of material nature, but who is making research on how to stop death? From *Bhagavad-gītā* we learn that death is not really natural for us. It is artificially imposed upon us, and we have to become deathless again. That is the perfection of human life, but no one cares about it. We have become so dull that we cannot avoid birth, old age, disease and death. We are actually experiencing them because we are not alert. For this reason, when Sanātana Gosvāmī approached Caitanya Mahāprabhu, he said, "My dear Lord, somehow or other You have dragged me to Your lotus feet. I am now asking You what my actual position is. Why am I forced to suffer the threefold miseries of material life?" No one is interested in inquiring about this matter. *Mokṣa*, liberation, means getting free from the threefold miseries of life as well as birth, old age, disease and death. Sometimes, when people are a little interested, they take to a path that is not even approved, or they invent something. But nothing need be invented. By this Kṛṣṇa consciousness process, everyone can be elevated. Everyone can be delivered, regardless of his situation or culture. We have spread this Kṛṣṇa consciousness movement throughout the world, and people are becoming happy because of it.

According to *Bhagavad-gītā* (9.32), anyone can take shelter of Kṛṣṇa. Kṛṣṇa never denies anyone, and similarly, Kṛṣṇa's devotee never denies anyone. That is this Kṛṣṇa consciousness movement. We tell everyone, "Yes, you are welcome. Take this education and spiritual life and become a devotee of Kṛṣṇa." Sometimes we are criticized because of this, but

Kṛṣṇa specifically says in *Bhagavad-gītā* that even those who are lowborn can take shelter of Him and become elevated for liberation. What, then, to speak of pious people born in brahminical families? Unfortunately, in this age people born in rich or brahminical families often don't care for spiritual realization. They misuse their chance and exhaust the results of their pious activities. Society needs first-class *sādhus* in order to improve. If everyone is a *śūdra* and debauchee, how can society be peaceful? Therefore in order to organize society, Kṛṣṇa recommends the *varṇāśrama-dharma.* There must be ideal *brāhmaṇas, kṣatriyas, vaiśyas* and *śūdras.* However, no one cares about this now.

One may ask, "What is a *sādhu?*" A *sādhu* is one who serves Kṛṣṇa and engages in Kṛṣṇa consciousness without reservation. In *Bhagavad-gītā* (9.30), Śrī Kṛṣṇa says:

api cet sudurācāro
bhajate mām ananya-bhāk
sādhur eva sa mantavyaḥ
samyag vyavasito hi saḥ

"Even if one commits the most abominable actions, if he is engaged in devotional service, he is to be considered saintly because he is properly situated."

It is the *sādhu's* business to be very tolerant. When one becomes a devotee, many people become one's enemy, because in this age people are asuric, demoniac. Even one's father may turn into an enemy like Hiraṇyakaśipu, the father of Prahlāda Mahārāja. Prahlāda was only five years old and was chanting Hare Kṛṣṇa, but his father was prepared to kill him because he was a devotee. Hiraṇyakaśipu was saying, "Why are you chanting Hare Kṛṣṇa? Why are you speaking of a separate God? I am God." That is the meaning of asuric, demoniac. Rascals who claim to be God themselves are simply demons. Although Prahlāda's father was insisting that he was God, Prahlāda Mahārāja could not accept this. He simply accepted his father as an *asura*, and consequently there was a quarrel between them. When Hiraṇyakaśipu asked Prahlāda Mahārāja, "What is the best thing you have learned from your teachers?" Prahlāda replied, "O best of the *asuras*, as far as I can understand, because we have accepted this material body, we have to accept death. But this is not the object of human life. Human life is meant for *mokṣa*, liberation." Unfortunately, foolish people do not understand this. Kṛṣṇa says, *mṛtyuḥ sarva-haraś cāham:* "I am death, and I will take away everything you possess." (Bg. 10.34) Hiraṇyakaśipu was such a powerful demon that even the demigods were afraid of him, but Kṛṣṇa took everything away in a second. Hiraṇyakaśipu was looking for security, and he was thinking, "I will not die in this way, and I will not die in that way." But he did not think that he would be killed by the Lord in the form of Nṛsiṁha. However intelligent we may be, and however much we may try to cheat Kṛṣṇa, Kṛṣṇa is always more intelligent. When mother Yaśodā tried to bind Kṛṣṇa with a rope, she found that the rope was always two inches too short. Our intelligence is like that. We want to cheat God and surpass Him, but this is not possible. People think themselves very advanced in knowledge, but actually, due to their pride, their knowledge is taken away by *māyā*. Kṛṣṇa actually takes the knowledge away from atheistic, demoniac people like Hiraṇyakaśipu. Atheists do not know that Kṛṣṇa's intelligence is always at least two inches greater than anyone else's.

In material life, we simply struggle for existence. We want to exist, and we do not want to die. Nor do we want to undergo the pains of birth, catch diseases or grow old. There are so many miseries in material life that we do not want, but they are forced upon us. Unfortunately, we are not intelligent enough to make a solution to all these problems. We should be inquiring like Sanātana Gosvāmī about how to put an end to them all. Instead, we are working in such a way that we have to accept another material body. We are experiencing the difficulties arising from this material body, but we are not working in a way to become free. This Kṛṣṇa consciousness movement is giving information on how to become liberated.

Those who are *mahātmās* are always engaged in chanting Hare Kṛṣṇa, Hare Kṛṣṇa, Kṛṣṇa Kṛṣṇa, Hare Hare/ Hare Rāma, Hare Rāma, Rāma Rāma, Hare Hare. *Bhajana* is the chanting of Hare Kṛṣṇa. If we serve a *mahātmā* like Haridāsa Ṭhākura, who was always engaged in chanting Hare Kṛṣṇa, our path of liberation is opened. However, if we associate with materialistic people, who are simply mad for sense gratification, we take the way of darkness. *Tamo-dvāraṁ yoṣitāṁ saṅgi-saṅgam.* The *Vedas* enjoin that we not remain in darkness but that we go to the light. We have accepted a body, but we will not be allowed to remain in that body permanently. We will have to give it up and accept another, and then another and another. What is this business? The material world is in such darkness, and people are taking on one body after another. The Kṛṣṇa consciousness movement is therefore here to give enlightenment and liberation, and it is offering not only the simplest process of chanting Hare Kṛṣṇa but also the most sublime philosophy.

CHAPTER ELEVEN

The Symptoms of a Sādhu

TEXT 21

titikṣavaḥ kāruṇikāḥ
suhṛdaḥ sarva-dehinām
ajāta-śatravaḥ śāntāḥ
sādhavaḥ sādhu-bhūṣaṇāḥ

TRANSLATION

The symptoms of a sādhu are that he is tolerant, merciful and friendly to all living entities. He has no enemies, he is peaceful, he abides by the scriptures, and all his characteristics are sublime.

PURPORT

A *sādhu,* as described above, is a devotee of the Lord. His concern, therefore, is to enlighten people in devotional service; that is his mercy. He knows that without devotional service, human life is spoiled. A devotee travels all over the country, from door to door, preaching, "Be Kṛṣṇa conscious. Be a devotee of Lord Kṛṣṇa. Don't spoil your life in simply fulfilling your animal propensities. Human life is meant for self-realization, or Kṛṣṇa consciousness." These are the preachings of a *sādhu.* He is not satisfied with his own liberation. He always thinks about others. He is the most compassionate personality toward all fallen souls. One of his qualifications, therefore, is *kāruṇika,* great mercy to the fallen souls. While engaged in preaching work, he has to meet with so many opposing elements, and therefore the *sādhu* has to be very tolerant. Someone may ill-treat him because the conditioned souls are not prepared to receive the transcendental knowledge of devotional service. They don't like it; that is their disease. The *sādhu* has the thankless task of impressing upon them the importance of devotional service. Sometimes devotees are personally attacked with violence. Lord Jesus Christ was crucified, Haridāsa Ṭhākura was caned in twenty-two marketplaces, and Lord Caitanya's principal assistant, Nityānanda, was violently attacked by Jagāi and Mādhāi. But still they were tolerant because their mission was to deliver fallen souls. A *sadhu* is merciful because he is the well-wisher of all living entities. He is not only a well-wisher of human society, but a well-wisher of animal society as well. The word *sarva-dehinām* refers to all living entities who have accepted material bodies. Not only does the human being have a material body, but other living entities as well. The devotee of the Lord is merciful to everyone—cats, dogs, trees, etc. He treats all living entities in such a way that they can ultimately get salvation from this material entanglement. Śivānanda Sena, one of the disciples of Lord Caitanya, gave liberation to a dog by treating the dog transcendentally. There are many instances where a dog got salvation by association with a *sādhu,* because a *sādhu* engages in the highest philanthropic activities for the benediction of all living entities. Yet although a *sādhu* is not inimical toward anyone, the world is so ungrateful that even a *sādhu* has many enemies.

What is the difference between an enemy and a friend? It is a difference in behavior. A *sādhu* behaves with all conditioned souls for their ultimate relief from material entanglement. Therefore, no one can be more friendly than a *sādhu* in relieving a conditioned soul. A *sādhu* is calm, and he quietly and peacefully follows the principles of scripture. A *sādhu* is also one who follows the principles of scripture and at the same time is a devotee of the Lord. One who actually follows the principles of scripture must be a devotee of God because all the *śāstras* instruct us to obey the orders of the Personality of Godhead. A *sādhu,* therefore, is a follower of the scriptural injunctions and a devotee of the Lord. All good characteristics are prominent in a devotee, and he develops all the good qualities of the demigods, whereas a nondevotee, even though academically qualified, has no good qualifications or good characteristics according to the standard of transcendental realization.

There are 8,400,000 life forms according to the *Padma Purāṇa,* and the *ātmā* is the same in all of them. The *sādhu* can understand this, as *Bhagavad-gītā* (5.18) indicates:

vidyā-vinaya-sampanne
brāhmaṇe gavi hastini
śuni caiva śvapāke ca
paṇḍitāḥ sama-darśinaḥ

"The humble sage, by virtue of true knowledge, sees with equal vision a learned and gentle *brāhmaṇa*, a cow, an elephant, a dog and a dog-eater [outcaste]."

It is not that a *brāhmaṇa* is the same as a dog, but that the *brāhmaṇa* is a spirit soul, and the dog is also a spirit soul. We are conditioned according to our different bodies, which are given by superior forces. Yamarāja offers the living entity a body according to his *karma. Karmaṇā daiva-netreṇa.* We have already discussed the point that bodies are awarded according to one's qualifications. If we acquire the qualities of a *brāhmaṇa* and work as a *brāhmaṇa,* we become a *brāhmaṇa.* If we act as a dog and do the work of a dog, we become a dog. Nor should one think that simply because one is born as a *brāhmaṇa,* one is automatically a *brāhmaṇa.* There are characteristics mentioned in *Bhagavad-gītā* by which one can tell to which caste one belongs. Śrīdhara Svāmī has also noted that birth is not everything. One has to acquire the qualities. Whatever body we may have, our position is temporary. We cannot remain in any position indefinitely. We may think that at present we are Americans and are very happy, and that's all right. We may chalk out our plans for continued happiness, but nature will not allow us to stay indefinitely. As soon as nature calls, we die and give up our post. Then we have to take the post of a dog, a cat, a demigod, a human being or whatever. We are now given a most exalted life form, that of a human being, but if we do not act accordingly, we have to take a lower body. This is *karmaṇā daiva-netreṇa.*

We should therefore be very careful in this human form that our aim is to become devotees of Lord Kṛṣṇa. That is the path of liberation. Previously, great personalities in India used to go to the forest in order to meditate to stop the repetition of birth and death. That is the highest occupation for man, and actually every man is meant for that. Unless we conquer repeated birth and death, we simply waste our lives like animals—eating, sleeping, defending and mating. People in this age especially cannot distinguish between animal life and human life. They think the difference is that animals sleep in the street and human beings sleep in nice apartments. However, the *śāstras* do not define civilization in this way. Whether one sleeps in the street or in an apartment, the activity is the same. A dog may eat out of a garbage can, and a human being may eat on a golden plate, but this does not mean that they are engaged in different activities. In either case, both the dog and the man are taking food into their bodies. A dog may have sex in the street, and a human being may have sex in a very nice bed in a secluded place, but that does not change the activity. People are thinking that advancement of civilization means improving eating, sleeping, mating and defending, but actually these activities have nothing to do with civilization. They simply tighten our bondage to material life.

Human life is meant for *yajña*, sacrifice for the satisfaction of the Supreme Person. We may perfect our activities, but our success lies in satisfying Kṛṣṇa by our talents. Presently we may be attached to material activity, but we should transfer that attachment to a *sādhu*. Then our lives will be successful. Presently we are attached to money, women, nice houses, country, society, friends, family and so forth. This attachment is called *arjanaṁ pāśu*. The word *pāśu* means "rope." When we are bound with a rope, we are helpless, and now we are bound by the *guṇas*, or the three modes of material nature. The word *guṇa* also means "rope." We cannot free ourselves, for we are conditioned. We cannot move freely without the sanction of the supreme authority. It is generally said that not a blade of grass moves without God's sanction. Similarly, we cannot do anything without the supervision of a superior authority.

It is not that God has to take personal supervision of this. *Parāsya śaktir vividhaiva śrūyate . . . na tasya kāryaṁ karaṇaṁ ca vidyate:* in the *Śvetāśvatara Upaniṣad* (6.8), it is thus stated that the Supreme Lord does not have to act personally. He has many agents to perform everything for Him. We are so controlled that we are not even free to blink our eyes. We may be moving our hands very freely, but at any moment they can be immediately paralyzed. Presently I am claiming, "This is my hand." But what is this? The hand could be paralyzed immediately. This is conditioned life, and how can we improve it? Our business is to become liberated from all this conditioning. How is this possible? *Sa eva sādhuṣu kṛto mokṣa-dvāram apāvṛtam* (*Bhāg.* 3.25.20). We have to turn our attachment from material things to a *sādhu*. *'Sādhu-saṅga', 'sādhu-saṅga'*—

sarva-śāstre kaya: this is the advice of Śrī Caitanya Mahāprabhu. All *śāstras* advise us to associate with a *sādhu.* Even Cāṇakya Paṇḍita, the great politician, recommended: *tyaja durjana-saṁsargaṁ bhaja sādhu-samāgamam.* One Vaiṣṇava householder asked Caitanya Mahāprabhu what the duty of a householder is, and Śrī Caitanya Mahāprabhu immediately replied, *asat-saṅga-tyāga,—ei vaiṣṇava-ācāra:* "Don't associate with nondevotees, but search out a *sādhu.*" (Cc. *Madhya* 22.87)

At the present moment it is very difficult to avoid the company of *asādhus,* those who are not *sādhus.* It is very difficult to find a *sādhu* for association. We have therefore started this Kṛṣṇa consciousness movement to create an association of *sādhus* so that people may take advantage and become liberated. There is no other purpose for this society.

Kṛṣṇa states in *Bhagavad-gītā* (6.47) that the first-class *sādhu* is one who is always thinking of Him. This process is not very difficult. We should always think of Kṛṣṇa, but how is this possible? We think of our business, our dog, our family, our lovable object and so many other things. We have to think of something; without thinking, we cannot remain. We simply have to divert our thoughts to Kṛṣṇa. It is the *sādhu's* business to teach this, and one can learn this in the association of a *sādhu.* Actually a *sādhu* will not teach anything else. *Ādau śraddhā tataḥ sādhu-saṅgaḥ* (*Bhakti-rasāmṛta-sindhu* 1.4.15). This is the way to make spiritual advancement. One has to associate with a *sādhu.* Often the *sādhu's* task is a thankless one, but he has to be tolerant. Despite all the trouble a *sādhu* may encounter, he is very merciful upon fallen conditioned souls. He sees that people are suffering due to a lack of Kṛṣṇa consciousness, and because he is always thinking of the welfare of others, he is *suhṛt.* Other people are always envious, but the *sādhu* is always thinking how to save others from the clutches of *māyā.* A *sādhu* is kind not only to human beings but to cats, dogs, trees, plants and insects; he will hesitate even to kill one mosquito. He does not simply think, "I shall just take care of my brother." He looks on all living beings as his brothers because Kṛṣṇa says that He is the father of all living entities.

Because a *sādhu* lives in this way, he does not create enemies. If there are enemies, they become enemies out of their own character, not out of any provocation on the part of a *sādhu.* A *sādhu* simply teaches, "My dear human being, my dear friend, just surrender to Kṛṣṇa." Enemies arise due to man's envious nature. Cāṇakya Paṇḍita says that there are two envious animals—serpents and men. Although you may be faultless, either may kill you. Of the two, Cāṇakya Paṇḍita says that the envious man is more dangerous because a serpent can be subdued by chanting a *mantra* or by some herbs, but an envious man cannot be so subdued. In Kali-yuga, practically everyone is envious, but we have to tolerate this.

Envious people create many impediments to the Kṛṣṇa consciousness movement, but we have to tolerate them. There is no alternative. One must be peaceful and depend on Kṛṣṇa in all circumstances. These are the ornaments of a *sādhu*. We should find a *sādhu* and associate with him. Then our path of liberation will be open.

In the next verse, Lord Kapila further explains the activities of a *sādhu*.

TEXT 22

mayy ananyena bhāvena
bhaktiṁ kurvanti ye dṛḍhām
mat-kṛte tyakta-karmāṇas
tyakta-svajana-bāndhavāḥ

TRANSLATION

Such a sādhu engages in staunch devotional service to the Lord without deviation. For the sake of the Lord he renounces all other connections, such as family relationships and friendly acquaintances within the world.

PURPORT

A person in the renounced order of life, a *sannyāsī*, is also called a *sādhu* because he renounces everything—his home, his comfort, his friends, his relatives and his duties to friends and to family. He renounces everything for the sake of the Supreme Personality of Godhead. A *sannyāsī* is generally in the renounced order of life, but his renunciation will be successful only when his energy is employed in the service of the Lord with great austerity. It is said here, therefore, *bhaktiṁ kurvanti ye dṛḍhām*. A person who seriously engages in the service of the Lord and is in the renounced order of life is a *sādhu*. A *sādhu* is one who has given up all responsibility to society, family and worldly humanitarianism, simply for the service of the Lord. As soon as he takes his birth in the world, a person has many responsibilities and obligations—to the public, demigods, great sages, general living beings, parents, forefathers and many others. When he gives up all these obligations for the service of the Supreme Lord, he is not punished for his renunciation. But if for sense gratification a person renounces these obligations, he is punished by the law of nature.

Kṛṣṇa and all the *śāstras* say that our only obligation is to the Supreme Personality of Godhead. If we take to His service, we are no longer obliged to anyone. We are free. How is this possible? By almighty God's power. A man may be condemned to death, but if a president or a king excuses him, he is saved. Kṛṣṇa's final instruction in *Bhagavad-gītā* is to surrender everything to Him. We can sacrifice our life, wealth and intelligence, and this is called *yajña*. Everyone has some intelligence, and everyone uses his intelligence in one way or another. Generally people use their intelligence in trying to gratify their senses, but even an ant can do this. We should try to gratify not our senses but Kṛṣṇa's senses. Then we become perfect.

We have to learn this purificatory process from a *sādhu*. Inasmuch as we try to gratify our senses, we become attached to the material world. We may render service to the *sādhu* or to Kṛṣṇa. The *sādhu* is the representative of Kṛṣṇa. He will never say, "Serve me," but will say, "Serve Kṛṣṇa." Therefore we have to approach Kṛṣṇa through the *sādhu*. This is confirmed by the Vaiṣṇava *ācārya* Narottama dāsa Ṭhākura: *chāḍiyā vaiṣṇava-sevā nistāra pāyeche kebā*. We cannot directly approach Kṛṣṇa; we have to go through the transparent via media, Kṛṣṇa's representative.

Those who are after material concessions go to different demigods. They take something from Śiva, Durgā, Kālī, Gaṇeśa, Sūrya and whomever. However, it was the goddess Pārvatī who asked Lord Śiva, "What is the best type of worship?" Lord Śiva advised, *ārādhanānāṁ sarveṣāṁ viṣṇor ārādhanaṁ param* (*Padma Purāṇa*). "My dear Pārvatī, of all kinds of worship, worship of Lord Viṣṇu is the best." Then he added: *tasmāt parataraṁ devi tadīyānāṁ samarcanam*. "And even better than the worship of Lord Viṣṇu is the worship of a Vaiṣṇava, a devotee."

Spiritual life begins with the association of a devotee, a *sādhu*. One cannot progress an inch without the mercy of a *sādhu.* Prahlāda Mahārāja has also indicated this:

naiṣāṁ matis tāvad urukramāṅghriṁ
spṛśaty anarthāpagamo yad-arthaḥ
mahīyasāṁ pāda-rajo-'bhiṣekaṁ
niṣkiñcanānāṁ na vṛṇīta yāvat

"Unless they smear upon their bodies the dust of the lotus feet of a Vaiṣṇava completely freed from material contamination, persons very much inclined toward materialistic life cannot be attached to the lotus feet of the Lord, who is glorified for His uncommon activities. Only by becoming Kṛṣṇa conscious and taking shelter at the lotus feet of the Lord in this way can one be freed from material contamination." (*Bhāg.* 7.5.32) Hiraṇyakaśipu asked Prahlāda Mahārāja, "My dear son Prahlāda, how have you become so advanced in Kṛṣṇa consciousness?" Although Hiraṇyakaśipu was a demon, he was nonetheless inquisitive. Prahlāda Mahārāja replied, "My dear father, O best of the *asuras*, one can receive Kṛṣṇa consciousness only from the instructions of a *guru.* One cannot attain it simply by speculating. Ordinary men do not know that their ultimate destination is to return to Viṣṇu." In the material world, people are always hoping for something. They hope against hope, yet their hopes will never be fulfilled. People are trying to become happy by adjusting the external energy, but they do not know that happiness cannot be achieved without approaching God. People are thinking, "I must first of all see to my own interest." That's all right, but what is that interest? That they do not know. People are thinking that by adjusting the material energy they will be happy, and everyone is trying this individually, collectively or nationally. In any case, it is not possible. People will ultimately be frustrated. Why attempt a process that will ultimately meet with frustration? It is therefore said: *adānta-gobhir viśatāṁ tamisraṁ punaḥ punaś carvita-carvaṇānām* (*Bhāg.* 7.5.30). People are being baffled in so many ways because they cannot control their senses. Their only possibility of rescue is Kṛṣṇa. Therefore in this verse it is said: *mayy ananyena bhāvena bhaktiṁ kurvanti ye dṛḍhām.*

Prahlāda Mahārāja simply thought of Kṛṣṇa. Because of this, he had to undergo a great deal of trouble given by his father. Material nature will not give us freedom very easily. If we become strong enough to try to capture the lotus feet of Kṛṣṇa, *māyā* will try to keep us under her clutches. However, if one gives up everything for Kṛṣṇa's sake, *māyā* can have no effect. The most excellent example of this is the *gopīs.* They gave up everything—family, prestige and honor—just to follow Kṛṣṇa. That is the highest perfection, but that is not possible for ordinary living entities. We should, however, follow the Gosvāmīs in their determination to worship Kṛṣṇa.

Sanātana Gosvāmī was an important minister in the government of Hussain Shah, but he gave up everything to follow Śrī Caitanya Mahāprabhu. He adopted the life of a mendicant and lived under a different tree every night. One may ask, "After giving up material enjoyment, how can one live?" The Gosvāmīs lived by dipping into the ocean of the transcendental loving affairs between Kṛṣṇa and the *gopīs.* Since that was their asset, they could live very peacefully. We cannot simply give up everything. We will become mad if we try to give up everything without having staunch faith in Kṛṣṇa. Yet if we find Kṛṣṇa's association, we can easily give up our opulent positions—our family, business and everything. However, that requires *sādhu-saṅga,* association with a *sādhu,* a devotee. When we associate with a devotee, the day will eventually come when we can give up everything and become liberated persons, fit to return home, back to Godhead.

Presently we are attached to material enjoyment, and Kṛṣṇa even gives us a chance to gratify our senses. He lets us enjoy ourselves to the fullest extent because we have come to this material world to enjoy sense gratification. However, this is called *māyā,* illusion. It is not really enjoyment, but simply struggle. When one realizes that he is simply struggling life after life, that there is actually no real enjoyment in the material world, one becomes a devotee of Kṛṣṇa. That realization requires knowledge, and that knowledge can be acquired by association with a *sādhu,* a devotee.

Freedom from this struggle with material existence is further explained by Lord Kapila in the next verse.

TEXT 23

mad-āśrayāḥ kathā mṛṣṭāḥ
śṛṇvanti kathayanti ca

tapanti vividhās tāpā
naitān mad-gata-cetasaḥ

TRANSLATION

Engaged constantly in chanting and hearing about Me, the Supreme Personality of Godhead, the sādhus do not suffer from material miseries because they are always filled with thoughts of My pastimes and activities.

PURPORT

There are multifarious miseries in material existence—those pertaining to the body and the mind, those imposed by other living entities and those imposed by natural disturbances. But a *sādhu* is not disturbed by such miserable conditions because his mind is always filled with Kṛṣṇa consciousness, and thus he does not like to talk about anything but the activities of the Lord. Mahārāja Ambarīṣa did not speak of anything but the pastimes of the Lord. *Vacāṁsi vaikuṇṭha-guṇānuvarṇane.* He engaged his words only in glorification of the Supreme Personality of Godhead. Ordinary conditioned souls, being forgetful of the activities of the Lord, are always full of anxieties and material tribulations. On the other hand, since the devotees always engage in the topics of the Lord, they are forgetful of the miseries of material existence. Thus they differ from other living entities, who are simply suffering.

There is no one in the world materially engaged who can boldly say, "I am not suffering." I challenge anyone to say this. Everyone in the material world is suffering in some way or another. If not, why are so many drugs being advertised? On the television they are always advertising tranquilizers and pain killers, and in America and in other Western countries they are so advanced that there are dozens of tablets for various pains. Therefore there must be some suffering. Actually, anyone who has a material body has to accept suffering. There are three types of suffering in the material world: *ādhyātmika, ādhibhautika* and *ādhidaivika.* *Ādhyatmika* refers to the body and mind. Today I have a headache or some pain in my back, or my mind is not very quiet. These are sufferings called *ādhyātmika.* There are other forms of suffering called *ādhibhautika,* which are sufferings imposed by other living entities.

Apart from this, there are sufferings called *adhidaivika*, over which we have no control whatsoever. These are caused by the demigods or acts of nature, and include famine, pestilence, flood, excessive heat or excessive cold, earthquakes, fire and so on. Nonetheless, we are thinking that we are very happy within this material world, although in addition to these threefold miseries there is also birth, old age, disease and death. So where is our happiness? Because we are under the spell of *māyā*, we are thinking that our position is very secure. We are thinking, "Let us enjoy life," but what kind of enjoyment is this?

Obviously we have to tolerate suffering. One of the characteristics of a *sādhu* is tolerance. Everyone is tolerant to a degree, but a *sādhu's* tolerance and an ordinary man's tolerance are different. This is because a *sādhu* knows that he is not the body. According to a Bengali Vaiṣṇava song: *deha-smṛti nāhi yāra saṁsāra-bandhana kāhāḥ tāra.*

If we properly understand that we are not the body, although we may suffer, we will not feel the suffering as acutely. For instance, if one thinks, "This is my car," and is very attached to it, he suffers more when it is wrecked than a person who thinks, "It can be repaired, or I can leave it." It is a question of mental absorption. Because he is more like an animal, a materialist suffers more. The devotee, on the other hand, takes Kṛṣṇa's advice in *Bhagavad-gītā* (2.14):

mātrā-sparśās tu kaunteya
śītoṣṇa-sukha-duḥkha-dāḥ
āgamāpāyino 'nityās
tāṁs titikṣasva bhārata

"O son of Kuntī, the nonpermanent appearance of happiness and distress and their disappearance in due course are like the appearance and disappearance of winter and summer seasons. They arise from sense perception, O scion of Bharata, and one must learn to tolerate them without being disturbed."

In summer we suffer, and in winter we suffer. In the summer, fire brings suffering, and in the winter the same fire is pleasing. Similarly, in the winter, water is suffering, but in the summer it is pleasing. The water and the fire are the same, but sometimes they are pleasing, sometimes they are not. This is due to the touch of the skin. We all have some "skin disease," which is the body, and therefore we are suffering. Because we have become such rascals, we are thinking, "I am this body." According to the Āyur-vedic system, the body is composed of three material elements: *kapha-pitta-vāyu.* The more we are in the bodily conception, the more we suffer.

Presently so many "ism's" are being developed according to the bodily conception—nationalism, communism, socialism, communalism and so on. In Calcutta during the 1947 Hindu-Muslim riots, there was more suffering because everyone was thinking, "I am a Hindu" or "I am a Muslim." But, if one is advanced in Kṛṣṇa consciousness, he will not fight according to such conceptions. A Kṛṣṇa conscious person knows that he is neither Hindu nor Muslim but the eternal servant of Kṛṣṇa. Because people are being educated to become more body conscious, their sufferings are increasing. If we reduce the bodily conception, suffering will also be reduced. Those who are Kṛṣṇa conscious, who are always thinking of Kṛṣṇa within their minds and within their hearts, are not suffering as much because they know that whatever they might suffer is due to Kṛṣṇa's desire. Therefore they welcome suffering. For instance, when Kṛṣṇa was leaving, Queen Kuntī said, "My dear Kṛṣṇa, when we were in a dangerous situation, You were always present as our friend and adviser. Now we are well situated with our kingdom, and now You are leaving for Dvārakā. This is not good. It is better that we again suffer so that we can always remember You." Thus the devotee sometimes welcomes suffering as an opportunity to remember Kṛṣṇa constantly. When a devotee suffers, he thinks, "This is due to my past misdeeds. Actually I should be suffering a great deal, but due to Kṛṣṇa's grace I am suffering just a little. After all, suffering and enjoyment are in the mind." In this way, a devotee is not greatly affected by suffering, and this is the difference between a devotee and a nondevotee.

Prahlāda Mahārāja, a five-year-old boy, had to undergo a great deal of suffering at the hands of his father, who was torturing him for being a devotee. The boy was trampled by elephants, thrown from a mountain, placed in burning oil and thrown into a snake pit, yet he was silent during this whole ordeal. Similarly, Haridāsa Ṭhākura, a Muhammadan by birth, was a very great devotee and was always chanting Hare Kṛṣṇa. That was his only fault. However, the Muslim Kazi called him forth and said, "You are a Muhammadan, born in a great Muhammadan family, yet you are chanting this Hindu Hare Kṛṣṇa *mantra.* What is this?" Haridāsa Ṭhākura mildly replied, "My dear sir, there are many Hindus who have become Muhammadans. Suppose I have become a Hindu? What is wrong with this?" The Kazi became very angry and ordered Haridāsa Ṭhākura to be whipped in twenty-two bazaars. This essentially meant that he was to be beaten to death, but because he was such a great devotee he did not actually feel the pain. Although a devotee may sometimes have to suffer, he tolerates the suffering. At the same time, he is very kind to conditioned souls and tries to elevate them to Kṛṣṇa consciousness. This is one of the primary features of a devotee's life. People are always putting a *sādhu* into difficulties, but he does not give up his job, which is to spread Kṛṣṇa consciousness so that others may become happy. It was Prahlāda Mahārāja who said: "My Lord, I am not suffering, for I know the art of being happy." How is this? "Simply by hearing about You and chanting about You I am happy." This is the business of a devotee—hearing and chanting about the Lord. This is *śravaṇaṁ kīrtanaṁ viṣṇoḥ smaraṇam.* Now this *śravaṇaṁ kīrtanam* is taking place all over the world through the Kṛṣṇa consciousness movement.

Even in ordinary life it is possible for the mind to be absorbed in such a way that even a surgical operation may not disturb a man. Years ago, when Stalin had to undergo a surgical operation, he refused the use of chloroform. If this is possible even in an ordinary materialistic life, what to speak of spiritual life? One's mind should always be absorbed in Kṛṣṇa consciousness, in thinking of Kṛṣṇa. It is Kṛṣṇa's injunction, "Always think of Me." The European and American youths in the Kṛṣṇa consciousness movement have been accustomed to many bad habits since birth, but now they have given these up. Many people think that it is impossible to live without illicit sex, intoxication, meat-eating and gambling. One famous Marquess told one of my Godbrothers, "Please make me a *brāhmaṇa.*" My Godbrother said, "Yes, it is not a very difficult thing. Simply give up these bad habits—intoxication, illicit sex, meat-eating and gambling. Then you can become a *brāhmaṇa.*" The Marquess then said, "Impossible! This is our life." Actually we have seen that in Western countries older men cannot give up these habits, and because of this they are suffering, yet many young boys and girls have given them up, and there is no suffering. This is due to Kṛṣṇa consciousness.

This process is open to everyone. Everyone has heard of the

Bhagavad-gītā. We can attain perfection simply by following the instructions given in this book. It is not necessary to abandon our responsibilities. Mahārāja Ambarīṣa was a great emperor administering to his kingdom, yet at the same time he spoke only of Kṛṣṇa. Caitanya Mahāprabhu requested that His devotees only talk about Kṛṣṇa. If we simply talk about Kṛṣṇa and hear about Him, the stage will come when we will no longer suffer. This is called *ānandamayo 'bhyāsāt* in the *Vedānta-sūtra.* The living entity and Kṛṣṇa are both *ānandamaya,* transcendentally blissful. On that platform, there is no possibility of material suffering. It is not a question of displaying some magical feats. The greatest magic is freedom from suffering, and this is the freedom of a devotee. When we feel pleasure from hearing about Kṛṣṇa and talking about Him, we should know that we are making progress on the path of perfection. At that time, material suffering will not be felt at all. This is the practical effect of rendering devotional service, which Lord Kapila is pointing out to His mother.

TEXT 24

ta ete sādhavaḥ sādhvi
sarva-saṅga-vivarjitāḥ
saṅgas teṣv atha te prārthyaḥ
saṅga-doṣa-harā hi te

TRANSLATION

O My mother, O virtuous lady, these are the qualities of great devotees who are free from all attachment. You must seek attachment to such holy men, for this counteracts the pernicious effects of material attachment.

PURPORT

Kapila Muni herein advises His mother, Devahūti, that if she wants to be free from material attachment, she should increase her attachment for the *sādhus,* or devotees who are completely freed from all material attachment. In *Bhagavad-gītā* (15.5) it is stated, *nirmāna-mohā jita-saṅga-doṣāḥ.* This refers to one who is completely freed from the puffed-up condition of material possessiveness. A person may be materially very rich or respectable, but if he at all wants to transfer himself to the spiritual kingdom, back home, back to Godhead, he has to be freed from material possessiveness because that is a false position.

The word *moha* used here means the false understanding that one is rich or poor. In this material world, the conception that one is very rich or very poor—or any such consciousness in connection with material existence—is false, because this body itself is temporary. A pure soul who is prepared to be freed from this material entanglement must first be free from the association of the three modes of nature. Our consciousness at the present moment is polluted because of association with the three modes of nature; therefore in *Bhagavad-gītā* the same principle is stated. It is advised, *jita-saṅga-doṣāḥ:* one should be freed from the contaminated association of the three modes. Here also, in the *Śrīmad-Bhāgavatam,* this is confirmed: a pure devotee, who is preparing to transfer himself to the spiritual kingdom, is also freed from the association of the three modes. We have to seek the association of such devotees. For this reason we have begun the International Society for Krishna Consciousness. There are many mercantile and scientific associations in human society established to develop a particular type of education or consciousness, but there is no association which helps one to get free from all material association. If anyone wishes to become free from this material contamination, he has to seek the association of devotees, wherein Kṛṣṇa consciousness is exclusively cultured.

Because a devotee is freed from all contaminated material association, he is not affected by the miseries of material existence, even though he appears to be in the material world. How is it possible? A cat carries her kittens in her mouth, and when she kills a rat, she also carries the booty in her mouth. Thus both are carried in the mouth of the cat, but they are in different conditions. The kitten feels comfort in the mouth of the mother, whereas when the rat is carried in the mouth of the cat, the rat feels the blows of death. Similarly, those who are *sādhus,* or devotees engaged in the transcendental service of the Lord, do not feel the contamination of material miseries, whereas those who are not devotees in Kṛṣṇa consciousness actually feel the miseries of material existence. One should therefore give up the association of materialistic persons and seek the association of those engaged in Kṛṣṇa consciousness. By such association one will be benefited by spiritual advancement. By their words and instructions, one will be able to cut off his attachment to material existence.

In this Kali-yuga, the present age, the dangerous modes of *rajo-guṇa* and *tamo-guṇa*, passion and ignorance, are especially prominent. Practically everyone in this age is contaminated by lusty desire, greed and ignorance. It is said in the *śāstras* that in this age of Kali, *sattva-guṇa*, the mode of goodness, is practically nonexistent.

The Fourteenth Chapter of *Bhagavad-gītā* nicely explains how one can free oneself of contamination by the material modes. Now Kapiladeva advises, "Mother, if you want to get rid of the contamination of material nature, you should associate with a *sādhu.*" Attachment to the material modes brings about our bondage. If we want to be free from this bondage, we have to transfer our attachment to a *sādhu.*

Actually everyone is attached to something. No one can say that he is free from attachment. The Māyāvāda and Buddhist philosophies tell us to become detached, but this in itself is not possible. A child is attached to playing in so many ways, but gradually his attachments should be transferred to reading and going to school to acquire an education. It is a question not of stopping attachment but of transferring it. If one simply tries to put an end to attachment, he will become mad. Something must be given in the place of attachment. For instance, we tell our disciples to stop eating meat, but how is this meat-eating stopped? In the place of meat, we are supplying *kacaurīs*, *rasagullā* and many other palatable things. In this way, detachment is possible. First of all, nullify the inferior attachment, and then supply a better attachment. There is no question of forcing a living entity. This must be done gradually. A child may have some attachment, but by the system of replacing attachment, his attachment is overturned. Similarly, our consciousness has somehow or other become contaminated. Now it has to be purified. Then Kṛṣṇa consciousness will automatically arise and awaken.

Kṛṣṇa consciousness is our original consciousness, but somehow or other it has become covered by material attachment. The question is how to give up material attachment and become attached to Kṛṣṇa. The process is *sādhu-saṅga*, association with a *sādhu.* We have many attachments in this material world, but we cannot make these attachments void. We simply have to purify them. Some say that if the eye is diseased,

His Divine Grace A.C. Bhaktivedanta Swami Prabhupāda

The Founder-Ācārya of the International Society for Krishna Consciousness and the greatest exponent of Kṛṣṇa consciousness in the modern world.

PLATE ONE: Lord Kapiladeva teaches His mother, Devahūti, the science of *sāṅkhya-yoga*. (*p.* 2)

PLATE TWO: Within every atom of creation resides an expansion of Lord Kṛṣṇa known as the Paramātmā, or Supersoul. (*p. 34*)

PLATE THREE: In Goloka Vṛndāvana, His personal, spiritual abode, Kṛṣṇa enjoys a daily festival of happiness in the company of His beloved cowherd boyfriends and girlfriends. (*p. 84*)

PLATE FOUR: Lord Kṛṣṇa appears as the Deity form in the temple to give us a chance to see Him and serve Him. As shown here, in Vedic times Deity worship was extremely opulent. (*p. 163*)

PLATE FIVE: By means of His glance, Mahā-Viṣṇu impregnates the living entities into the material nature, personified as Goddess Durgā. (*p. 154*)

PLATE SIX: Lord Caitanya teaches His intimate associates the process of *yoga* for the modern age: devotional service, beginning with the congregational chanting of the holy names of God. (*p. 97*)

PLATE SEVEN: Countless universes emanate from the body of Mahā-Viṣṇu as He reclines in the Causal Ocean. (*p. 224*)

it should be plucked out, but that is not treatment. Treatment is removing the disease. Somehow or other there is a cataract, and if the cataract is removed, one's eyesight will be revived. We have many desires, but we have to divert these desires to Kṛṣṇa's service. For instance, we may be very attached to making money; therefore Kṛṣṇa says, "Yes, go ahead and conduct your business. There is no harm. Simply give Me the results." As stated in *Bhagavad-gītā* (9.27):

yat karoṣi yad aśnāsi
yaj juhoṣi dadāsi yat
yat tapasyasi kaunteya
tat kuruṣva mad-arpaṇam

"O son of Kuntī, all that you do, all that you eat, all that you offer and give away, as well as all austerities that you may perform, should be done as an offering unto Me."

This is the beginning of *bhakti-yoga*. If we conduct business and earn money, we should spend it for Kṛṣṇa. This is a form of *bhakti*. Another vivid example is Arjuna, who was a fighter. By fighting, he became a devotee. He did not become a devotee by chanting Hare Kṛṣṇa but by fighting in the Battle of Kurukṣetra. Kṛṣṇa advised him to fight, but because Arjuna was a Vaiṣṇava, in the beginning he was unwilling. A Vaiṣṇava does not like to kill anything, but if Kṛṣṇa orders him, he must fight. He does not fight out of his own will, because a Vaiṣṇava's natural instinct is not to do harm to anyone. However, when a Vaiṣṇava knows that Kṛṣṇa wants a particular thing done, he does not care for his own considerations. In any case, everyone has some particular type of duty, an occupation. If we perform our occupation in the worship of Kṛṣṇa, our life will be perfect. This is also the instruction given in *Śrīmad-Bhāgavatam* (1.2.13):

ataḥ pumbhir dvija-śreṣṭhā
varṇāśrama-vibhāgaśaḥ
svanuṣṭhitasya dharmasya
saṁsiddhir hari-toṣaṇam

"O best of the twice-born, it is therefore concluded that the highest perfection one can achieve by discharging the duties prescribed for one's own occupation according to caste divisions and orders of life is to please the Personality of Godhead."

Formerly, the *varṇāśrama-dharma* was prominent, and everyone had a particular duty according to his position in society. Now the occupational duties have expanded, but it doesn't matter whether one is an engineer, a doctor or whatever. Simply try to serve Kṛṣṇa by the results of work. That is *bhakti.* It is not the philosophy of this Kṛṣṇa consciousness movement to disengage people from their activities. One should engage in his occupation, but one should never forget Kṛṣṇa. Kṛṣṇa advises us to always become Kṛṣṇa conscious, and we should always think that we are acting for Kṛṣṇa. Of course, we should work by the order of Kṛṣṇa or His representative, not whimsically. If we perform some nonsensical action and think, "I am doing this for Kṛṣṇa," that will not be accepted. The work must be verified by Kṛṣṇa's acceptance or by the acceptance of Kṛṣṇa's representative. Arjuna did not fight without Kṛṣṇa's order; therefore we must receive our orders also. We may say, "I cannot find Kṛṣṇa. How can I follow His order?" It is the role of the *sādhu* to impart Kṛṣṇa's orders. Since Kṛṣṇa's representative is the *sādhu,* Kapiladeva advises His mother to associate with *sādhus.*

We have described the symptoms of a *sādhu,* and we have stated that a *sādhu* should be accepted by his characteristics. It is not that we accept anyone who comes along and says, "I am a *sādhu.*" The characteristics of a *sādhu* have to be present. Similarly, it is not that anyone is accepted who comes along and says, "I am an incarnation of God." There are characteristics of God given in the *śāstras. Sādhu-saṅga,* association with a *sādhu,* is very essential in Kṛṣṇa consciousness. People are suffering due to contamination by *tamo-guṇa* and *rajo-guṇa.* The *sādhu* teaches one how to remain purely in *sattva-guṇa* by truthfulness, cleanliness, mind control, sense control, simplicity, tolerance, and full faith and knowledge. These are some of the characteristics of *sattva-guṇa.*

Instead of thinking, "Unless I have a drink, I will go mad," one should think, "Unless I associate with a *sādhu,* I will go mad." When we can think in this way, we will become liberated. Caitanya Mahāprabhu has stated that He wants every village in the entire world to be a center for Kṛṣṇa consciousness so that people can take advantage of *sādhus* and in turn become *sādhus.* This is the mission of this Kṛṣṇa consciousness movement. We simply have to voluntarily undergo some penance in the beginning. It may be a little painful in the beginning to refrain from illicit sex, intoxication, meat-eating and gambling, but one has to be tolerant. To be cured of a disease, we may have to agree to undergo some surgical operation. Although the operation may be very painful, we have to tolerate it. This is called *titikṣavaḥ.* At the same time, we have to be *kāruṇikāḥ*—that is, we have to take compassion upon fallen souls by going from town to town to enlighten others in Kṛṣṇa consciousness. This is a *sādhu's* duty. Those who are preachers are superior to those who go to the Himalayas to meditate. It is good to go to the Himalayas to meditate for one's personal benefit, but those who undergo many difficulties in order to preach are superior. They are actually fighting for Kṛṣṇa's sake, and they are certainly more compassionate. Those *sādhus* who leave Vṛndāvana to go fight in the world, to spread Kṛṣṇa consciousness, are superior *sādhus.* This is the opinion of Kṛṣṇa in *Bhagavad-gītā* (18.68–69):

ya idaṁ paramaṁ guhyaṁ
mad-bhakteṣv abhidhāsyati
bhaktiṁ mayi parāṁ kṛtvā
mām evaiṣyaty asaṁśayaḥ

na ca tasmān manuṣyeṣu
kaścin me priya-kṛttamaḥ
bhavitā na ca me tasmād
anyaḥ priyataro bhuvi

"For one who explains the supreme secret to the devotees, devotional service is guaranteed, and at the end he will come back to Me. There is no servant in this world more dear to Me than he, nor will there ever be one more dear."

If we want to be quickly recognized by Kṛṣṇa, we should become preachers. This is also the message of Śrī Caitanya Mahāprabhu. It is not that one should remain in India; rather, one should travel all over the world to preach Kṛṣṇa consciousness. The *sādhu* is *suhṛt;* he is the well-wisher of everyone. This does not mean that he is a well-wisher for an

Indian nationalist or whatever. No, he is a well-wisher even of cats and dogs. A devotee even wishes to benefit cats and dogs by giving them *prasāda.* Once, when devotees from Bengal were going to see Caitanya Mahāprabhu, a dog began to follow them, and the leader of the party, Śivānanda Sena, was giving *prasāda* to the dog. When they had to cross a river, the boatman would not take the dog, but Śivānanda Sena paid him more money and said, "Please take this dog. He is a Vaiṣṇava, for he has joined our company. How can we leave him behind?" Caitanya Mahāprabhu Himself actually threw some of His food to the dog, and in this way the dog attained Vaikuṇṭha.

Not only is a *sādhu* everyone's well-wisher, but he is not an enemy of anyone. He is also *śānta,* peaceful. These are the preliminary characteristics of a *sādhu.* He is also attached to no one but Kṛṣṇa. *Mayy ananyena bhāvena.* These are the external and internal symptoms of a devotee. A devotee also respects the demigods because he knows their position in relation to Kṛṣṇa. In *Brahma-saṁhitā* (5.44), the goddess Durgā is worshiped as the external energy, or potency, of Kṛṣṇa.

sṛṣṭi-sthiti-pralaya-sādhana-śaktir ekā
chāyeva yasya bhuvanāni bibhārti durgā
icchānurūpam api yasya ca ceṣṭate sā
govindam ādi-puruṣaṁ tam ahaṁ bhajāmi

"The external potency, *māyā,* who is of the nature of the shadow of the *cit,* spiritual, potency, is worshiped by all people as Durgā, the creating, preserving and destroying agency of this mundane world. I adore the primeval Lord Govinda, in accordance with whose will Durgā conducts herself."

The goddess Durgā is so powerful that she can create, maintain and annihilate. However, she cannot act independent of Kṛṣṇa. She is like a shadow of Kṛṣṇa. A *sādhu* knows that *prakṛti,* nature, is working under Kṛṣṇa's direction. Similarly, a policeman knows that he is not working independently but under government orders. This knowledge is required in order that the policeman, who has some power, will not think that he has become God. No, God is not so cheap. God has multienergies, and one of these energies is Durgā. It is not that she is all and all, for there are many millions of Durgās, just as there are many millions of Śivas and millions of universes. Although there are millions of demigods, God is one. It is not that there are a million Gods. Of course, God can expand in millions of forms, but that is different. A devotee offers respects to the demigods as the assistants of the Supreme Personality of Godhead, not as the supreme power. One who does not know God as He is considers the demigods to be supreme. Such people are less intelligent. A devotee offers respects to the demigods, but he knows that the Supreme Lord is Kṛṣṇa. *Kṛṣṇas tu bhagavān svayam.* Actually a *sādhu*, a Vaiṣṇava, offers respects to everyone, and he is ready to give up relatives and everything else for Kṛṣṇa's sake. A *sādhu* simply takes pleasure in hearing about Kṛṣṇa and talking about Him.

There are many pastimes enacted by Kṛṣṇa. He fights and kills demons, and He performs His pastimes with the *gopīs.* He plays as a cowherd boy in Vṛndāvana and as King of Dvārakā. There are many books about Kṛṣṇa, *kṛṣṇa-kathā,* and this Kṛṣṇa consciousness movement has already published many of them. Apart from *Bhagavad-gītā,* which is spoken by Kṛṣṇa, we can read these other books. In this way, one can learn the art of becoming a *sādhu.* Simply by hearing about Kṛṣṇa and speaking about Him, we will be immediately relieved from the suffering of this material condition.

As stated in this verse:

ta ete sādhavaḥ sādhvi
sarva-saṅga-vivarjitāḥ

These symptoms are visible when one no longer has material attachment. A *sādhu* does not think himself Hindu, Muslim, Christian, American, Indian or whatever. A *sādhu* simply thinks, "I am the servant of Kṛṣṇa." Śrī Caitanya Mahāprabhu has said, "I am not a *brāhmaṇa, kṣatriya, vaiśya, śūdra, brahmacārī* or whatever. I am simply the servant of the servant of the servant of Kṛṣṇa." One need only learn this process in order to render the best service to humanity.

CHAPTER TWELVE

Association With the Supreme Lord Through Hearing

TEXTS 25–26

satāṁ prasaṅgān mama vīrya-saṁvido
bhavanti hṛt-karṇa-rasāyanāḥ kathāḥ
taj-joṣaṇād āśv apavarga-vartmani
śraddhā ratir bhaktir anukramiṣyati

bhaktyā pumāñ jāta-virāga aindriyād
dṛṣṭa-śrutān mad-racanānucintayā
cittasya yatto grahaṇe yoga-yukto
yatiṣyate ṛjubhir yoga-mārgaiḥ

TRANSLATION

In the association of pure devotees, discussion of the pastimes and activities of the Supreme Personality of Godhead is very pleasing and satisfying to the ear and the heart. By cultivating such knowledge one gradually becomes advanced on the path of liberation, and thereafter he is freed, and his attraction becomes fixed. Then real devotion and devotional service begin.

Thus consciously engaged in devotional service in the association of devotees, a person gains distaste for sense gratification, both in this world and in the next, by constantly thinking about the activities of the Lord. This process of Kṛṣṇa consciousness is the easiest process of mystic power; when one is actually situated on that path of devotional service, he is able to control the mind.

PURPORT

The process of advancing in Kṛṣṇa consciousness and devotional service is described here. The first point is that one must seek the association of persons who are Kṛṣṇa conscious and who engage in devotional service. Without such association one cannot advance. Simply by theoretical knowledge or study one cannot make any appreciable advancement. One must give up the association of materialistic persons and seek the association of devotees because without such association one cannot understand the activities of the Lord. Generally, people are convinced of the impersonal feature of the Absolute Truth. Because they do not associate with devotees, they cannot understand that the Absolute Truth can be a person and have personal activities. This is a very difficult subject matter, and unless one has personal understanding of the Absolute Truth, there is no meaning to devotion. Service or devotion cannot be offered to anything impersonal. Service must be offered to a person. Nondevotees cannot appreciate Kṛṣṇa consciousness by reading the *Śrīmad-Bhāgavatam* or any other Vedic literature wherein the activities of the Lord are described; they think that these activities are fictional, because spiritual life is not explained to them in the proper mood. To understand the personal activities of the Lord, one has to seek the association of devotees, and by such association, when one contemplates and tries to understand the transcendental activities of the Lord, the path to liberation is open, and he is freed. One who has firm faith in the Supreme Personality of Godhead becomes fixed, and his attraction for association with the Lord and the devotees increases. Association with devotees means association with the Lord. The devotee who makes this association develops the consciousness for rendering service to the Lord, and then, being situated in the transcendental position of devotional service, he gradually becomes perfect.

In all scriptures people are encouraged to act in a pious way so that they can enjoy sense gratification not only in this life but also in the next. For example, one is promised promotion to the heavenly kingdom of higher planets by pious fruitive activities. But a devotee in the association of devotees prefers to contemplate the activities of the Lord—how He has created this universe, how He is maintaining it, how the creation dissolves, and how in the spiritual kingdom the Lord's pastimes are enacted. There are full literatures describing these activities, especially *Bhagavad-gītā*, *Brahma-saṁhitā* and *Śrīmad-Bhāgavatam.* The sincere devotee who associates with devotees gets the opportunity to hear and contemplate these subjects, and the result is that he feels distaste for so-called happiness in this or that world, in heaven or on other planets. The devotees are simply interested in being transferred to the personal association of the Lord; they are no longer attracted to temporary so-called happiness. That is the position of one who is *yoga-yukta.* One who is fixed in mystic power is not disturbed by the allurement of this world or that world; he is interested in spiritual understanding. This is very easily attained by the easiest process, *bhakti-yoga. Ṛjubhir yoga-mārgaiḥ.* A very suitable word used here is *ṛjubhiḥ,* or "very easy." There are different processes of *yoga-mārga,* attaining *yoga* perfection, but this process, devotional service to the Lord, is the easiest. Not only is it the easiest process, but the result is sublime. Everyone, therefore, should try this process of Kṛṣṇa consciousness and reach the highest perfection.

Sat means "existence," and *asat* means "that which does not exist," that which is temporary. The material world is *asat;* therefore the *Vedas* enjoin: *asato mā sad gama:* "Do not remain within this material world." Those who are interested in materialistic life are also called *asat.* When asked how a Vaiṣṇava behaves, Caitanya Mahāprabhu replied, *asat-saṅga-tyāga,*—*ei vaiṣṇava-ācāra:* "A devotee first of all avoids the company of *asat,* those who are materially interested." (Cc. *Madhya* 22.87) We have established this Kṛṣṇa consciousness movement in order to avoid *asat-saṅga,* association with those who are interested in material things. Because we are associating with Kṛṣṇa, we do not wish to talk about anything but Kṛṣṇa. Everyone is interested in this business or that, and we are exclusively interested in our Kṛṣṇa consciousness business. Those who are *asat* are very much attached to sense gratification, and the culmination of sense gratification is sex.

In addition, Śrī Sanātana Gosvāmī in his *Hari-bhakti-vilāsa* recommends that one should not hear *Bhagavad-gītā,* the *Purāṇas,* the *Śrīmad-Bhāgavatam* or any *hari-kathā* from anyone who is not a Vaiṣṇava in his actions. That means that we should not hear these Vedic literatures from the Māyāvādīs, who actually do not accept Kṛṣṇa as the Supreme Personality of Godhead. How can one not accept Kṛṣṇa as the Supreme Lord and yet dare to speak on *Bhagavad-gītā?* We will never derive any benefit from listening to the commentaries of such people. *Bhagavad-gītā* and *Śrīmad-Bhāgavatam* should be heard from the devotees. We can hear *Bhagavad-gītā* from Māyāvādīs for hundreds of years and yet never understand Kṛṣṇa. It is therefore forbidden for Vaiṣṇavas to hear talks given by Māyāvādīs.

Hari-kathā, talks about Śrī Hari, or Kṛṣṇa, are *amṛta*, nectar. If one hears them from the right source, he attains *amṛta* (*so 'mṛtatvāya kalpate*). *Mṛta* means "birth and death," and *amṛta* means "the cessation of birth and death." Spiritual life means putting an end to birth, old age, disease and death. Getting *amṛta*, nectar, means getting relief from birth and death, and that is the real aim of spiritual life. Lord Kṛṣṇa says in *Bhagavad-gītā* (7.16) that spiritual life begins when one is pious:

catur-vidhā bhajante māṁ
janāḥ sukṛtino 'rjuna
ārto jijñāsur arthārthī
jñānī ca bharatarṣabha

"O best among the Bhāratas [Arjuna], four kinds of pious men render devotional service unto Me—the distressed, the desirer of wealth, the inquisitive, and he who is searching for knowledge of the Absolute."

If we actually want to become pious and develop our devotional life, we have to associate unflinchingly with a *sādhu*. Then we can acquire some taste for Kṛṣṇa. When we discuss Kṛṣṇa with a *sādhu*, the discussion becomes very pleasing, and we develop some taste, which is called *rasa*, or mellow. *Rasa* is the enjoyment we derive from drinking something very nice when we are thirsty. Kṛṣṇa has instructed us to think of Him when drinking water. This is not very difficult. Kṛṣṇa also tells us to think of Him when we see sunlight in the morning. Why do we say, "Can you show me God?" God is showing us Himself. Why do we close our eyes to try to see Him? He says, "I am this, and I am that." It is not that suddenly we can expect to see God, but we can become qualified to see God through the association of a *sādhu*. Presently many people are interested in receiving degrees from big universities, but education without God consciousness is simply an expansion of *māyā's* influence. Because knowledge is taken away by illusion, the universities are simply presenting impediments on the path of God consciousness. The living entity is already illusioned when he comes into the material world, and so-called advanced education simply increases his illusion. Trying to become happy in this temporary, material life, the living entity has forgotten that he is the eternal servant of Kṛṣṇa. Even if one becomes happy in this temporary life, his happiness is an illusion because no one is allowed to stay and enjoy his happiness. These points have to be understood in the association of devotees. A devotee knows everything because he has seen the Supreme Absolute Truth, Kṛṣṇa.

What is the goal of *vedānta-darśana? Veda* means "knowledge," and *anta* means "ultimate." What is that ultimate knowledge? In *Bhagavad-gītā* (15.15) Śrī Kṛṣṇa says:

vedaiś ca sarvair aham eva vedyo
vedānta-kṛd veda-vid eva cāham

"By all the *Vedas*, I am to be known; indeed, I am the compiler of *Vedānta*, and I am the knower of the *Vedas.*"

If we listen to Kṛṣṇa and understand what and who He is, we can actually understand *Vedānta.* If we do not understand Kṛṣṇa but advertise ourselves as Vedāntists, we are just being illusioned. Without understanding Kṛṣṇa, one is actually a *mūḍha*, a fool. People do not know it, but actually anyone in the material world is more or less a *mūḍha.* We are all *mūḍhas*, for unless we are *mūḍhas*, we do not come into the material world. From Brahmā down to the smallest ant, we are all *mūḍhas* of different degrees. In order to become really learned, we have to associate with devotees. Then we can actually relish *kṛṣṇa-kathā.* When discussed among devotees, *kṛṣṇa-kathā* is pleasing to the heart and ear. This requires a little training, and this training is given by the devotees. We should follow the devotees in their practical daily life, in their routine work and behavior. Cultivation means practice, and the great *ācāryas* have given a routine we can cultivate. For instance, *The Nectar of Devotion* by Śrīla Rūpa Gosvāmī deals with the cultivation of devotional service, and this book, which we have translated, has been very well received in European and American universities. *Bhakti-rasāmṛta-sindhu, The Nectar of Devotion*, is the actual science of *bhakti. Bhakti* is not sentiment; it is a great science, and we have to learn it scientifically. It is not that we have to wait for another life to cultivate devotional service. We can read *The Nectar of Devotion*, live with devotees, rise early in the morning to attend *maṅgala-ārati,* study Vedic literature, take *prasāda* and preach Kṛṣṇa consciousness.

Māyā is very strong, and to begin devotional service is to declare war against *māyā.* Some of the devotees in this Kṛṣṇa consciousness movement may fall down, but whatever is done sincerely is to their permanent credit. This is confirmed in *Bhagavad-gītā.* If one renders a little devotional service, he does not fall down into the lower species but again attains a human form. There are 8,400,000 species, but the fallen devotee is guaranteed a human life. If one becomes Kṛṣṇa conscious, he is assured of a good birth in the next life. However, if one completes his Kṛṣṇa consciousness in this life, he will not take birth again but will go to Kṛṣṇa. This is what is actually wanted. Why take the chance of being born into a rich family or a *brāhmaṇa* family? Actually, such a birth is quite risky because there is really no guarantee. Generally, those who are rich don't care at all for Kṛṣṇa consciousness, and those who are born in *brāhmaṇa* families generally become puffed-up, thinking, "I am a *brāhmaṇa.* I am born in a very high family." Thinking this brings about their falldown. It is said that pride precedes a fall. A Vaiṣṇava is by nature very humble.

These are the chances one takes when one becomes a human being. Kṛṣṇa is personally advising us to take up the opportunities offered by the Kṛṣṇa consciousness movement. We should take them and not run the risk of committing spiritual suicide.

This is the process for understanding the Absolute Truth, the Supreme Person, the Supreme Being. In the Absolute, there are no contradictions. Kṛṣṇa's name, form, activities, paraphernalia and attributes are identical with Kṛṣṇa. This is the meaning of absolute. There is no difference between Kṛṣṇa's form and Kṛṣṇa. Kṛṣṇa's hands and Kṛṣṇa's legs are nondifferent. In the material world, there is a difference between our left hand and our right hand, between the nose and the ear, but these dualities do not exist in Kṛṣṇa. This is the meaning of absolute. As stated in *Brahma-saṁhitā* (5.32):

aṅgāni yasya sakalendriya-vṛttimanti
paśyanti pānti kalayanti ciraṁ jaganti
ānanda-cinmaya-sad-ujjvala-vigrahasya
govindam ādi-puruṣaṁ tam ahaṁ bhajāmi

"I worship Govinda, the primeval Lord, whose transcendental form is full of bliss, truth and substantiality, and is thus full of the most dazzling splendor. Each of the limbs of that transcendental figure possesses, in Himself, the full-fledged functions of all the organs, and eternally sees, maintains and manifests the infinite universes, both spiritual and mundane." The different parts of our bodies serve different purposes, but any limb of Kṛṣṇa's body can serve any purpose. Kṛṣṇa can eat through His eyes, or Kṛṣṇa can go somewhere simply by thinking. The Absolute is *advaita.* There is no duality in the Absolute. Everything is one.

Our material disease lies in wanting to satisfy our senses. We have stated before that advancement of civilization means advancement of sense gratification, but *bhakti* means just the opposite. As long as we are interested in sense gratification, there is no question of *bhakti.* We have to reduce our tendency for sense gratification and increase our devotional activities. We have also stated that material bondage means accepting one body and creating another. Kṛṣṇa, through nature, will give us full facility to enjoy our senses. Presently in the Western countries it has become fashionable to run around naked. Therefore nature will give these people an opportunity to stand naked like trees for many years. Why are we receiving different bodies? Because we have different tendencies for sense gratification. We actually have to come to detest sense gratification before our spiritual life begins. This is made possible through *bhakti.* Although Kṛṣṇa is beyond our vision, He has agreed to be seen by us through the *arcā-vigraha,* the Deity. We should not think that the Deity is made of stone. Even if it is stone, we should think that Kṛṣṇa has made Himself visible before us like a stone because we cannot see beyond stone. That is Kṛṣṇa's mercy. Because our eyes and other senses are imperfect, we cannot see Kṛṣṇa present everywhere in His original spiritual form. Because we are imperfect, we see the difference between things spiritual and material, but Kṛṣṇa, being absolute, knows no such distinctions. He can become spiritual or material, however He likes, and it does not make any difference to Him. Being almighty and omnipotent, Kṛṣṇa can change matter into spirit and spirit into matter. Therefore we should not think, as the atheists do, that we are worshiping idols. Even if it is an idol, it is still Kṛṣṇa. That is the absolute nature of Kṛṣṇa. Even if we think that the Deity is a stone, or a piece of metal or some wood, He is still Kṛṣṇa. The understanding of this requires *bhakti* on our part. If we are a little thoughtful and philosophical, and if we are at all inclined toward *bhakti*, we can understand that Kṛṣṇa is present in stone.

Actually, nothing is different from Kṛṣṇa because everything is Kṛṣṇa's energy. The Māyāvādī philosophers say that since everything is God, the personality of Kṛṣṇa is finished. But actually Kṛṣṇa is Kṛṣṇa, and at the same time He is everything. We can understand this by *bhakti*, but not by any other process. When a *bhakta* sees a tree, he sees Kṛṣṇa. As explained in *Caitanya-caritāmṛa* (*Madhya* 8.274):

sthāvara-jaṅgama dekhe, nā dekhe tāra mūrti
sarvatra haya nija iṣṭa-deva-sphūrti

The advanced devotee does not see living entities as moving and not moving. He sees Kṛṣṇa. This is also stated in the *Brahma-saṁhitā* (5.38):

premāñjana-cchurita-bhakti-vilocanena
santaḥ sadaiva hṛdayeṣu vilokayanti

Because his eyes are always smeared with the ointment of devotion, the devotee always sees Kṛṣṇa and nothing else. He sees Kṛṣṇa and Kṛṣṇa's energy everywhere. For instance, if you love your child, when you see your child's shoe, you immediately see your child. Or if you see your child's toy, you immediately see your child and hear his voice. Similarly, if we have actually developed love of Kṛṣṇa, nothing exists but Kṛṣṇa. When our love for Kṛṣṇa is actually developed, whatever we see, we will see Kṛṣṇa.

Unless one is advanced in *kṛṣṇa-premā*, love of Kṛṣṇa, he cannot see or understand. By the blunt material senses, we cannot even understand the name of Kṛṣṇa. People are always asking, "Why are these people chanting Hare Kṛṣṇa?" They cannot understand, although Kṛṣṇa realization begins with the name. The name of Kṛṣṇa and Kṛṣṇa are nondifferent, but we cannot realize this intellectually. We have to practice chanting Hare Kṛṣṇa to realize it. When we actually advance in devotional service and chant the Hare Kṛṣṇa *mahā-mantra* offenselessly, we will realize that Kṛṣṇa and His name are nondifferent. Thus *kṛṣṇa-bhakti* begins with the tongue, for we can utilize the tongue to chant, and to taste *kṛṣṇa-prasāda.* In this way we can become a Kṛṣṇa *bhakta.*

When we see the Deity of Kṛṣṇa in the temple, we should think that the Deity is Kṛṣṇa. In this way Kṛṣṇa has agreed to be seen by us and even dressed by us. However, if we think of Kṛṣṇa's *virāṭ-rūpa,* His universal form, what can we do? How can we dress the *virāṭ-rūpa?* His many heads cover the sky, and we cannot even conceive of Him. Kṛṣṇa can become bigger than the biggest and smaller than the smallest. Therefore this verse states: *bhaktyā pumāñ jāta-virāga aindriyāt.* The more we serve Kṛṣṇa, give Him things to eat and dress Him nicely, the less we become interested in our own bodies. In the material world everyone is very busy dressing himself very nicely in order to be sexually attractive, but if we try to dress Kṛṣṇa nicely, we will forget our own material dress. If we feed Kṛṣṇa nice food, we will forget to satisfy our own tongue by going to this or that restaurant.

Kṛṣṇa was teaching *Bhagavad-gītā,* and Arjuna was seeing Him face to face, but seeing Kṛṣṇa and reading *Bhagavad-gītā* are the same. Some people say that Arjuna was fortunate to have seen Kṛṣṇa face to face and take instructions from Him, but Kṛṣṇa can be seen immediately, provided one has the eyes to see. There is the example in *Caitanya-caritāmṛta* of a *brāhmaṇa* in South India who was reading *Bhagavad-gītā,* although he was illiterate. The people in the neighborhood knew that he was illiterate, and they made jokes, asking him, "Well, how is it you are reading *Bhagavad-gītā?*" One day Caitanya Mahāprabhu happened to be in a temple nearby, and He could understand that this man was a devotee. He therefore approached him and asked, "My dear *brāhmaṇa,* what are you reading?" The *brāhmaṇa* replied, "I am reading *Bhagavad-gītā,* or, rather, I am trying to read *Bhagavad-gītā.* I happen to be illiterate, but my *guru-mahārāja* has said that I must read the eighteen chapters of *Bhagavad-gītā* daily. I am simply trying to carry out his order, and therefore I am opening and closing the pages." Caitanya Mahāprabhu then said, "I see that you are crying sometimes. Why is this?" The *brāhmaṇa* replied, "Yes, I am crying because when I take up this book, I see a picture of Kṛṣṇa driving Arjuna's chariot. Śrī Kṛṣṇa is so kind that He has accepted the position of a servant to His devotee. Therefore when I see this picture, I weep." Lord Caitanya Mahāprabhu then immediately embraced the *brāhmaṇa* and said, "You have actually read *Bhagavad-gītā.*"

It is not that a wealth of education is required. One does not even have to understand the language. The only ingredient needed is *bhakti,* love. If one becomes a pure *bhakta,* he will forget all material sense enjoyment. Being a *bhakta* doesn't simply mean wearing *tilaka* and robes. One is not a *bhakta* if he has a taste for material sense enjoyment. A true *bhakta* wants to satisfy not his senses but the senses of Kṛṣṇa. That is the spiritual world. In the spiritual world, Vṛndāvana, everyone—mother Yaśodā, Nanda Mahārāja, Śrīmatī Rādhārāṇī, the *gopīs,* the cowherd boys, Śrīdāmā, Sudāmā, the land, the water, the trees, the birds—all are trying to satisfy Kṛṣṇa. That is the real meaning of Vṛndāvana. When Kṛṣṇa left Vṛndāvana for Mathurā, everyone in Vṛndāvana fell dead out of separation from Him. Similarly, we can always live in Vṛndāvana, in Vaikuṇṭha, if we are mad after Kṛṣṇa. This is the teaching of Caitanya Mahāprabhu, and He illustrated this by His very life. When He was in Jagannātha Purī, He was always mad after Kṛṣṇa day and night. The last twelve years of His life were passed in madness. Sometimes He threw Himself into the ocean, and He wandered about like a madman. Of course, this is not possible for ordinary living entities. However, if we become *bhaktas,* we will find intelligence behind everything in the creation. If we take a flower and see its constitution, how it is made and how its colors are displayed and how it comes into existence, we can see Kṛṣṇa. We can see how Kṛṣṇa has created such a beautiful thing so intelligently. We should not consider like rascals that such a thing has come into being automatically. Fools cannot see, but those who are intelligent can see that the hand of the Supreme Lord is in everything within the creation. *Īśāvāsyam idaṁ sarvam.*

Actually, nothing comes about automatically. Everything comes about through the intelligence of Kṛṣṇa, through His fine and accurate powers. If we paint a picture of a flower, we have to arrange many facets, and still the picture will not be absolutely perfect. Yet the flower created by Kṛṣṇa has come out perfectly. What rascal can say that there is no brain behind it? Kṛṣṇa specifically says that we should not think that *prakṛti,* nature, is working automatically. He says, "Nature is working under My direction." One simply has to develop the eyes to see how these things are going on. This is possible if we engage the senses in the service of Kṛṣṇa.

We first of all must engage the tongue in chanting Hare Kṛṣṇa and in eating *bhagavat-prasāda.* Nothing else is required. Therefore the Kṛṣṇa consciousness movement is distributing *prasāda* and engaging people in chanting the Hare Kṛṣṇa *mahā-mantra.*

TEXT 27

asevayāyaṁ prakṛter guṇānāṁ
jñānena vairāgya-vijṛmbhitena
yogena mayy arpitayā ca bhaktyā
māṁ pratyag-ātmānam ihāvarundhe

TRANSLATION

Thus by not engaging in the service of the modes of material nature but by developing Kṛṣṇa consciousness, knowledge in renunciation, and by practicing yoga, in which the mind is always fixed in devotional service unto the Supreme Personality of Godhead, one achieves My association in this very life, for I am the Supreme Personality, the Absolute Truth.

PURPORT

When one engages in the nine different processes of *bhakti-yoga* enunciated in authoritative scriptures, such as hearing (*śravaṇam*), chanting (*kīrtanam*), remembering, worshiping, praying and offering personal service—either in one of them or two or three or all of them—he naturally has no opportunity to engage in the service of the three modes of material nature. Unless one has good engagements in spiritual service, it is not possible to become detached from material service. Those who are not devotees, therefore, are interested in so-called humanitarian or philanthropic work, such as opening a hospital or charitable institution. These are undoubtedly good works in the sense that they are pious activities, and the performer may get some opportunities for sense gratification, either in this life or in the next. Devotional service, however, is beyond the boundary of sense gratification. It is a completely spiritual activity. When one engages in the spiritual activities of devotional service, he does not engage in sense gratificatory activities. Kṛṣṇa conscious activities are performed not blindly but with the perfect understanding of knowledge and renunciation. This kind of *yoga* practice, in which the mind is always fixed upon the Supreme Personality of Godhead in devotion, results in liberation in this very life. The person who performs such acts gets in touch with the Supreme Personality of Godhead. Lord Caitanya, therefore, approved the process of hearing from realized devotees about the pastimes of the Lord. It does not matter to what mundane category the audience belongs. If one meekly and submissively hears about the activities of the Lord from a realized soul, he will be able to conquer the Supreme Personality of Godhead, who is unconquerable by any other process. Hearing and associating with devotees are the most important functions for self-realization.

In Goloka Vṛndāvana, the living entities are serving Kṛṣṇa as friends, cowherd boys, *gopīs*, lovers, fathers, mothers and so on. Even the trees, water, flowers, land, calves and cows serve Kṛṣṇa in Goloka Vṛndāvana. This is also our business, but somehow or other we do not like to serve Kṛṣṇa; therefore we have been put into the service of *māyā*, in the three modes of material nature. When a criminal does not like to obey the laws of the state, he is placed into prison and forced to abide by the laws. Our constitutional position is to render service to Kṛṣṇa as His part and parcel, and as soon as we refuse to render Him service, *māyā* is immediately there to capture us and say, "Serve me." It is not our nature to become master. Even if we become master, we will not be happy, because that is artificial. For instance, if the hand thinks, "Oh, now I have some nice sweets. Now I can eat," the hand will ultimately be frustrated. It is the duty and nature of the hand to place the food in the mouth. In this way the hand is nourished; otherwise everything is spoiled. Similarly, we are part and parcel of Kṛṣṇa, and our business is to satisfy Kṛṣṇa. From the *Vedas* we understand that God, who is one, has become many. We are the many parts and parcels of Kṛṣṇa. *Svāṁśas* are His personal expansions, and we are His differential expansions, *vibhinnāṁśas*. In any case, all expansions are meant to serve Kṛṣṇa. This is explained in the *Caitanya-caritāmṛta* (*Ādi* 5.142): *ekale īśvara kṛṣṇa, āra saba bhṛtya.* "Lord Kṛṣṇa alone is the supreme controller, and all others are His servants."

It is our natural propensity to enjoy ourselves with Kṛṣṇa. As stated before, Kṛṣṇa is *ānanda-maya*, and, being part and parcel of Kṛṣṇa, we are also *ānanda-maya*. Now we are seeking *ānanda* (bliss) in different atmospheres. Because we have a little independence, we have decided to go to the prison house of material nature and try to serve our senses instead of Kṛṣṇa. Now we have to learn how to forget to serve this material nature, and that process is *bhakti-mārga*, the path of devotional service. When we come to the understanding that we are actually no one's servant but Kṛṣṇa's, we attain self-realization. We must come to this understanding not by sentiment but by real knowledge. After many births and deaths, when one realizes that *vāsudevaḥ sarvam iti*—Vāsudeva is all—he surrenders unto Kṛṣṇa. This is real knowledge—*jñāna* and *vairāgya*, knowledge and detachment from material things.

Once one engages fully in Kṛṣṇa's service, he comes to the *brahma-bhūta* platform. Presently we are on the *māyā-bhūta* platform, identifying ourselves with *māyā* and working according to the modes of material nature. However, when one comes to the realization that he is spirit (*ahaṁ brahmāsmi*), he will immediately become happy.

Under the modes of material nature, we are being carried away by the waves of material nature, and we have no control over where we are going. Bhaktivinoda Ṭhākura has stated: *māyāra vaśe, yāccha bhese', khāccha hābuḍubu, bhāi.* We are like straws on the waves of the ocean, and we are fully under the control of the waves. Atheists shudder when they think that there is a next life, because their lives are sinful and they fear punishment in the next. There is a Bengali proverb about a person who thought, "I have committed so many sinful acts that Yamarāja will come and punish me. How can I avoid him?" Thinking about this some time, he decided, "Let me smear my body with stool. Then Yamarāja will not touch me." However, this is simply foolishness. We are under the control of *māyā*, material nature, and it is not possible to avoid it. We have become infected by the disease of material nature, and no artificial means will save us. There is no way out other than surrender to Kṛṣṇa. Kṛṣṇa says that He will save us, even though we are very sinful.

If we turn our attention to Kṛṣṇa's service, to *bhakti-yoga*, we can force ourselves to give up all *anarthas*, unwanted things. We should get up early in the morning and engage ourselves in the service of Kṛṣṇa;

then gradually we will forget the service of *māyā*. *Bhakti-yoga* is so strong that if we engage in it, *māyā's* service will automatically be negated. This is called *vairāgya*.

Kṛṣṇa is the original *puruṣa*, the original spirit, the original person. Everything has come from Kṛṣṇa, and therefore He is *purāṇa*, the oldest. No one is older than Kṛṣṇa, but He is always young. That is Bhagavān. He is *ādi*, the original source, the cause of all causes. Yet we never see Kṛṣṇa as an old man. He is always fresh and youthful. Although Kṛṣṇa was a great-grandfather at the Battle of Kurukṣetra, He did not appear any older than a young man of twenty. Kṛṣṇa is always a young boy, and those living entities in the spiritual universe also have spiritual bodies the same as Kṛṣṇa's. In the Sixth Canto of *Śrīmad-Bhāgavatam* we read that when the Vaikuṇṭha-dūtas came to take Ajāmila, they were four-handed and very beautiful. In the spiritual world, there are four-handed living entities, and they are all *nitya-mukta*, eternally liberated.

Unfortunately, we are now prisoners in this material world, and we presently have material bodies. These bodies are changing. Sometimes they are young and sometimes old. However, if we become Kṛṣṇa conscious, we will not get another material body after leaving this body. We will go home, back to Godhead, and attain our original, spiritual body, which is the same kind of beautiful body that Kṛṣṇa, Nārāyaṇa, has. We should take this opportunity to become devotees of Kṛṣṇa by following the processes of *bhakti-yoga—śravaṇaṁ kīrtanaṁ viṣṇoḥ smaraṇaṁ pāda-sevanaṁ arcanam*. We can take one or all of the nine processes of devotional service and make our lives successful. Caitanya Mahāprabhu has prescribed the most important process—*śravaṇam*. We need only hear, and that will make our lives successful.

CHAPTER THIRTEEN

Perfect Knowledge Through Surrender

TEXT 28

devahūtir uvāca
kācit tvayy ucitā bhaktiḥ
kīdṛśī mama gocarā
yayā padaṁ te nirvāṇam
añjasānvāśnavā aham

TRANSLATION

On hearing this statement of the Lord, Devahūti inquired: What kind of devotional service is worth developing and practicing to help me easily and immediately attain the service of Your lotus feet?

PURPORT

It is stated in *Bhagavad-gītā* that no one is barred from rendering service to the Lord. Whether one is a woman or a laborer or a merchant, if he engages himself in the devotional service of the Lord, he is promoted to the highest perfectional state and goes back home, back to Godhead. The devotional service most suitable for different types of devotees is determined and fixed by the mercy of the spiritual master. Therefore in order to become free from the miseries of material nature, one should approach a bona fide spiritual master inquisitively and submissively. When Arjuna submitted to Kṛṣṇa, he said, "My dear Kṛṣṇa, now I no longer care to talk to You as a friend because friendly talks will not benefit me now." Generally we talk to a friend just to spend time, but when we approach a spiritual master, we should be submissive. Friends approach one another on an equal basis, but this is not the way to approach a spiritual master. Unless one is submissive, one cannot accept sublime instructions. Arjuna teaches us submission by giving up his friendly relationship with Kṛṣṇa, the Supreme Personality of Godhead. He says, "I have now become Your disciple. Please instruct me."

We can speculate for many births, for many years, and yet not be able to understand the ultimate goal of life. Therefore the *śāstras* all advise that we search out a *guru*. The word *guru* means "heavy" or "weighty." One who has much knowledge is heavy with knowledge. One should consider the bona fide *guru* in this way, and one should not think, "I know everything. Who can teach me?" No one can say such a thing, for everyone needs instruction.

According to the Vedic system, a child is sent to a *guru-kula* to learn spiritual knowledge from the very beginning. When a child goes to a *guru-kula*, he becomes a *brahmacārī* and works like a menial servant. He may be the son of a great *brāhmaṇa* or a great king; it doesn't matter. When one goes to a *guru-kula*, he immediately becomes the menial servant of the *guru*. If the *guru* orders him to perform some lowly service, he is prepared to do it. This is the business of a *brahmacārī*. Even Kṛṣṇa went to a *guru-kula* to teach us. There was no need for Kṛṣṇa, the Supreme Personality of Godhead, to go to a *guru-kula*, but He did this simply to set an example. Caitanya Mahāprabhu also accepted a *guru*.

Prakāśānanda Sarasvatī was a very learned scholar, and he knew that Caitanya Mahāprabhu was also a great scholar, yet he criticized Caitanya Mahāprabhu for chanting and dancing, for Prakāśānanda Sarasvatī felt that a *sannyāsī* should devote his entire attention to the reading of *Vedānta*. He therefore considered Caitanya Mahāprabhu a sentimentalist, not a bona fide *sannyāsī*. Prakāśānanda Sarasvatī inquired, "Why aren't you reading *Vedānta-sūtra?* Why are you chanting and dancing?" Caitanya Mahāprabhu replied:

prabhu kahe—śuna, śrīpāda, ihāra kāraṇa
guru more mūrkha dekhi' karila śāsana

"Actually, I am not very learned, and my *guru* has stated that I am fool number one. He said that because of this I cannot possibly read *Vedānta-sūtra*, for *Vedānta-sūtra* is not meant for an ordinary person. My *guru* therefore advised me to chant this Hare Kṛṣṇa *mahā-mantra*, and now I am doing this and getting the results." (Cc. *Ādi* 7.71)

At the present moment in Kali-yuga, people are not well educated. They are simply engaged in earning money to fill the belly. Vedānta philosophy is not meant for an ordinary person, nor even for an ordinary learned person. It requires great knowledge of Sanskrit and philosophy. Of course Caitanya Mahāprabhu, being the Supreme Personality of Godhead, knew all things, but at that moment He had assumed the role of an ordinary person in order to instruct an illiterate, ignorant society. In this age people are not even interested in reading *Vedānta-sūtra.* People are so badly infected by the influence of *māyā* that they do not even care to understand that there is life after death or that there are 8,400,000 life forms. Sometimes if people hear that by acting in such a way they will become a tree, a dog, a cat, an insect or even a human being, they say that they do not even care to know this. Sometimes they say, "Never mind if I become a dog. What's wrong with that? I will simply forget everything." Many university students in the Western countries speak this way. They have become so ignorant that they are described as *manda.* Previously, in India, the *brāhmaṇas* were interested in understanding Brahman. *Athāto brahma-jijñāsā.* However, at the present moment everyone is a *śūdra,* and no one is interested in understanding Brahman. People are simply interested in getting more money and going to the cinemas.

Human life is meant for understanding our situation, and we should take instructions from *Bhagavad-gītā.* Arjuna is personally teaching us by accepting Kṛṣṇa as his *guru.* He asks Kṛṣṇa to become his spiritual master and teach him. The lessons given by Śrī Kṛṣṇa are not simply meant for Arjuna but for everyone. Kṛṣṇa tells us in *Bhagavad-gītā* that we should search out a *guru.* The first *guru* is Śrī Kṛṣṇa Himself, and whoever represents Śrī Kṛṣṇa is also a *guru.* If I am a businessman, and someone goes to canvass for my business and take orders for me, he is my representative. If he simply says that he is my representative and yet takes some orders but uses the money for something else, he is not really my representative.

Kṛṣṇa's representative does not say, "I have become Kṛṣṇa." Such a person is neither a representative nor a *guru.* He is simply a cheater. Kṛṣṇa's representative is one who canvasses for Kṛṣṇa. Kṛṣṇa says, "Give up everything and surrender unto Me." Kṛṣṇa's representative says, "Give up everything and simply surrender unto Kṛṣṇa." This is certainly not very difficult to understand. Anyone can become Kṛṣṇa's representative. Nonetheless, for the past two hundred years, many *yogīs* and *svāmīs* have gone to foreign countries, but no one has spoken about Kṛṣṇa. They have simply presented a hodgepodge of Indian philosophy. No one has actually presented Vedic culture as it is.

We should read *Bhagavad-gītā* as it is and understand the philosophy as Arjuna understood it. Arjuna was a friend of Kṛṣṇa's. He was sitting with Kṛṣṇa and speaking to Him as a friend speaks to a friend. In the Eleventh Chapter, after having seen the universal form, Arjuna tells Kṛṣṇa: "I have in the past addressed You as 'O Kṛṣṇa,' 'O Yādava,' 'O my friend,' without knowing Your glories. Please forgive whatever I may have done in madness or in love."

Arjuna understood that although Kṛṣṇa was his friend, He was the Supreme Personality of Godhead and therefore the proper person to be his *guru.* He therefore told Kṛṣṇa at the beginning of *Bhagavad-gītā* (2.7), *śiṣyas te 'haṁ śādhi māṁ tvāṁ prapannam:* "Now I am Your disciple and a soul surrendered unto You. Please instruct me."

These are the instructions we get from *Bhagavad-gītā*, and whoever reads *Bhagavad-gītā* has to accept Kṛṣṇa as the *guru.* We have to render service to a *guru* and surrender ourselves. It is not that one should accept just any person as a *guru.* The *guru* must be the representative of Kṛṣṇa; then one can surrender oneself. Surrender means that one will accept whatever the *guru* says. It is not that one thinks, "I do not care for my *guru's* order. Still I am a disciple." That is not actually accepting a *guru.* Of course, it has become a fashion to accept a *guru* in this way, but this will not help anyone. As soon as Kṛṣṇa became Arjuna's *guru*, Kṛṣṇa immediately chastised him. Śrī Kṛṣṇa told him:

aśocyān anvaśocas tvaṁ
prajñā-vādāṁś ca bhāṣase
gatāsūn agatāsūṁś ca
nānuśocanti paṇḍitāḥ

"While speaking learned words, you are mourning for what is not worthy of grief. Those who are wise lament neither for the living nor the dead." (Bg. 2.11)

In this way Kṛṣṇa essentially told Arjuna that he was fool number one for lamenting for those things for which one should not lament. Arjuna was lamenting for the body, thinking that it was horrible that his relatives would be killed in war. This was not the proper subject matter for him to be contemplating. The real subject matter for a wise man to contemplate is the salvation of the soul. Therefore Śrī Kṛṣṇa first explained the distinction between the body and the soul.

This Kṛṣṇa consciousness movement is also concerned with the soul, and therefore we have used the word "consciousness" because consciousness belongs to the soul. Consciousness is the symptom of the soul's presence. Because the soul is in the body, the body feels pleasure and pain. When the soul leaves the body, the body can be hacked to pieces, and yet it will not protest. This is because the consciousness is gone. We feel pleasure and pain because consciousness is present, and Kṛṣṇa advises us that it is this consciousness that is eternal, not the body. We have to purify our consciousness in order to understand that consciousness is eternal. If we can do this, our lives will be successful. At the time of death, our consciousness carries us into another body. There are the mind, the intelligence and the ego, which constitute the subtle body, and there is also the spirit soul, which is even more subtle. We know that we possess a mind, although we cannot see it. Nor can we see the intelligence, the ego or the soul. We can only see the gross material body, and when this gross material body ends, we say that everything is finished. In order to understand these things, we have to approach a *guru*, just as Arjuna approached Śrī Kṛṣṇa.

Śrī Kṛṣṇa told Arjuna in very gentlemanly language that he was not a learned man. In essence, He said, "You are not a *paṇḍita.* Just try to understand that the real life is the life of the soul." Vedic education means taking care of the soul. Presently the soul is encaged, embodied, entangled in material affairs. The soul is suffering, and it is to our benefit to rescue him from these material clutches. This is real education. To receive this education, one has to approach a proper *guru.* The *guru* is there—Kṛṣṇa. The *guru* is also there as Kapiladeva, the incarnation of Kṛṣṇa. Kṛṣṇa informs us that He is the owner of the body, and He has explained this in many different ways. He has stated that the soul can never be cut to pieces, burned by fire, moistened by water nor withered by the wind. Matter interacts with matter, but the soul does not belong to the material world. This means that the soul is above material action and reaction. In the material world even iron and stone can be melted, but the laws of material nature do not apply to the spirit soul.

To understand these subjects, we should be careful to approach Kṛṣṇa's representative. We should not approach a bogus *guru,* who is like a blind man trying to lead other blind men. We must go to one who has open eyes, to one who has seen the Absolute Truth. The Absolute Truth is there, just as the sun is there for everyone to see. The sun does not hide, but a person can try to hide from the sun by closing his door. One must open the door in order to see the sun. Similarly, Kṛṣṇa is there, God is there, and we have to come to Kṛṣṇa and take the lessons of *Bhagavad-gītā* to learn who and what God is. Rascals will not do this, but will simply manufacture some philosophy or other. There is actually no difficulty because Kṛṣṇa's instructions are there, and Kṛṣṇa Himself is there. Kṛṣṇa is so kind that He says, "All right, if you cannot understand Me in this way, just see Me in water. Come on, if you do not understand Me in that way, just see Me in the sunshine." Is this very difficult? There is nothing difficult about it, but we are very obstinate. *Māyā* is also very strong, and as soon as we try to accept Kṛṣṇa as the Supreme Lord, *māyā* will whisper in our ear, "No, no. There are many gods. Why are you accepting Kṛṣṇa?" However, the *śāstras* say, *kṛṣṇas tu bhagavān svayam . . . īśvaraḥ paramaḥ kṛṣṇaḥ.* "Kṛṣṇa is the Supreme Personality of Godhead." We should take our lessons from the *ācāryas* and the *śāstras.* At least in India there are many great *ācāryas*—Rāmānujācārya, Madhvācārya, Viṣṇusvāmī, and even Śaṅkarācārya and Guru Nanak. All of these have accepted Kṛṣṇa as the Supreme Personality of Godhead. Why, then, should we reject Him? Why should we accept a competitor? We should not simply engage in mental speculation but should accept Kṛṣṇa in full consciousness and be happy. This is made possible by the help of the *guru;* therefore Devahūti is further questioning her son, Kapiladeva.

TEXT 29

yo yogo bhagavad-bāṇo
nirvāṇātmaṁs tvayoditaḥ
kīdṛśaḥ kati cāṅgāni
yatas tattvāvabodhanam

TRANSLATION

The mystic yoga system, as you have explained, aims at the Supreme Personality of Godhead and is meant for completely ending material existence. Please let me know the nature of that yoga system. How many ways are there by which one can understand in truth that sublime yoga?

PURPORT

There are different kinds of mystic *yoga* systems aiming for different phases of the Absolute Truth. The *jñāna-yoga* system aims at the impersonal Brahman effulgence, and the *haṭha-yoga* system aims at the localized personal aspect, the Paramātmā feature of the Absolute Truth, whereas *bhakti-yoga,* or devotional service, which is executed in nine different ways, headed by hearing and chanting, aims at complete realization of the Supreme Lord. There are different methods of self-realization. But here Devahūti especially refers to the *bhakti-yoga* system, which has already been primarily explained by the Lord. The different processes of the *bhakti-yoga* system are hearing, chanting, remembering, offering prayers, worshiping the Lord in the temple, accepting service to Him, carrying out His orders, making friends with Him and ultimately surrendering everything for His service.

The word *nirvāṇātman* is very significant in this verse. Unless one accepts the process of devotional service, one cannot end the continuation of material existence. As far as *jñānīs* are concerned, they are interested in *jñāna-yoga,* but even if one elevates oneself, after a great performance of austerity, to the Brahman effulgence, there is a chance of falling down again to the material world. Therefore, *jñāna-yoga* does not actually end material existence. Similarly, regarding the *haṭha-yoga* system, which aims at the localized aspect of the Lord, Paramātmā, it has been experienced that many *yogīs,* such as Viśvāmitra, fall down. But *bhakti-yogīs,* once approaching the Supreme Personality of Godhead, never come back to this material world, as confirmed in the *Bhagavad-gītā. Yad gatvā na nivartante:* upon going, one never comes back. *Tyaktvā dehaṁ punar janma naiti:* after giving up this body, he never comes back again to accept a material body. *Nirvāṇa* does not finish the existence of the soul. The soul is everexisting. Therefore *nirvāṇa* means to end one's material existence, and to end material existence means to go back home, back to Godhead.

Sometimes it is asked how the living entity falls down from the spiritual world to the material world. Here is the answer. Unless one is elevated to the Vaikuṇṭha planets and is directly in touch with the Supreme Personality of Godhead, he is prone to fall down, either from the impersonal Brahman realization or from an ecstatic trance of meditation. Another word in this verse, *bhagavad-bāṇaḥ*, is very significant. *Bāṇaḥ* means "arrow." The *bhakti-yoga* system is just like an arrow aiming up to the Supreme Personality of Godhead. The *bhakti-yoga* system never urges one toward the impersonal Brahman effulgence or to the point of Paramātmā realization. This *bāṇaḥ*, or arrow, is so sharp and swift that it goes directly to the Supreme Personality of Godhead, penetrating the regions of impersonal Brahman and localized Paramātmā.

We must understand the Supreme Person, *tattvataḥ*, in truth. Generally people are not interested in knowing about God or their relationship with Him. However, the entire Vedic instruction is for this purpose. First of all we have to know God, then we have to know our relationship with God. The next step is acting on the basis of that relationship. Kṛṣṇa states that out of many millions of people, one may be interested in knowing the purpose of life. Human life is meant for this end, and if one does not come to this understanding, he is no better than an animal. We not only have to understand God and our relationship with Him but also how to act in that relationship. In this way we can perfect our lives. When one is a *siddha*, one understands himself—that is, one understands, *ahaṁ brahmāsmi:* "I am not this body." This is Brahman realization, the *brahma-bhūta* platform. When one attains this stage, he becomes very happy. However, we must progress beyond this and come to the platform of *bhakti-yoga*. On that platform, there is variety and *ānanda*, bliss. As stated previously, we are seeking spiritual variety, and if we do not enter the spiritual world, we will again fall down into the material atmosphere.

The varieties of the spiritual world are mentioned in the *Brahma-saṁhitā* (5.29–30):

cintāmaṇi prakara-sadmasu kalpa-vṛkṣa-
lakṣāvṛteṣu surabhīr abhipālayantam

lakṣmī-sahasra-śata-sambhrama-sevyamānaṁ
govindam ādi-puruṣaṁ tam ahaṁ bhajāmi

veṇuṁ kvaṇantam aravinda-dalāyatākṣaṁ
barhāvataṁsam asitāmbuda-sundarāṅgam
kandarpa-koṭi-kamanīya-viśeṣa-śobhaṁ
govindam ādi-puruṣaṁ tam ahaṁ bhajāmi

"I worship Govinda, the primeval Lord, the first progenitor, who is tending the cows, yielding all desires, in abodes built with spiritual gems and surrounded by millions of purpose trees. He is always served with great reverence and affection by hundreds and thousands of goddesses of fortune.

"I worship Govinda, the primeval Lord, who is adept in playing on His flute, with blooming eyes like lotus petals, with head decked with peacock's feather, with the figure of beauty tinged with the hue of blue clouds, and His unique loveliness charming millions of Cupids."

We should not consider Kṛṣṇa's form to be imagined by some artist. He is described in the *Vedas* as *veṇuṁ kvaṇantam aravinda-dalāyatākṣam.* He plays a flute, and His eyes are like the petals of a lotus flower. He wears a peacock feather, and His complexion is very beautiful, like a dark cloud. He is so beautiful that He attracts many hundreds of thousands of Cupids (*kandarpa-koṭi-kamanīya-viśeṣa-śobham*). These are descriptions of Govinda found in the *śāstras.*

In the material world we are simply chewing the chewed, throwing it away, picking it up and then chewing it again. Spiritual variety is not like this. Spiritual variety is *ānandāmbudhi-vardhanam:* it is constantly increasing. It is even greater than the ocean, because the ocean does not increase. The shores of the ocean are set; they have certain limits. However, the ocean of bliss is constantly increasing. The more we enter into that spiritual bliss, the more we become joyful.

The young people in the Hare Kṛṣṇa movement chant the Hare Kṛṣṇa *mantra* all the time. If this *mantra* were material, how long would they chant it? It is not possible to chant a material name for very long because the chanting would become hackneyed and very tiresome. No one could be satisfied simply by chanting Hare Kṛṣṇa unless Hare Kṛṣṇa itself were spiritual. We may chant, "Mr. John, Mr. John, Mr. John," but after an hour we will be fed up. However, the more we become spiritually advanced, the more bliss we will derive from chanting Hare Kṛṣṇa.

We can experience *ānanda* perfectly in the association of Kṛṣṇa. We can associate with Kṛṣṇa as a servant, a friend, a father, a mother or a conjugal lover. There are five basic *rasas—śānta, dāsya, sakhya, vātsalya* and *mādhurya.* In this material world, we experience the same *rasas,* or relationships. We are related to someone as a father, a son, a lover, a beloved, a master, a servant or whatever. These are perverted reflections of the relationship with Kṛṣṇa found in the spiritual world. Today in the material world I may be relishing my love for my son, but tomorrow my son may be my greatest enemy. There is no eternity in this kind of love. Or, if my son does not become my enemy, he may die. Today I may love some man or woman, but tomorrow we may break up. All of this is due to the defects of the material world. However, in the spiritual world these relationships never break up. They simply increase and increase, and this is called perfection.

Kṛṣṇa is very fond of tending *surabhi* cows, but the Māyāvādīs cannot understand this. They say, "What is this Kṛṣṇa?" Even Lord Brahmā was bewildered. He said, "How is it that this Kṛṣṇa, this boy of Vṛndāvana, is being worshiped? He is called the Supreme Personality of Godhead. How is that?" Lord Indra was also bewildered. Therefore if we do not wish to be bewildered we have to understand Kṛṣṇa in truth from Kṛṣṇa Himself or His bona fide representative.

The activities of Kṛṣṇa are not ordinary but divine. If we can understand this, we immediately become liberated. We need only understand the pastimes of Kṛṣṇa with the *gopīs.* These pastimes are not ordinary. In the material world, a young man wants to dance with many young girls, but Kṛṣṇa's dancing with the *gopīs* is different. Because people cannot understand Kṛṣṇa, when they hear about Kṛṣṇa's dancing with the *gopīs,* they take this as some kind of concession, and say, "Now let us dance with young girls." In this way they go to hell. Therefore we have to learn from the proper person about Kṛṣṇa's activities. We should not immediately try to understand Kṛṣṇa's dealings with the *gopīs,* for they are very confidential. These dealings are given in the Tenth Canto of *Śrīmad-Bhāgavatam,* and this indicates that we have to understand Kṛṣṇa as He is by first reading the preceding nine cantos. When we have understood these nine cantos, we can go on to the tenth. In this way we can understand that Kṛṣṇa's activities are not ordinary but divine, and we can immediately become liberated.

We may either hear about Kṛṣṇa, chant His names, worship Him or offer prayers. In any case, we should work under the directions of our spiritual master or Śrī Kṛṣṇa Himself. For instance, Hanumān simply carried out Lord Rāmacandra's orders. Hanumān apparently had no education, and he was not capable of teaching Vedānta, but he simply carried out the orders of Lord Rāmacandra and attained perfection. Arjuna, on the other hand, took Kṛṣṇa as his most intimate friend. Arjuna was not a Vedāntist but a fighter, a warrior. He had no time to study Vedānta because he had to deal with war and politics, but still he was the greatest devotee. People may say, "Oh, Arjuna was not a Vedāntist, nor even a *brāhmaṇa* or a *sannyāsī*. How could Kṛṣṇa accept him as a devotee?" Nonetheless, in *Bhagavad-gītā* (4.3), Kṛṣṇa says that Arjuna is His very dear friend and devotee: *bhakto 'si me sakhā ceti*. If one becomes a devotee, there is no material impediment.

Actually *bhakti* should be automatic and spontaneous. There should be no motive in serving Kṛṣṇa, but even if there is a motive, service rendered unto Kṛṣṇa is good. Even if one approaches Kṛṣṇa with some ulterior motive, one is considered pious. For instance, Dhruva Mahārāja initially worshiped Kṛṣṇa with a motive, but after attaining perfection in devotional service, his ulterior motive vanished. When he actually saw Kṛṣṇa, he said, "I do not want anything from You. I don't want any benediction other than Your service." After hearing about the many transcendental qualities of Kṛṣṇa, if we somehow or other become attracted to Kṛṣṇa consciousness, our lives will be successful. *Tasmāt kenāpy upāyena manaḥ kṛṣṇe niveśayet:* "Somehow or other we have to attach our minds to Kṛṣṇa consciousness." (*Bhāg*. 7.1.32) Then Kṛṣṇa will help us and give us intelligence from within, as He indicates in *Bhagavad-gītā* (10.10):

teṣāṁ satata-yuktānāṁ
bhajatāṁ prīti-pūrvakam
dadāmi buddhi-yogaṁ taṁ
yena mām upayānti te

"To those who are constantly devoted and worship Me with love, I give the understanding by which they can come to Me." This is actual *buddhi-yoga. Bhakti-yoga* means *buddhi-yoga*, because one who is highly intelligent decides to take to Kṛṣṇa consciousness. In this way, one can perfect his life by engaging in devotional service under the directions of the *śāstras* and the spiritual master. Devahūti understands this and is thus submitting to her son just as Arjuna submitted to Śrī Kṛṣṇa on the battlefield.

TEXT 30

tad etan me vijānīhi
yathāhaṁ manda-dhīr hare
sukhaṁ buddhyeya durbodhaṁ
yoṣā bhavad-anugrahāt

TRANSLATION

My dear son, Kapila, after all, I am a woman. It is very difficult for me to understand the Absolute Truth because my intelligence is not very great. But if You will kindly explain it to me, even though I am not very intelligent, I can understand it and thereby feel transcendental happiness.

PURPORT

Knowledge of the Absolute Truth is not very easily understood by ordinary, less intelligent men; but if the spiritual master is kind enough to the disciple, however unintelligent he may be, then by the divine grace of the spiritual master everything is revealed. Viśvanātha Cakravartī Ṭhākura therefore says, *yasya prasādād*, by the mercy of the spiritual master, the mercy of the Supreme Personality of Godhead, *bhagavat-prasādaḥ*, is revealed. Devahūti requested her great son to be merciful toward her because she was a less intelligent woman and also His mother. By the grace of Kapiladeva it was quite possible for her to understand the Absolute Truth, even though the subject matter is very difficult for ordinary persons, especially women.

In this verse Devahūti shows us the process for understanding transcendental subject matters. It is not by challenge but by submission. The entire *bhakti* process is a process of submission. That is also Caitanya Mahāprabhu's teaching:

tṛṇād api sunīcena
taror iva sahiṣṇunā
amāninā mānadena
kīrtanīyaḥ sadā hariḥ
(*Śikṣāṣṭaka* 3)

If one is interested in advancing in chanting Hare Kṛṣṇa, Caitanya Mahāprabhu advises that one be humbler than the grass and more tolerant than the trees. One should not be very proud of his intelligence but should give all respect to others. In this way, one can chant Hare Kṛṣṇa offenselessly. Although Devahūti was the mother of Kapiladeva, she presented herself as a humble woman. It was not that she considered herself superior because she was His mother.

We have to please the spirtiual master by service, and the entire *bhakti* process depends on the attitude of service. The transcendental nature of Kṛṣṇa is not possible to understand with our blunt material senses. Kṛṣṇa's name, form, qualities and pastimes are all *divya*, divine. Our present material senses have to be purified by engagement in the Lord's service, and our first engagement begins with the tongue. It is with the tongue that we can chant the transcendental names of the Lord. This is not very difficult, and this path is open to everyone—even women, *vaiśyas* and *śūdras*. After describing all the faults of Kali-yuga, *Śrīmad-Bhāgavatam* (12.3.51) states:

kaler doṣa-nidhe rājann
asti hy eko mahān guṇaḥ
kīrtanād eva kṛṣṇasya
mukta-saṅgaḥ paraṁ vrajet

"There is one special advantage about this age of Kali-yuga, and that is that people can attain liberation and return home, back to Godhead, simply by chanting the Hare Kṛṣṇa *mahā-mantra.*" Śrī Caitanya Mahāprabhu said:

harer nāma harer nāma
harer nāmaiva kevalam
kalau nāsty eva nāsty eva
nāsty eva gatir anyathā

"Chant Hare Kṛṣṇa, chant Hare Kṛṣṇa. There is no other way, no other way at all in Kali-yuga."

We should try to avoid the ten offenses in chanting the holy name, but anyone who chants Hare Kṛṣṇa sincerely is purified. *Ceto-darpaṇa-mārjanaṁ bhava-mahā-dāvāgni-nirvāpaṇam* (*Śikṣāṣṭaka* 1). This is the easiest process by which the mirror of the mind can be cleansed. If Kṛṣṇa sees that someone is sincerely chanting Hare Kṛṣṇa, He will help. He is within everyone, and He can understand whether one is sincere or not. Kṛṣṇa helps a sincere devotee internally and externally. Internally He helps as Paramātmā by giving intelligence from within. *Dadāmi buddhi-yogaṁ tam.* Externally He helps as His representative, the spiritual master. Therefore Caitanya Mahāprabhu says: *guru-kṛṣṇa-prasāde pāya bhakti-latā-bīja.* "By the grace of Kṛṣṇa, one gets a bona fide *guru*, and by the grace of the *guru*, one gets Kṛṣṇa." (Cc. *Madhya* 19.151) Thus the *śāstras* have given us a very easy way to appreciate our transcendental life. That is the Kṛṣṇa consciousness movement.

Devahūti has submissively accepted her son as her *guru.* She wants to understand Kṛṣṇa perfectly, by the grace of Kapiladeva. It is very important to receive the causeless mercy of Kṛṣṇa and the spiritual master. By Kṛṣṇa's mercy, we receive a spiritual master, and by the spiritual master's mercy, we receive Kṛṣṇa.

Śrīla Viśvanātha Cakravatī Ṭhākura has greatly stressed the mercy of the *guru,* and it is an actual fact that if we satisfy the *guru* by our service, he will give us his blessings. This is a very great opportunity, for the *guru* is the confidential servant of Kṛṣṇa. The *guru* never claims that he is Kṛṣṇa, although he is worshiped as Kṛṣṇa: *sākṣād dharitvena samasta-śāstrair uktas tathā bhāvyata eva sadbhiḥ* (*Gurv-aṣṭaka* 7).

All the *śāstras* describe the *guru* as being on an equal basis with Kṛṣṇa, for he is the representative of Kṛṣṇa. Therefore he is worshiped as Kṛṣṇa. Being the most confidential servant of Kṛṣṇa, the *guru* is very dear to Kṛṣṇa; therefore if he recommends someone to Kṛṣṇa, Kṛṣṇa accepts the person. The *guru* is the confidential servant of Kṛṣṇa because he canvasses from door to door, saying, "Please become Kṛṣṇa conscious and surrender unto Kṛṣṇa." Kṛṣṇa tells Arjuna that such a person is very dear to Him. The bona fide *guru* tells people to surrender not unto him but unto Kṛṣṇa. Thus one has to surrender unto Kṛṣṇa through the via media of the *guru*, not directly. This is the process. The *guru* does not accept respect from his disciple for his personal self but conveys this respect to Kṛṣṇa. If we cannot receive the mercy of the *guru*, Kṛṣṇa is very difficult to approach directly.

It is stated in *Bhagavad-gītā* that knowledge of Kṛṣṇa is received through the *paramparā*, the disciplic succession. *Evaṁ paramparā-prāptam.* The *guru* offers the same respects to his *guru*, and his *guru* offers respects to his, and so it goes all the way to Kṛṣṇa. Thus the mercy of Kṛṣṇa comes down through the *paramparā* system, and the respect offered to Kṛṣṇa is offered up through the *paramparā* system. One has to learn to approach the Supreme Personality of Godhead in this way. Thus if we want to approach God, we have to take shelter of the *guru* in the beginning. Devahūti is begging the mercy of Kapiladeva in order to understand the way to approach Kṛṣṇa. She approaches Him very humbly saying, "My dear Kapila, You are the Supreme Personality of Godhead, but I am a woman, and my intelligence is not very sharp. Nonetheless, I want to understand these sublime transcendental subjects from You. It is possible by Your mercy."

The process of approaching and understanding the Supreme Personality of Godhead was also discussed between Rāmānanda Rāya and Caitanya Mahāprabhu. First, Rāmānanda Rāya explained the process in terms of *varṇāśrama-dharma.* He said first of all that human life is meant for approaching Lord Viṣṇu through the rules and regulations governing *varṇāśrama-dharma.* Caitanya Mahāprabhu replied that it is very difficult in this age to execute the rules and regulations of *varṇāśrama-dharma.* It is very difficult to be a *brāhmaṇa* in this age, and it is practically impossible to revive the old *varṇāśrama-dharma* culture. Caitanya Mahāprabhu therefore said that this method is not very practical. Caitanya Mahāprabhu has been called by Śrīla Rūpa Gosvāmī "the most munificent *avatāra*" because He distributes love of Kṛṣṇa free of charge. First of all, we cannot even understand Kṛṣṇa; therefore there is no question of loving Him. If we do not understand someone, how can we love him? The love is very far away, but Caitanya Mahāprabhu is so kind that He distributes *kṛṣṇa-premā*, love of Kṛṣṇa, to whomever will take it. In His life, Caitanya Mahāprabhu cried for Kṛṣṇa and showed how one should be mad after Him.

yugāyitaṁ nimeṣeṇa
cakṣuṣā prāvṛṣāyitam
śūnyāyitaṁ jagat sarvaṁ
govinda-viraheṇa me

"O Govinda! Feeling Your separation, I am considering a moment to be like twelve years or more. Tears are flowing from my eyes like torrents of rain, and I am feeling all vacant in the world in Your absence." (*Śikṣāṣṭaka* 7)

Without Kṛṣṇa, one should see everything as vacant. This is Rādhārāṇī's frame of mind, but this is not possible for an ordinary living being. It was possible for Caitanya Mahāprabhu and a few devotees, His immediate disciples like the six Gosvāmīs, who were following in His footsteps. They worshiped Kṛṣṇa in separation and sought Kṛṣṇa everywhere.

he rādhe vraja-devike ca lalite he nanda-sūno kutaḥ
śrī-govardhana-kalpa-pādapa-tale kālindī-vanye kutaḥ
ghoṣantāv iti sarvato vraja-pure khedair mahā-vihvalau
vande rūpa-sanātanau raghu-yugau śrī-jīva-gopālakau

"I offer my respectful obeisances to the six Gosvāmīs, namely Śrī Rūpa Gosvāmī, Śrī Sanātana Gosvāmī, Śrī Raghunātha Bhaṭṭa Gosvāmī, Śrī Raghunātha dāsa Gosvāmī, Śrī Jīva Gosvāmī and Śrī Gopāla Bhaṭṭa Gosvāmī, who were chanting very loudly everywhere in Vṛndāvana, shouting, 'Queen of Vṛndāvana, Rādhārāṇī! O Lalitā! O son of Nanda Mahārāja! Where are you all now? Are you just on the hill of Govardhana, or are you under the trees on the bank of the Yamunā? Where are you?' These were their moods in executing Kṛṣṇa consciousness." (*Ṣaḍ-gosvāmy-aṣṭaka* 8)

The Gosvāmīs never said, "We have seen Kṛṣṇa." This is the recommended process—worship in separation. We should awaken our lost

Kṛṣṇa consciousness in this way and become mad after Kṛṣṇa in our separation from Him. This is called *kṛṣṇa-premā*, and this love was distributed by Caitanya Mahāprabhu. We should not try to understand Kṛṣṇa by our small knowledge. Since we are imperfect, how can we speculate on Kṛṣṇa? There are many people like *jñānīs* and theosophists who try to understand the Absolute Truth by speculation, but this is not possible.

athāpi te deva padāmbuja-dvaya-
prasāda-leśānugṛhīta eva hi
jānāti tattvaṁ bhagavan-mahimno
na cānya eko 'pi ciraṁ vicinvan

"My Lord, if one is favored by even a slight trace of the mercy of Your lotus feet, he can understand the greatness of Your personality. But those who speculate in order to understand the Supreme Personality of Godhead are unable to know You, even though they continue to study the *Vedas* for many years." (*Bhāg.* 10.14.29) Even if one speculates for many years, he cannot understand Kṛṣṇa. One has to receive the mercy of Kṛṣṇa through the spiritual master, and this is the path recommended by Śrī Caitanya Mahāprabhu. *Sthāne-sṭhitāḥ śruti-gatāḥ tanu-vāṅ-manobhiḥ* (*Bhāg.* 10.14.3). Another name for Kṛṣṇa is Ajita. No one can conquer Kṛṣṇa, but Kṛṣṇa can be conquered by His devotee. One should be submissive and say, "Kṛṣṇa, I am very poor. I have no means to understand You. Please be merciful upon me. Please allow me to understand You and surrender." This is wanted. Kṛṣṇa is very merciful, and when He sees that someone has surrendered, He will help from within.

CHAPTER FOURTEEN

Bhakti as Ultimate Liberation

TEXT 31

maitreya uvāca
viditvārthaṁ kapilo mātur itthaṁ
jāta-sneho yatra tanvābhijātaḥ
tattvāmnāyaṁ yat pravadanti sāṅkhyaṁ
provāca vai bhakti-vitāna-yogam

TRANSLATION

Śrī Maitreya said: After hearing His mother's statement, Kapila could understand her purpose, and He became compassionate toward her because of having been born from her body. He then described the Sāṅkhya system of philosophy, which is a combination of devotional service and mystic realization, as received by disciplic succession.

PURPORT

The philosophy propounded by the atheist Kapila is an analysis of the material elements and is very much appreciated by Western philosophers. The *sāṅkhya-yoga* explained by Lord Kapiladeva, the son of Devahūti, is practically unknown in the West. The *sāṅkhya-yoga* propounded herein is actually *bhakti.* It is stated here that the proper way to receive this knowledge is by disciplic succession, not by philosophical speculation. Speculation is an improper way to understand the Absolute Truth. Generally Western philosophers try to understand the Absolute Truth by the ascending process of mental speculation. This is the process of inductive logic. The other process is the descending process, and this is the *paramparā* process. By this method, knowledge descends from a higher source.

In *Bhagavad-gītā*, many *yoga* systems are explained, but the *bhakti-yoga* system is considered highest of all. Ultimately, all *yogas* end in *bhakti-yoga*. The ultimate conclusion of *jñāna-yoga* and *haṭha-yoga* is *bhakti-yoga*. In the Sixth Chapter of *Bhagavad-gītā*, the *haṭha-yoga* system of meditation is explained, and Arjuna, who was highly elevated, said that he could not concentrate his mind in this way. If the *haṭha-yoga* system was so difficult five thousand years ago for a person so elevated that he was Kṛṣṇa's friend, how is it possible today? Arjuna frankly said that this system of *yoga* was impossible to execute because the mind is as difficult to control as the wind.

The *haṭha-yoga* system is basically meant for those who are overly attached to the body; otherwise, the preferred *yoga* is *sāṅkhya-yoga* or *bhakti-yoga*. When Arjuna told Śrī Kṛṣṇa that the *haṭha-yoga* system was too difficult to execute, the Lord pacified him by saying that the first-class *yogī* is one "who is always thinking of Me." (Bg. 6.47) Arjuna did not know anything but Kṛṣṇa, and Arjuna requested that Kṛṣṇa be present on his side in the battle. When Duryodhana approached Kṛṣṇa with Arjuna and requested Him to take sides, Kṛṣṇa said, "I have eighteen military divisions. These divisions will take one side, and I personally will take another. However, I will not fight in this battle." At first Arjuna thought it wise to take the eighteen divisions with their many thousands of elephants and horses, but then he considered that if he simply had Kṛṣṇa on his side, that would be sufficient. He would not need ordinary soldiers. Duryodhana, on the other hand, decided to take Kṛṣṇa's soldiers. Thus in order to pacify Arjuna, Kṛṣṇa told him not to worry, although he could not execute the *aṣṭāṅga-yoga* system.

"The first-class *yogī* is he who always thinks of Me." One should always remember that Kṛṣṇa is within his heart and think of Him. This is the proper system of meditation. If we always chant the Hare Kṛṣṇa *mahā-mantra*, we will always remember Kṛṣṇa, and immediately the form of Kṛṣṇa will be awakened within our hearts. The process of always thinking of Kṛṣṇa is the process of Kṛṣṇa consciousness. The first-class *yogī* is he who is always conscious of Kṛṣṇa. One can be conscious of Kṛṣṇa by hearing about Him submissively.

We have to accept Kṛṣṇa through the disciplic succession. There are four *sampradāyas*, disciplic successions. One comes from Lord Brahmā (the Brahma-sampradāya), and another comes from Lakṣmī, the goddess of fortune, (the Śrī-sampradāya). There are also the Kumāra-sampradāya and the Rudra-sampradāya. At the present moment, the Brahma-sampradāya is represented by the Madhva-sampradāya, and we belong to the Madhva-gauḍīya-samprādaya. Our original *sampradāya* stems from Madhvācārya. In that *sampradāya* there was Mādhavendra Purī, and Mādhavendra Purī's disciple was Śrī Īśvara Purī. Śrī Īśvara Purī's disciple was Lord Caitanya Mahāprabhu. Thus we are coming in the disciplic succession from Śrī Caitanya Mahāprabhu, and therefore our *sampradāya* is called the Madhva-gauḍīya-sampradāya. It is not that we have manufactured a *sampradāya;* rather, our *sampradāya* stems from Lord Brahmā. There is also the Rāmānuja-sampradāya, which comes from the Śrī-sampradāya, and there is the Viṣṇusvāmī-sampradāya, which comes from the Rudra-sampradāya. The Nimbāditya-sampradāya comes from the Kumāra-sampradāya. If we do not belong to any *sampradāya,* our conclusion is fruitless. It is not that one should think, "I am a big scholar, and I can interpret *Bhagavad-gītā* in my own way. All these *sampradāyas* are useless." We cannot manufacture our own comments. There are many commentaries made in this way, and they are all useless. They have no effect. We have to accept the philosophy as it was contemplated by Lord Brahmā, Nārada, Madhvācārya, Mādhavendra Purī and Īśvara Purī. These great *ācāryas* are beyond the imperfections of so-called scholars. Mundane scientists and philosophers use the words "perhaps" and "maybe" because they cannot arrive at a proper conclusion. They are simply speculating, and mental speculation cannot be perfect.

Bhakti-yoga is at the top of the stairs of all the *yogas.* The first step is *karma-yoga,* and then *jñāna-yoga* and *dhyāna-yoga,* but the ultimate is *bhakti-yoga.* Everyone is trying to reach the ultimate Absolute Truth, but the other *yogas* end in partial understanding. The understanding derived from *bhakti-yoga* is complete, and even if partially executed, it has potency. It is also recommended by the great *mahājanas* like Lord Brahmā, Lord Śiva and Kapiladeva. Since the path of perfection is very difficult to understand, the *śāstras* recommend that we follow the *mahājanas,* who are thus described in *Śrīmad-Bhāgavatam* (6.3.20):

svayambhūr nāradaḥ śambhuḥ
kumāraḥ kapilo manuḥ

prahlādo janako bhīṣmo
balir vaiyāsakir vayam

Another name for Lord Brahmā is Svayambhū because he was born from a lotus flower emanating from the navel of Lord Viṣṇu. Since he was not born of a father and mother, he is therefore called Svayambhū. Nārada Muni is also a *mahājana*, and Śambhu is Lord Śiva. Kumāra refers to the four Kumāras—Sanaka, Sanandana, Sanātana and Sanat-kumāra. There are twelve authorities following the Sāṅkhya philosophy, or *bhakti-yoga*, and these include Lord Brahmā, Lord Śiva, Kapiladeva, Manu, Bhīṣmadeva, Janaka Mahārāja, Śukadeva Gosvāmī and Prahlāda Mahārāja. If we simply accept one of these *mahājanas*, we will be successful in understanding the Absolute Truth, but if we try to understand the Absolute Truth by logic and argument, we will ultimately be frustrated. One philosopher may be a better logician than another, and one philosophical argument may counteract another, but this process goes on and on. It is simply a useless waste of time. Even if we approach Vedic scriptures, there are difficulties. There are so many scriptures—*Yajur Veda*, *Ṛg Veda*, *Sāma Veda*, *Atharva Veda*, the *Upaniṣads*, the *Purāṇas*, *Brahma-sūtra*, *Rāmāyaṇa*, *Mahābhārata* and so forth. Different people read them and arrive at different conclusions. There are also the Bible and the Koran. According to so many different men, there are so many interpretations. One philosopher defeats another philosopher on the basis of scripture. It is even stated that one cannot become a *ṛṣi*, a philosopher, unless one propounds a different system of philosophy. *Nāsāv ṛṣir yasya mataṁ na bhinnam.* Thus the truth of spiritual life is very complicated and difficult to understand. The conclusion is that one should follow one of these twelve *mahājanas* in order to be successful. Kṛṣṇa is the original *mahājana*, and He instructed Lord Brahmā. Lord Brahmā is also a *mahājana*. Actually, Kṛṣṇa instructed everyone in *Bhagavad-gītā*, and thus everyone has learned from Kṛṣṇa.

In *Śrīmad-Bhāgavatam* (1.1.1) it is also stated: *tene brahma hṛdā ya ādi-kavaye*. Thus Kṛṣṇa gives His personal instructions just as Kapiladeva gave His personal instructions. There is no contradiction between Kṛṣṇa's philosophy in *Bhagavad-gītā* and Kapiladeva's philosophy. We need only receive the transcendental knowledge through the *mahājanas*, and the results will be beneficial. Kapiladeva explained this

Sāṅkhya philosophy to His mother, and although He had a natural affection for His mother, we should not think that Devahūti was an ordinary woman. She was very submissive, and when Kapiladeva saw this, He became very compassionate. He saw that she was eager to know about the Absolute Truth, and He considered that, after all, He had received His body from her. Therefore He concluded that He should try to give her the ultimate conclusion of philosophical knowledge, which is this Sāṅkhya philosophy.

TEXT 32

śrī-bhagavān uvāca
devānāṁ guṇa-liṅgānām
ānuśravika-karmaṇām
sattva evaika-manaso
vṛttiḥ svābhāvikī tu yā
animittā bhāgavatī
bhaktiḥ siddher garīyasī

TRANSLATION

Lord Kapila said: The senses are symbolic representations of the demigods, and their natural inclination is to work under the direction of the Vedic injunctions. As the senses are representatives of the demigods, so the mind is the representative of the Supreme Personality of Godhead. The mind's natural duty is to serve. When that spirit of service is engaged in devotion to the Personality of Godhead, without any motive, that is far better than salvation.

PURPORT

The senses of the living entity are always engaged in some occupation, either in activities prescribed in the Vedic injunctions or in material activities. The natural inclination of the senses is to work for something, and the mind is the center of the senses. The mind is actually the leader of the senses; therefore it is called *sattva.* Similarly, the leader of all the demigods who are engaged in the activities of this material world—in managing the sun, moon, etc.—is the Supreme Personality of Godhead.

It is stated in the Vedic literature that the demigods are different limbs of the universal body of the Supreme Personality of Godhead. Our senses are also controlled by different demigods; our senses are representations of various demigods, and the mind is the representation of the Supreme Personality of Godhead. The senses, led by the mind, act under the influence of the demigods. When the service is ultimately aimed at the Supreme Personality of Godhead, the senses are in their natural position. The Lord is called Hṛṣīkeśa, for He is actually the proprietor and ultimate master of the senses. The senses and the mind are naturally inclined to work, but when they are materially contaminated, they work for some material benefit or for the service of the demigods, although actually they are meant to serve the Supreme Personality of Godhead. The senses are called *hṛṣīka*, and the Supreme Personality of Godhead is called Hṛṣīkeśa. Indirectly, all the senses are naturally inclined to serve the Supreme Lord. That is called *bhakti.*

Kapiladeva said that in devotional service the senses, without desire for material profit or other selfish motives, are engaged in the service of the Supreme Personality of Godhead. That spirit of service is far better than *siddhi,* salvation. *Bhakti,* the inclination to serve the Supreme Personality of Godhead, is in a transcendental position far superior to *mukti,* or liberation. Thus *bhakti* is the stage after liberation. Unless one is liberated, one cannot engage the senses in the service of the Lord. When the senses are engaged either in material activities of sense gratification or in the activities of the Vedic injunctions, there is some motive, but when the same senses are engaged in the service of the Lord without ulterior motive, that is called *animittā* and is the natural inclination of the mind. The conclusion is that when the mind, undeviated either by Vedic injunctions or by material activities, is fully engaged in Kṛṣṇa consciousness, or devotional service to the Supreme Personality of Godhead, one is situated far above mere liberation from material entanglement.

Bhakti, devotional service, is transcendental even to *mukti,* liberation. Generally people are concerned with *dharma, artha, kāma* and *mokṣa.* In the beginning, there is *dharma* (religion), then *artha* (economic development), *kāma* (sense gratification), then *mokṣa* (merging into the Supreme One). However, *bhakti* is above all these. *Mukti* is not very important for a *bhakta.* In the words of Bilvamaṅgala Ṭhākura: *muktiḥ svayaṁ mukulitāñjali sevate 'smāt.* "*Mukti* herself is standing with folded hands, waiting to serve the devotee." (*Kṛṣṇa-karṇāmṛta* 107) This is the experience of Bilvamaṅgala Ṭhākura, who was a very rich South Indian *brāhmaṇa.* Due to bad association, Bilvamaṅgala Ṭhākura became a very staunch prostitute hunter, and he spent all his money on a prostitute named Cintāmaṇi. One night, during a terrible rainstorm, Bilvamaṅgala went to see Cintāmaṇi, but the prostitute was thinking, "Surely tonight Bilvamaṅgala will not come. This is a terrible storm." Nonetheless, Bilvamaṅgala came, despite all difficulties. Somehow he managed to cross the raging river, and when he saw the gates of Cintāmaṇi's house closed, he somehow managed to jump over them. Despite all the dangers, he reached Cintāmaṇi's house, and the prostitute, being very astonished, said, "How is it you have come tonight? Oh, you are so attracted to this skin! If you just had this much attraction for Kṛṣṇa, it would certainly be to your benefit." Bilvamaṅgala then immediately left the prostitute's house and went to Vṛndāvana. The fact was that in his previous life he had executed devotional service up to *bhāva-bhakti.* Thus the prostitute Cintāmaṇi actually became his *guru.* While in Vṛndāvana, Bilvamaṅgala Ṭhākura wrote a book named *Kṛṣṇa-karṇāmṛta,* which has been recommended by Śrī Caitanya Mahāprabhu. In that book, Bilvamaṅgala Ṭhākura writes: "If we have devotion fixed on You, My Lord Bhagavān, then we can easily see Your divine form as *kaiśora-mūrti,* a young boy."

Another name for Kṛṣṇa is Kaiśora. The word *kaiśora* refers to the age before marriage—that is, it refers to a boy between the ages of eleven and sixteen. Śrī Kṛṣṇa is always *kaiśora-mūrti.* By devotional service, one can see the *kaiśora-mūrti* of Kṛṣṇa very easily.

When Bilvamaṅgala Ṭhākura was going to Vṛndāvana, he was still attracted to women. One night he stayed at the house of a very rich merchant, and the merchant's wife told her husband that Bilvamaṅgala Ṭhākura was attracted to her. She asked her husband what to do, and the merchant simply said, "Serve him." Finally Bilvamaṅgala Ṭhākura came to his senses, and he thought, "These eyes are my enemies." When the beautiful woman approached him, Bilvamaṅgala Ṭhākura said, "Mother, please give me the pins out of your hair. I am very mad after the beauty of women. So let me pluck out my eyes." In this way, he blinded himself.

Although he could not see, in Vṛndāvana he was supplied milk by Kṛṣṇa Himself. Thus he personally realized Kṛṣṇa through *bhakti* and wrote of his personal experience. He wrote, "*Mukti* is not a very important thing. She is always at my service with folded hands, saying, 'My dear sir, what can I do for you?' " Thus a devotee is not very anxious for *mukti* because he is already liberated. If a man has a million dollars, why should he hanker after ten rupees?

Bhakti should be *animittā*, without motive. Actually Kṛṣṇa can fulfill all of our wishes without difficulty because He is almighty and full of all opulences. If we want material happiness from Kṛṣṇa, it is certainly not difficult for Him to grant it. He can also give us *mukti*, liberation, but it is foolishness to ask anything from Kṛṣṇa except *bhakti*. Śrīla Bhaktisiddhānta Sarasvatī Ṭhākura used to say that asking God for *mukti* or anything else other than *bhakti* is like going to a rich man and asking for ashes. There is another story, about an old woman who was carrying a bundle of dry wood through the forest. Somehow or other the bundle, which was very heavy, fell to the ground. The old woman became very disturbed, and thought, "Who will help put this bundle back on my head?" She then began to call on God, saying, "God help me." Suddenly God appeared and said, "What do you want?" She said, "Please help me put this bundle back on my head." So this is our foolishness. When God comes to give us some benediction, we simply ask Him to load us down again with all these material bundles. We ask Him for more material things, for a happy family, for a large amount of money, for a new car or whatever.

Caitanya Mahāprabhu teaches us that we should only beg God for His service life after life. This is the actual meaning of the Hare Kṛṣṇa *mahā-mantra.* When we are chanting Hare Kṛṣṇa, Hare Kṛṣṇa, Kṛṣṇa Kṛṣṇa, Hare Hare/ Hare Rāma, Hare Rāma, Rāma, Rāma, Hare Hare, we are actually addressing God and His energy, Harā. Harā is Kṛṣṇa's internal potency, Śrīmatī Rādhārāṇī or Lakṣmī. *Jaya rādhe!* This is *daivī prakṛti*, and the devotees take shelter of the *daivī prakṛti*, Śrīmatī Rādhārāṇī. Thus the Vaiṣṇavas worship Rādhā-Kṛṣṇa, Lakṣmī-Nārāyaṇa and Sītā-Rāma. In the beginning of the Hare Kṛṣṇa *mahā-mantra* we first address the internal energy of Kṛṣṇa, Hare. Thus we say, "O Rādhārāṇī! O Hare! O energy of the Lord!" When we address someone in this way, he usually says, "Yes, what do you want?" The answer is,

"Please engage me in Your service." This should be our prayer. We should not say, "O energy of the Lord, O Kṛṣṇa, please give me money. Please give me a beautiful wife. Please give me many followers. Please give me some prestigious position. Please give me the presidency." These are all material hankerings, which should be avoided. Lord Buddha advocated that we give up all material desires. It is not possible to become desireless, but it is possible to give up material desires. It is the nature of the living entity to desire; it is not possible to be desireless. If one is desireless, he is dead. Desirelessness means purifying one's desire, and desire is purified when we only desire the service of Kṛṣṇa.

Lord Caitanya Mahāprabhu teaches:

na dhanaṁ na janaṁ na sundarīṁ
kavitāṁ vā jagad-īśa kāmaye
mama janmani janmanīśvare
bhavatād bhaktir ahaitukī tvayi

"O almighty Lord, I have no desire to accumulate wealth, nor do I desire beautiful women, nor do I want any number of followers. I only want Your causeless devotional service birth after birth." (*Śikṣāṣṭaka* 4) He requests Lord Kṛṣṇa's service birth after birth. It is not that He is seeking salvation; rather, He simply wants to serve Kṛṣṇa one life after another. The devotees are not anxious to merge into the existence of the Supreme. The Buddhist philosophy advocates *nirvāṇa*, the negation of all material desires. Buddha does not offer more than this. Śaṅkarācārya gives a little more, saying that we should become desireless in this material world and then enter into the Brahman effulgence. This is called *brahma-nirvāṇa*. According to the Vaiṣṇava philosophy, however, we should negate material desires and be situated on the Brahman platform, but in addition we should engage in the devotional service of the Lord. This is called *bhakti*. Māyāvādī philosophers cannot understand this, but Kṛṣṇa says that this devotional service is on the transcendental platform.

The Sāṅkhya philosophy of the atheist Kapila, which is a material philosophy, is simply the study of the twenty-four elements. However, the real Sāṅkhya philosophy, propounded by Kapiladeva, is transcendental to the twenty-four elements and material activity. Thus in this Sāṅkhya philosophy, which is actually *bhakti-yoga*, there is no desire for material benefits. On the material platform, a person works for his own personal sense gratification or for some expanded sense gratification. One may work for himself, family, wife, children, society, community, nation or humanity at large. This is simply expanded sense gratification. Whether one steals for himself, family, community or whatever, the fact remains that he is a thief. It is said that when Alexander the Great arrested a common thief, the thief told Alexander, "What is the difference between us? I am a small plunderer, and you are a great plunderer." Being very sensible, Alexander released him, saying, "Yes, there is no difference." Regardless whether the sense gratification is for oneself, one's family, one's nation or whatever, it is, after all, sense gratification. The quality changes only when we work for the sense gratification of Kṛṣṇa.

It is noteworthy that *Bhagavad-gītā* or *Śrīmad-Bhāgavatam* never states that *kṛṣṇa uvāca* ("Kṛṣṇa says") or *kapiladeva uvāca* ("Kapiladeva says"). Rather, it states *bhagavān uvāca* ("the Supreme Personality of Godhead says"). This means that the version is perfect. If we receive knowledge from an ordinary man, there will be many defects. An ordinary person is subject to illusion, and he also has the tendency to cheat. Although an ordinary person may be a very advanced scholar, he does not possess perfect knowledge. Perfection is something totally different from what we find in the material world. Perfection means that there is no mistake, no illusion, no cheating, no imperfection. Therefore it is stated *bhagavān uvāca*, for Bhagavān is all-perfect. We should therefore take knowledge from Bhagavān or from one who speaks according to the version of Bhagavān.

The Kṛṣṇa consciousness movement is based on this principle. We are not presenting anything that we ourselves could manufacture. Whatever we manufacture is sure to be defective or deficient. What is the value of my philosophy? What is the value of my thought? Generally, people say, "In my opinion," thinking that "my opinion" really means something. People do not think, "I am simply a rascal." People value their opinion, thinking it something very big. Everyone in this material world has imperfect senses; therefore whatever knowledge has been gathered through the senses is necessarily imperfect. As we have stressed over and over, we have to receive knowledge from the disciplic succession. Knowledge has to be received from Bhagavān, the perfect one. If we simply follow this system, we can become a *guru* for the whole world.

The devotee never thinks that he is a great *bhakta.* Kṛṣṇadāsa Kavirāja Gosvāmī, the author of *Caitanya-caritāmṛta,* has stated, *purīṣera kīṭa haite muñi se laghiṣṭha:* "I am lower than the worms in stool." (*Ādi* 5.205) This is the Vaiṣṇava conception. A Vaiṣṇava is by nature very humble. He never says, "I am the Supreme; I have become God." Kṛṣṇa says, "I am God. Worship Me." The Vaiṣṇava says, "Kṛṣṇa is God. Worship Kṛṣṇa." It is not difficult to become a *guru,* provided that we repeat what Kṛṣṇa says. Whatever Kṛṣṇa states in *Bhagavad-gītā* is *dharma. Dharma* is one. It cannot be different. *Dharma* means abiding by the orders of God. However, if we do not know God or His orders, we can only set about manufacturing some rubbish and fighting among ourselves. This is not *dharma* but philosophical speculation. All of this speculation and manufactured *dharma* has been kicked out of *Śrīmad-Bhāgavatam* because it is all cheating. *Bhāgavata-dharma* is not cheating, for it is related to the Supreme Lord. *Bhakti* can be applied only to Bhagavān, and if there is no Bhagavān, there is no *bhakti.* If Bhagavān is zero, where is *bhakti? Bhakti* is the transaction between Bhagavān and the *bhakta.* Bhagavān is there, and the *bhaktas* are there, and the *bhaktas* address Bhagavān, feed Bhagavān, chant Bhagavān's names, invoke people to hear about Bhagavān, publish books about Bhagavān and worship Bhagavān, and in this way they are constantly absorbed in Bhagavān. This is the process of *bhakti.*

TEXT 33

jarayaty āśu yā kośaṁ
nigīrṇam analo yathā

TRANSLATION

Bhakti, devotional service, dissolves the subtle body of the living entity without separate effort, just as fire in the stomach digests all that we eat.

PURPORT

Bhakti is in a far higher position than *mukti* because a person's endeavor for liberation from the material encagement is automatically realized in devotional service. If the digestive power is sufficient, then whatever we eat will be digested by the fire in the stomach. Similarly, a devotee doesn't have to try separately to attain liberation. That very service to the Supreme Personality of Godhead is the process of liberation because to engage in the service of the Lord is to liberate oneself from material entanglement.

For a devotee, liberation is no problem at all. Liberation takes place without separate endeavor. *Bhakti*, therefore, is far better than *mukti* or the impersonalist position. The impersonalists undergo severe penances and austerities to attain *mukti*, but the *bhakta*, simply by engaging in the *bhakti* process, especially in chanting Hare Kṛṣṇa, Hare Kṛṣṇa, Kṛṣṇa Kṛṣṇa, Hare Hare/ Hare Rāma, Hare Rāma, Rāma Rāma, Hare Hare, immediately develops control over the tongue by chanting, and accepting the remnants of foodstuff offered to the Personality of Godhead. As soon as the tongue is controlled, all other senses are controlled automatically. Sense control is the perfection of the *yoga* principle, and one's liberation begins immediately as soon as he engages in the service of the Lord. It is confirmed by Kapiladeva that *bhakti*, or devotional service, is *garīyasī*, more glorious than *siddhi*, liberation.

It is stated in this verse that *bhakti* dissolves the subtle body. The spirit soul has two coverings—subtle and gross. The gross body is composed of earth, water, fire, air and ether. The subtle body is composed of mind, intelligence and ego. Of the eight material elements, five are gross and three are subtle. We cannot see the subtle, and the soul is even more subtle. Anyone with eyes can see the body, but not everyone can perceive the soul, the actual person. When we understand that the soul, or the person, has left the body, we cry, "Oh, my friend has left." We can perceive that the body is there, but something is obviously missing. Thus one's friend is actually different from the body. At the present moment when we say, "This is my friend," we refer to the body, but that is simply the vision of an animal. Animals think, "This is my dog friend, and this is my mother dog." They cannot see beyond the gross body. Similarly, we cannot see the soul, and if we cannot see the minute soul, how can we hope to see God with these blunt eyes? We cannot actually see one another. How, then, can we hope to see God? It is stated: *ataḥ śrī-kṛṣṇa-nāmādi na bhaved grāhyam indriyaiḥ*. "Material senses cannot appreciate Kṛṣṇa's holy name, form, qualities and pastimes."

Our present senses are incapable of seeing God. Generally, at death we can understand that something has gone. We understand that what we were seeing was not actually our friend but a lump of matter. This is knowledge. However, one who understands before death that the body is simply a lump of matter is called a wise man. He sees the soul through the eyes of knowledge. Those who are on the gross platform, who are like animals, can see neither the soul nor Bhagavān. The *karmīs*, the gross fruitive workers, do not understand the distinction between the body and the soul. Out of many millions of *karmīs*, there may be one *jñānī*, one wise man who can understand. The *jñānī* knows that he is not the body, and out of many millions of *jñānīs*, one may be actually liberated. The Māyāvādīs think that because they are spirit soul, they are one with the Supreme. Being equal in quality does not mean that one is the Supreme Soul. Because the Māyāvādīs think that they have become one with Nārāyaṇa, they address one another as Nārāyaṇa. They say, "You are Nārāyaṇa, I am Nārāyaṇa, everyone is Nārāyaṇa." From this misconception, the idea of *daridra-nārāyaṇa* (poor Nārāyaṇa) arises. The devotees fully engaged in the service of the lotus feet of the Supreme Lord do not think in this way. They think, "If I am one with the Supreme, how is it I have fallen into this condition?" They know that a drop of seawater is one in quality with the vast ocean, but they also know that a drop of water is never equal to the ocean itself.

Sometimes the Māyāvādīs worship Lord Viṣṇu, but they do not actually believe in the form of Lord Viṣṇu. They consider His image to be some imaginary form to utilize as a means for self-realization. Māyāvādīs say that the Absolute Truth has no *rūpa*, no form, but it is stated: *īśvaraḥ paramaḥ kṛṣṇaḥ sac-cid-ānanda-vigrahaḥ*. "Kṛṣṇa, who is known as Govinda, is the supreme controller. He has an eternal, blissful, spiritual body."

The word *vigraha* refers to the supreme form, but the Māyāvādīs do not understand this. There are also many so-called Vaiṣṇavas who worship Lord Viṣṇu with an aim of becoming one with the Supreme. They sometimes give the example of a drop of water merging into the great ocean itself. This is simply nonsense. The ocean is a combination of countless molecules of water, and it is impossible for one molecule to merge into the totality. The sunshine is a combination of countless trillions of small shining particles, and each particle has its individual identity as an atom. Because we do not have the eyes to see the small atomic divisions, we think that they are one, but actually they are not homogeneous. Similarly, although we are very small particles of the Supreme Personality of Godhead, we all have different identities. In *Bhagavad-gītā* (2.12) Śrī Kṛṣṇa says:

na tv evāhaṁ jātu nāsaṁ
na tvaṁ neme janādhipāḥ
na caiva na bhaviṣyāmaḥ
sarve vayam ataḥ param

"Never was there a time when I did not exist, nor you, nor all these kings; nor in the future shall any of us cease to be."

Kṛṣṇa never says that He, Arjuna, and all the soldiers shall eventually become one. Rather, He says that everyone will retain his own individuality.

Those who have complete knowledge never think that in the future they will become one with the Supreme. They simply want to remain in their constitutional position as part and parcel of Kṛṣṇa. Although we are now covered by the material body, the material body can be easily dissolved by the process of *bhakti-yoga.* If we are strong in *bhakti-yoga,* we actually no longer have a material body but a spiritual one. We are free.

When we are baffled, we want to become the husband of goddess Lakṣmī. The husband of goddess Lakṣmī is Nārāyaṇa, God Himself. In this material world, we are hankering after Lakṣmī, the goddess of fortune, but we are frustrated in our attempts. We think, "Now let me become the husband of Lakṣmī." Actually, no one can enjoy Lakṣmī but Nārāyaṇa. Even exalted demigods like Lord Brahmā and Lord Śiva are inferior to Lord Nārāyaṇa, but we are so foolish that we are thinking of assuming Nārāyaṇa's position, or making Nārāyaṇa into *daridra-nārāyaṇa,* the poor man in the street. The *śāstras* never equalize Nārāyaṇa with anyone, not even Lord Brahmā or Lord Śiva, what to speak of foolish rascals.

One may ask why Nārāyaṇa has created us, why it is we are part and parcel of Nārāyaṇa. *Eko bahu-syām.* Why has Nārāyaṇa become many? He has created us for enjoyment. *Ānandamayo 'bhyāsāt.* He has created us in the same way a gentleman accepts a wife. If one takes on a wife, he will beget children. A man takes on the responsibility of maintaining a wife and children because he thinks that through them he will enjoy life. In the material world we see that during the evening a man tries to enjoy life with his wife, children and friends. Therefore he takes on so many responsibilities. This is supposed to be *ānanda*, bliss, but because it takes place in the material world, the *ānanda* is converted into something distasteful. However, we can enjoy this *ānanda* when we are with our Supreme Father, Kṛṣṇa. We are all children of the Supreme Father, and in *Bhagavad-gītā* (14.4) Kṛṣṇa claims all species of life as His children:

sarva-yoniṣu kaunteya
mūrtayaḥ sambhavanti yāḥ
tāsāṁ brahma mahad yonir
ahaṁ bīja-pradaḥ pitā

"It should be understood that all species of life, O son of Kuntī, are made possible by birth in this material nature, and that I am the seed-giving father."

The Supreme Father, Śrī Kṛṣṇa, has created us for His enjoyment, not to create distress. Although we are Kṛṣṇa's children, we have given up our Supreme Father because we wish to enjoy ourselves independently. Consequently we are suffering. If a rich man's son gives up his home to try to enjoy life independently, he simply suffers. It is to our benefit to return home, back to Godhead, to enjoy ourselves with our original father, Kṛṣṇa. This will give us happiness. Kṛṣṇa is full of all opulence. He possesses in totality wealth, strength, beauty, fame, knowledge and renunciation. He possesses everything in unlimited quantity. If we return to our original father, we can enjoy ourselves with Him unlimitedly. It is not that we can enjoy ourselves independent of Kṛṣṇa. Nor can we say that to enjoy ourselves we have to become one with Kṛṣṇa. In the material world, our father gives us our birth, and we are an entity separate from him. If we are suffering, do we say, "My dear father, I am suffering. Will you please once again make me one with you?" Is this a very good proposal? A father says, "I have begotten you separately to enjoy yourself. You remain separate, and I remain separate, and in this way we will enjoy. Now you are asking to become one with me. What is this nonsense?"

The Māyāvādīs want to become one with the Supreme because they are suffering in the material world. Kṛṣṇa has created us to enjoy ourselves in His company, but due to our desire for independent enjoyment, we are not doing that. Consequently we are suffering in this material world, and because we are suffering we are thinking of becoming one with our father. It is *māyā's* business to try to build up the living entity, to puff him up, and *māyā's* last snare is to make the living entity think that he can become one with God. Māyāvādīs think that becoming one with the Supreme is the highest perfection, but this is not perfection because our original constitutional position is to enjoy the company of Kṛṣṇa. Friends sit together in a room and enjoy one another's company. What enjoyment can one have by himself? Variety is the mother of enjoyment, and real enjoyment is being in Kṛṣṇa's company. Therefore devotees never desire to become one with the Supreme. It is Caitanya Mahāprabhu who says:

mama janmani janmanīśvare
bhavatād bhaktir ahaitukī tvayi

"My dear Lord, I do not want to put an end to the process of birth and death. I am not anxious for *mukti.* Let Me go ahead and take one birth after another. It doesn't matter. Simply let Me engage in Your service birth after birth." (*Śikṣāṣṭaka* 4) This is real *ānanda.* Unless we are fully qualified devotees, we cannot enter into the Vaikuṇṭha planets. We have to live outside in the *brahmajyoti.* If we desire this, Kṛṣṇa will give us the opportunity. After all, Kṛṣṇa is everything. He is *brahmajyoti* and Paramātmā also. If we want to become one with the Supreme, we will be allowed to live outside the Vaikuṇṭha planets, in the *brahmajyoti.* However, that position is not eternal. As we have explained before, we cannot live eternally in the *brahmajyoti* because we want variety. Without variety, there is no enjoyment.

In all conditions, the pure devotee is liberated. He may engage in some occupation or business, but he is always thinking of how to serve Kṛṣṇa, and in this way he is automatically liberated. It is not that he thinks of becoming one with the Supreme and attaining liberation. Rather, his liberation lies in his personal relationship with the Supreme Lord Himself.

CHAPTER FIFTEEN

Meditation on the Lord's Transcendental Forms

TEXT 34

naikātmatāṁ me spṛhayanti kecin
mat-pāda-sevābhiratā mad-īhāḥ
ye 'nyonyato bhāgavatāḥ prasajya
sabhājayante mama pauruṣāṇi

TRANSLATION

A pure devotee who is attached to the activities of devotional service and who always engages in the service of My lotus feet never desires to become one with Me. Such a devotee, who is unflinchingly engaged, always glorifies My pastimes and activities.

PURPORT

There are five kinds of liberation stated in the scriptures. One is to become one with the Supreme Personality of Godhead, or to forsake one's individuality and merge into the Supreme Spirit. This is called *ekātmatām.* A devotee never accepts this kind of liberation. The other four liberations are: to be promoted to the same planet as God (Vaikuṇṭha), to associate personally with the Supreme Lord, to achieve the same opulence as the Lord and to attain His same bodily features. A pure devotee, as Kapila Muni will explain, does not aspire for any of the five liberations. He especially despises the attempt to become one with the Supreme Personality of Godhead. Śrī Prabodhānanda Sarasvatī, a great devotee of Lord Caitanya, said, *kaivalyaṁ narakāyate:* "The happiness of becoming one with the Supreme Lord, which is the aspiration of the Māyāvādīs, is considered hellish." That oneness is not for pure devotees.

There are many so-called devotees who think that in the conditioned state we may worship the Personality of Godhead but that ultimately there is no personality; they say that since the Absolute Truth is impersonal, one can imagine a personal form of the impersonal Absolute Truth for the time being, but as soon as one becomes liberated, the worship stops. That is the theory put forward by Māyāvāda philosophy. Actually the impersonalists do not merge into the existence of the Supreme Person but into His personal bodily luster, which is called *brahmajyoti.* Although that *brahmajyoti* is not different from His personal body, that sort of oneness (merging into the bodily luster of the Personality of Godhead) is not accepted by a pure devotee because the devotees engage in greater pleasure than merging into His existence. The greatest pleasure is to serve the Lord. Devotees are always thinking about how to serve Him; they are always designing ways and means to serve the Supreme Lord, even in the midst of the greatest material obstacles.

Māyāvādīs accept the description of the pastimes of the Lord as myths, but actually they are not; they are historical facts. Pure devotees accept the narrations of the pastimes of the Lord as Absolute Truth. The words *mama pauruṣāṇi* (My glorious activities) are significant. Devotees are very much attached to glorifying the activities of the Lord, whereas Māyāvādīs cannot even think of these activities. According to them, the Absolute Truth is impersonal, but without personal existence, how can there be activity? Because impersonalists take the activities mentioned in the *Śrīmad-Bhāgavatam*, *Bhagavad-gītā* and other Vedic literatures as fictitious stories, they interpret them most mischievously. They have no idea of the Personality of Godhead. They unnecessarily poke their noses into the scripture and interpret it in a deceptive way in order to mislead the innocent public. The activities of Māyāvāda philosophy are very dangerous to the public, and therefore Lord Caitanya warned His disciples never to hear from any Māyāvādī about any scripture. Māyāvādīs will spoil the entire process, and the person hearing them will never be able to come to the path of devotional service to attain the highest perfection. He only may be able to do so after a very long time.

It is clearly stated by Kapila Muni that *bhakti* activities are transcendental to *mukti.* This is called *pañcama-puruṣārtha.* Generally, people engage in the activities of religion, economic development and sense gratification, and ultimately they work with an idea that they are going to become one with the Supreme Lord (*mukti*). But *bhakti* is transcendental to all these activities. The *Śrīmad-Bhāgavatam*, therefore, begins by stating that all kinds of pretentious religiosity is completely eradicated from the *Bhāgavatam*. Ritualistic activities for economic development and sense gratification and, after frustration in sense gratification, the desire to become one with the Supreme Lord, are all completely rejected in the *Bhāgavatam*. The *Bhāgavatam* is especially meant for the pure devotees, who always engage in Kṛṣṇa consciousness, in the activities of the Lord, and always glorify these transcendental activities. Pure devotees worship the transcendental activities of the Lord in Vṛndāvana, Dvārakā and Mathurā as they are narrated in the *Śrīmad-Bhāgavatam* and other *Purāṇas*. The Māyāvādī philosophers completely reject them as myths, but actually they are great and worshipable subjects and thus are relishable only for devotees. That is the difference between a Māyāvādī and a pure devotee as they view scripture.

Actually Vedic scripture is *kṛṣṇa-kathā*, topics about Kṛṣṇa, and *kṛṣṇa-kathā* is not a subject matter for a debate club. It is meant for the devotees. Nondevotees simply waste their time reading *Bhagavad-gītā* and *Śrīmad-Bhāgavatam*, and we have often mentioned that so-called scholars, politicians and philosophers simply give misleading commentaries when they try to interpret *Bhagavad-gītā*. Śrīla Bhaktisiddhānta Sarasvatī Ṭhākura used to say that they are like people trying to lick at a bottle of honey that is sealed closed. If one does not know how to taste honey, one begins licking at the bottle, but for one to actually taste the honey, the bottle must be opened, and the key to its opening is the devotee. Therefore it is said:

satāṁ prasaṅgān mama vīrya-saṁvido
bhavanti hṛt-karṇa-rasāyanāḥ kathāḥ
taj-joṣaṇād āśv apavarga-vartmani
śraddhā ratir bhaktir anukramiṣyati

"In the association of pure devotees, discussion of the pastimes and activities of the Supreme Personality of Godhead is very pleasing and satisfying to the ear and the heart. By cultivating such knowledge one gradually becomes advanced on the path of liberation, and thereafter he is freed, and his attraction becomes fixed. Then real devotion and devotional service begin." (*Bhāg.* 3.25.25)

God is eternal, and His instructions and followers are also eternal. In *Bhagavad-gītā* (4.1) Kṛṣṇa tells Arjuna that millions of years ago He spoke *Bhagavad-gītā* to the sun-god. *Bhagavad-gītā* was spoken to Arjuna five thousand years ago, and if we read it today we will still find that it is fresh. *Bhagavad-gītā* and Kṛṣṇa are never old. Although Kṛṣṇa is the most ancient one, the oldest of all, He always remains like a young boy in His teens. He never appears older than twenty. Kṛṣṇa's words are absolute, as well as His form, qualities and activities. They are always fresh and new. If they were not, how could the devotees glorify them day after day with greater enthusiasm? The more one glorifies Kṛṣṇa, the more enthusiastic one becomes in glorifying, glorifying, glorifying. This is the meaning of spiritual. In the material world, if we repeat something once, twice, thrice or four times, it finally becomes hackneyed and disgusting. However, this Hare Kṛṣṇa *mahā-mantra* can be chanted twenty-four hours daily, and one will still feel fresh and enthusiastic. It is not a material sound like the sounds we hear on the radio. It is a spiritual sound that comes from the spiritual world. Even in the material world we can release a sound from one place, and it can be heard thousands of miles away. A spiritual sound can be released from many trillions of miles away, and it can be heard, provided that one has the machine to capture it. That machine is *bhagavat-premā.* Those who have developed love of Godhead can hear it.

Arjuna was neither a Vedāntist nor a *sannyāsī,* nor was he particularly advanced in spiritual understanding. However, he heard *Bhagavad-gītā* because he was a *bhakta.* Atheistic scholars and politicians cannot understand the transcendental vibration. They can only lick at the honey bottle. Fools and rascals eat and drink everything without restriction, thinking that they are doing so in the name of religion. There are many so-called *svāmīs* and *yogīs* who tell their disciples that they can do anything and still advance spiritually, but this is not possible. One has to become a pure *brāhmaṇa,* control the mind and senses and discuss the Supreme Personality of Godhead among *sādhus.* This may sound very difficult, but one can become a *sat,* a saintly person, within a second. If one is eager, one can immediately surrender to Kṛṣṇa.

When one approaches Kṛṣṇa, one should say, "My dear Kṛṣṇa, I have forgotten You. Now I am fully surrendered unto You. You may kill me as You like or, if You like, You can give me protection." When Prahlāda was asked by the Supreme Lord what benediction he desired, Prahlāda Mahārāja replied, "My dear Lord, why should I ask for some benediction simply because I have suffered for You? You are supremely powerful, and whatever I get, I get from You. I was born into a family of demons and was inclined toward material enjoyment. I have seen my powerful father, who was feared even by the demigods, annihilated within a second. Why should I ask for anything? Please engage me in the service of Your servant. This is all I want. I do not want anything else." In this way a devotee never asks for anything material from the Supreme Personality of Godhead. The devotees are simply satisfied in glorifying the Lord. This is the way of *bhakti-yoga*.

Kṛṣṇa descends to please His devotees and destroy the demons. From the very beginning of Kṛṣṇa's birth, demons were present. Kaṁsa advised his constables, "As soon as Kṛṣṇa is born, tell me. I shall immediately kill Him." He was always thinking of Kṛṣṇa in this way, negatively. Similarly, we will find so many so-called religionists whose only purpose is to kill Kṛṣṇa. Somehow or other they try to take Kṛṣṇa out of *Bhagavad-gītā*. They will comment on *Bhagavad-gītā*, but in their commentaries there will never be mention of Kṛṣṇa. They will never say that Kṛṣṇa is the Supreme Personality of Godhead and that He should be worshiped. This means that they are *asuras*, demons, although they may present themselves as big scholars. Somehow or other they try to evade *kṛṣṇa-bhakti*, and their entire propaganda is aimed toward this.

TEXT 35

paśyanti te me rucirāṇy amba santaḥ
prasanna-vaktrāruṇa-locanāni
rūpāṇi divyāni vara-pradāni
sākaṁ vācaṁ spṛhaṇīyāṁ vadanti

TRANSLATION

O My mother, My devotees always see the smiling face of My form, with eyes like the rising morning sun. They like to see My

various transcendental forms, which are all benevolent, and they also talk favorably with Me.

PURPORT

Māyāvādīs and atheists accept the forms of the Deities in the temple of the Lord as idols, but devotees do not worship idols. They directly worship the Personality of Godhead in His *arcā* incarnation. *Arcā* refers to the form we can worship in our present condition. Actually in our present state it is not possible to see God in His spiritual form because our material eyes and senses cannot conceive of a spiritual form. We cannot even see the spiritual form of the individual soul. When a man dies we cannot see how the spiritual form leaves the body. That is the defect of our material senses. In order to be seen by our material senses, the Supreme Personality of Godhead accepts a favorable form which is called *arcā-vigraha.* This *arcā-vigraha*, sometimes called the *arcā* incarnation, is not different from Him. Just as the Supreme Personality of Godhead accepts various incarnations, He takes on forms made out of matter—clay, wood, metal, jewels, etc.

There are many śāstric injunctions which give instructions for carving forms of the Lord. These forms are not material. If God is all-pervading, He is also in the material elements. There is no doubt about it. But the atheists think otherwise. Although they preach that everything is God, when they go to the temple and see the form of the Lord, they deny that He is God. According to their own theory, everything is God. Then why is the Deity not God? Actually, they have no conception of God. The devotees' vision, however, is different; their vision is smeared with love of God. As soon as they see the Lord in His different forms, the devotees become saturated with love, for they do not find any difference between the Lord and His form in the temple, as do the atheists. The smiling face of the Deity in the temple is beheld by the devotees as transcendental and spiritual, and the decorations on the body of the Lord are very much appreciated by the devotees. It is the duty of the spiritual master to teach his devotees how to decorate the Deity in the temple, how to cleanse the temple and how to worship the Deity. There are different procedures, rules and regulations followed in temples of Viṣṇu, and devotees go there and see the Deity, the *vigraha*, and spiritually enjoy the form, because all of the Deities are benevolent. The devotees express their minds before the Deity, and in many instances the Deity also gives answers. But one must be a very elevated devotee in order to be able to speak with the Supreme Lord. Sometimes the Lord informs the devotee through dreams. These exchanges between the Deity and the devotee are not understandable by atheists, but actually the devotee enjoys them.

Clearly, those who have the eyes to see Kṛṣṇa will see Him. When Caitanya Mahāprabhu entered the temple of Jagannātha, He immediately fainted upon seeing the Deity. He said, "Oh, here is My Lord! Here is My Lord!" In order to see, one has to become *santaḥ*, and one becomes *santaḥ* by culture. When we develop love of Kṛṣṇa, we will immediately see Kṛṣṇa and faint, saying, "Oh, here is my Lord!" However, those with no faith, those who are always trying to deny Kṛṣṇa, will simply say, "Oh, this is an idol. This is simply a piece of stone."

We must be eager to see Kṛṣṇa and talk with Him. He is actually waiting to see whether we are interested in talking with Him. In *Bhagavad-gītā* (10.10) Śrī Kṛṣṇa says:

teṣāṁ satata-yuktānāṁ
bhajatāṁ prīti-pūrvakam
dadāmi buddhi-yogaṁ taṁ
yena mām upayānti te

"To those who are constantly devoted and worship Me with love, I give the understanding by which they can come to Me."

If we want to talk to some important man, we must have some qualification. It is not that we can immediately talk to presidents or even to senators just because we want to talk to them. Somehow or other we must comply with certain rules and regulations. Kṛṣṇa is ready to talk to us, and for this purpose He has descended in the *arcā-mūrti*, the Deity, in order to be seen. We simply have to qualify ourselves to talk with Him. The nondevotees, Māyāvādīs, who are interested in denying Kṛṣṇa, say that God has no eyes, no legs, no hands, no ears and so on. This is indirectly saying that God is blind and deaf and that He cannot do this or that. In this way, they are indirectly insulting God. This is blasphemy. God does not want to hear such nonsense. Therefore it is said in this verse: *sākaṁ vācaṁ spṛhaṇīyāṁ vadanti.* By saying that Kṛṣṇa is blind, that He has no eyes, no hands, no nothing, we are indirectly saying that

Kṛṣṇa does not exist. This is certainly not a favorable way to talk about Kṛṣṇa. If we want to talk about Kṛṣṇa, we must consult the Vedic literatures. Then we can understand how Kṛṣṇa should be worshiped.

In *Brahma-saṁhitā* (5.29) it is stated: "Śrī Kṛṣṇa is playing on His flute, and His eyes are as beautiful as the petals of a lotus flower. He wears a peacock feather in His hair, and His form is very beautiful." The Māyāvādīs say, "Just imagine some form of God." But God's form cannot be imagined. God's form is not imaginary but factual. This factual information we receive from the *Vedas.* When Kṛṣṇa was present on this earth, He exhibited His form and activities. All of these are divine, not material. Kṛṣṇa's body is *sac-cid-ānanda-vigraha.* It has nothing to do with anything material. He descends as a favor to His devotees, who are always anxious to see Him. His first business is to give pleasure to His devotees, and His second business is to kill the demons, who are always giving the devotees trouble. It is the nature of demons to give devotees trouble, just as in the West, Lord Jesus Christ was crucified because he was preaching God consciousness. Similarly, Hiraṇyakaśipu tried to kill his five-year-old boy Prahlāda Mahārāja because his son was talking about Kṛṣṇa. There were many demons who tried to kill Kṛṣṇa Himself, great demons like Pūtanā, Aghāsura, Bakāsura and Kaṁsa. Nonetheless, Kṛṣṇa destroys them all by His omnipotence.

Actually everyone in the material world is more or less an *asura,* an atheist. If one preaches, one has to learn to tolerate the *asuras* and speak in such a way that they can also become devotees. We should always speak of Kṛṣṇa in a pleasing way; then we will be benefited. Another name for Kṛṣṇa is Uttamaśloka, which indicates that He is worshiped by the best selected words. It is not that we should use any words we choose. There are many prayers in the Vedic scriptures and also in the Bible and Koran. Although the Christians and Muhammadans do not worship the Deity, they offer prayers to the Lord, and that is also *bhakti. Arcanaṁ vandanam.*

There are nine different processes for worshiping the Lord, and one may accept one or all of them. We should use very selected words and surrender unto Kṛṣṇa, but we should not say things which do not please Him. We should not claim that God is formless and that He has no eyes, no head or whatever. Actually it is stated in the *Vedas* that Kṛṣṇa has no hand but that He can accept our offering. This means that He has no material hand. If He actually has no hand, how can He extend His hand millions of miles to accept an offering? Goloka Vṛndāvana is many trillions and trillions of miles away, but Kṛṣṇa can accept whatever we offer. When the *Vedas* say that God has no hands, it is meant that He has no material hands. His hands are *sac-cid-ānanda-vigraha.* If we can understand Kṛṣṇa's activities, form, qualities and pastimes in this way, we become fit to return home, back to Godhead.

TEXT 36

tair darśanīyāvayavair udāra-
vilāsa-hāsekṣita-vāma-sūktaiḥ
hṛtātmano hṛta-prāṇāṁś ca bhaktir
anicchato me gatim aṇvīṁ prayuṅkte

TRANSLATION

Upon seeing the charming forms of the Lord, smiling and attractive, and hearing His very pleasing words, the pure devotee almost loses all other consciousness. His senses are freed from all other engagements, and he becomes absorbed in devotional service. Thus in spite of his unwillingness, he attains liberation without separate endeavor.

PURPORT

There are three divisions of devotees—first-class, second-class and third-class. Even the third-class devotees are liberated souls. It is explained in this verse that although they do not have knowledge, simply by seeing the beautiful decoration of the Deity in the temple, they are absorbed in thought of Him and lose all other consciousness. By fixing oneself in Kṛṣṇa consciousness, engaging the senses in the service of the Lord, one is imperceptibly liberated. This is also confirmed in *Bhagavad-gītā.* Simply by discharging uncontaminated devotional service as prescribed in the scriptures, one becomes equal to Brahman. In *Bhagavad-gītā* it is said, *brahma-bhūyāya kalpate.* This means that the living entity in his original state is Brahman because he is part and parcel of the Supreme Brahman. Because of his forgetfulness of his real nature as an eternal servitor of the Lord, he is overwhelmed and captured by *māyā.* His forgetfulness of his real constitutional position is *māyā.* Otherwise he is eternally Brahman.

When one is trained to become conscious of his position, he understands that he is the servitor of the Lord. "Brahman" refers to a state of self-realization. Even the third-class devotee—who is not advanced in knowledge of the Absolute Truth but who offers obeisances with great devotion, thinks of the Lord, sees the Lord in the temple and brings forth flowers and fruits to offer to the Deity—becomes imperceptibly liberated. *Śraddhayānvitāḥ:* with great devotion the devotees offer worshipful respects and paraphernalia to the Deity. The Deities of Rādhā and Kṛṣṇa, Lakṣmī and Nārāyaṇa, and Rāma and Sītā, are very attractive to devotees, so much so that when they see the Deity decorated in the temple, they become fully absorbed in thinking of the Lord. That is liberation. In other words, it is confirmed herein that even a third-class devotee is in the transcendental position, above those who are striving for liberation by speculation or other methods. Even great impersonalists like Śukadeva Gosvāmī and the four Kumāras were attracted by the beauty of the Deities in the temple, by the decorations and by the aroma of *tulasī* offered to the Lord, and they became devotees. Even though they were in the liberated state, instead of remaining impersonalists they were attracted by the beauty of the Lord and became devotees.

Here the word *vilāsa* is very important. *Vilāsa* refers to the activities or pastimes of the Lord. It is a prescribed duty in temple worship that not only should one visit the temple to see the Deity nicely decorated, but at the same time he should hear the recitation of *Śrīmad-Bhāgavatam, Bhagavad-gītā* or some similar literature, which is regularly recited in the temple. In Vṛndāvana, in every temple, there is recitation of the *śāstras.* Even third-class devotees who have no literary knowledge or no time to read *Śrīmad-Bhāgavatam* or *Bhagavad-gītā* have the opportunity to hear about the pastimes of the Lord. In this way their minds may remain always absorbed in the thought of the Lord—His form, His activities and His transcendental nature. This state of Kṛṣṇa consciousness is a liberated stage. Lord Caitanya, therefore, recommended five important processes in the discharge of devotional service: (1) to chant the holy name of the Lord, Hare Kṛṣṇa, Hare Kṛṣṇa, Kṛṣṇa Kṛṣṇa, Hare Hare/ Hare Rāma, Hare Rāma, Rāma Rāma, Hare Hare, (2) to associate with devotees and serve them as far as possible, (3) to hear *Śrīmad-*

Bhāgavatam, (4) to see the decorated temple and the Deity and, if possible, (5) to live in a place like Vṛndāvana or Mathurā. These five items alone can help a devotee achieve the highest perfectional stage. This is confirmed in *Bhagavad-gītā* and in this verse of *Śrīmad-Bhāgavatam*. That third-class devotees can also imperceptibly achieve liberation is accepted in all Vedic literatures.

As far as meditation on the *arcā-vigraha* form of the Lord is concerned, we have to look at the Deity beginning with His lotus feet. It is not that we immediately look at His smiling face. We should first try to see the lotus feet of Kṛṣṇa, and when we are practiced in this way, we can look at His thighs, His waist and His chest. Then we can reach His smiling face. In this manner we should meditate on Kṛṣṇa's form, and thus we can associate with Kṛṣṇa by meditating on His smiling face, His flute, His hands, His dress, His consort Śrīmatī Rādhārāṇī and the other *gopīs* surrounding Him. Thus we should practice observing the Supreme Lord, and to this end He has appeared before us as the *arcā-vigraha*.

There are three kinds of devotee: *kaniṣṭha-adhikārī*, *madhyama-adhikārī* and *uttama-adhikārī*. The *uttama-adhikārī* is the most advanced; the *madhyama-adhikārī* is in the middle stage; and the *kaniṣṭha-adhikārī* is the neophyte. It is recommended that the neophyte meditate on the Deity daily. He should begin by meditating on the lotus feet, and then when he is practiced, he should turn his gaze toward Kṛṣṇa's smiling face. The neophyte should also read and hear *Bhagavad-gītā* and *Śrīmad-Bhāgavatam*. If we simply try to see and don't listen, the results will not be permanent. In some temples there are Deities but no discussion about Kṛṣṇa. People attend for some time, but after a while they lose interest. Thus there must be two activities. The Deities must be worshiped, and this is called *pāñcarātrikī-vidhi*. There must also be *bhāgavata-vidhi*, reading *Śrīmad Bhagavad-gītā* and *Śrīmad-Bhāgavatam*. *Pāñcarātrikī-vidhi* and *bhāgavata-vidhi* go hand in hand. By participating in these two processes, the neophyte can gradually attain the intermediate stage.

The spiritual master is supposed to be in the most advanced stage, but for preaching purposes he descends to the intermediate stage. The *uttama-adhikārī*, the most advanced devotee, does not discriminate between devotees and nondevotees. He sees everyone but himself as a devotee. The truly advanced devotee sees that he is not a devotee but that everyone else is a devotee. The *kaniṣṭha-adhikārī*, the neophyte, simply concentrates on the Deity, and that is required in the beginning:

arcāyām eva haraye
pūjāṁ yaḥ śraddhayehate
na tad-bhakteṣu cānyeṣu
sa bhaktaḥ prākṛtaḥ smṛtaḥ

"A person who is very faithfully engaged in the worship of the Deity in the temple, but who does not know how to behave toward devotees or people in general is called a *prākṛta-bhakta*, or *kaniṣṭha-adhikārī.*" (*Bhāg.* 11.2.47) According to the prescribed duties mentioned in the scriptures, one must care for the Deity, but when one is a little further advanced, he considers his functions with others. When one attains the *madhyama-adhikārī* stage, his vision is described thus:

īśvare tad-adhīneṣu
bāliśeṣu dviṣatsu ca
prema-maitrī-kṛpopekṣā
yaḥ karoti sa madhyamaḥ

"The *madhyama-adhikārī* is a devotee who worships the Supreme Personality of Godhead as the highest object of love, makes friends with the Lord's devotees, is merciful to the ignorant and avoids those who are envious by nature." (*Bhāg.* 11.2.46)

The *madhyama-adhikārī* is not only interested in the Deity, but he can also discern between devotees and nondevotees. He can also understand that this man is innocent and that this man is not. The innocent do not know what is to be done, and they do not know anything about God. They are not actually offenders, but there are others who are offenders. The offenders become immediately envious as soon as they hear about God or His devotees.

The *madhyama-adhikārī* knows that Kṛṣṇa is God: *kṛṣṇas tu bhagavān svayam.* He wants to develop his love for Kṛṣṇa. He also wants to see that not a moment is wasted without engagement in Kṛṣṇa consciousness. He is always careful not to spoil life's valuable time. That is the first qualification of a *madhyama-adhikārī.* We have a very short period to live, and we never know when we are going to die. There is no certainty. Foolish people think that they will go on living forever, but that is simply foolishness. Life is transient; therefore the devotee wants to utilize every moment for the advancement of Kṛṣṇa consciousness.

The *madhyama-adhikārī* also has a special taste for chanting the Hare Kṛṣṇa *mantra.* He is also very anxious to live in places like Vṛndāvana, Dvārakā and Mathurā, places where Kṛṣṇa lived. Of course it is a fact that Kṛṣṇa, being God, has His residence everywhere. He even resides within every atom. *Aṇḍāntara-stha-paramāṇu-cayāntara-stham.* Nonetheless, He has special places of residence like Vṛndāvana, Dvārakā and Mathurā; therefore a devotee is anxious to live in those places.

Increasing one's love for God is a gradual process, and the first ingredient is faith. Without faith, there is no question of progress in Kṛṣṇa consciousness. That faith is created after reading *Bhagavad-gītā* carefully and actually understanding it as it is. Unless one reads *Bhagavad-gītā,* there is no question of faith in Kṛṣṇa. One must have faith in the words of Kṛṣṇa, particularly when Kṛṣṇa says, "Abandon all *dharmas* and surrender to Me. I will give you all protection." If we study *Bhagavad-gītā* as a literary treatise and then throw it away, that is not faith. Faith is explained by Kṛṣṇadāsa Kavirāja Gosvāmī thus:

'śraddhā'-śabde——viśvāsa kahe sudṛḍha niścaya
kṛṣṇe bhakti kaile sarva-karma kṛta haya

"By rendering transcendental loving service to Kṛṣṇa, one automatically performs all subsidiary activities. This confident, firm faith, favorable to the discharge of devotional service, is called *śraddhā.*" (Cc. *Madhya* 22.62)

In *Bhagavad-gītā* Kṛṣṇa says that He is not only a person but the Supreme Personality of Godhead as well. He also says that there is no one superior to Him. If one believes these words, then one will have faith. Impersonalists read *Bhagavad-gītā,* but they do not accept Kṛṣṇa as a person. In the Twelfth Chapter of *Bhagavad-gītā,* Kṛṣṇa says that the impersonalist takes more trouble to come to Him. He will come later, but it will take some time. This is because impersonal understanding of the Supreme Absolute Truth is partial understanding. As Kṛṣṇa states:

kleśo 'dhikataras teṣām
avyaktāsakta-cetasām
avyaktā hi gatir duḥkhaṁ
dehavadbhir avāpyate

"For those whose minds are attached to the unmanifested, impersonal feature of the Supreme, advancement is very troublesome. To make progress in that discipline is always difficult for those who are embodied." (Bg. 12.5)

We have often given the example of impersonal understanding being like the understanding of the sunshine. One may see the sunshine entering through a window into his room, but this does not mean that one knows everything about the sun. Impersonal understanding of the Absolute Truth is like that. The sunshine is impersonal (Brahman), the sun itself is localized (Paramātmā) and the sun-god residing within the sun is a person (Bhagavān). Just as one can understand the three aspects of the sun—the sunshine, the sun itself and the sun-god—one can also understand the three aspects of the Supreme Absolute Truth—Brahman, Paramātmā and Bhagavān.

Impersonalists maintain that the sun is simply a fiery globe and nothing else, but in *Bhagavad-gītā* Kṛṣṇa specifically states that He spoke *Bhagavad-gītā* to the sun-god Vivasvān. Of course we can hardly imagine how the sun-god can be a person. The sun is a great fiery globe, and we think that it is impossible for anyone to live there, but this thinking is simply shortsighted. It does not follow that no one can live in fire just because we cannot live there. We cannot live in water, yet there are aquatics living there. We live on this planet, which is basically composed of earth, and our bodies are basically composed of earth in order to live here. Bodies are made in such a way that they can live in their environment. Similarly, the sun-god has a body capable of living in fire.

Kṛṣṇa is *sac-cid-ānanda-vigraha*, being, knowledge and bliss, with form. Impersonal understanding is understanding of the *sat* feature. Understanding Kṛṣṇa in full is understanding all of His features. The *ānanda* feature is realized in Bhagavān. Kṛṣṇa plays on His flute and is accompanied by His pleasure potency, *hlādinī śakti*, Śrīmatī Rādhārāṇī. Of Kṛṣṇa's many potencies, the *hlādinī śakti* is His pleasure-giving potency. That is *ānanda*. Although Kṛṣṇa is full in Himself, He expands

Himself when He wants to enjoy. That expansion is His pleasure potency, Rādhārāṇī. The *gopīs* are the expansions of Rādhārāṇī, and the various forms of Kṛṣṇa are manifest just to taste the mellow of transcendental bliss. *Ānanda-cinmaya-rasa.* Thus Brahman realization is realization of the *sat* portion, Paramātmā realization is realization of the *cit* portion, and Bhagavān realization is the realization of the *ānanda* portion. In the *Vedānta-sūtra* it is said that the Absolute Truth is *ānandamayo 'bhyāsāt.* Kṛṣṇa's *līlā* is always full of transcendental bliss—especially in Vṛndāvana, His original residence. It is in Vṛndāvana that Kṛṣṇa plays with His cowherd boy friends and dances with the *gopīs.* It is also in Vṛndāvana that Kṛṣṇa steals mother Yaśodā's butter. All His activities there are filled with transcendental bliss.

We can begin to experience this bliss by following the prescribed methods of devotional service. When we see the Deity, we can gradually realize how Kṛṣṇa is smiling, playing on His flute and enjoying the company of Śrīmatī Rādhārāṇī. Then we also have to hear about Kṛṣṇa. These two processes will increase in such a way that we will automatically become great devotees. *Anicchato me gatim aṇvīṁ prayuṅkte.* This is actually a scientific method. It is not imagination. People think that this is idol worship and imagination, but this method is prescribed in all the *śāstras* for developing God consciousness. It is an actual science.

śrī-bhagavān uvāca
jñānaṁ parama-guhyaṁ me
yad vijñāna-samanvitam
sa-rahasyaṁ tad-aṅgaṁ ca
gṛhāṇa gaditaṁ mayā

"The Personality of Godhead said: Knowledge about Me as described in the scriptures is very confidential, and it has to be realized in conjunction with devotional service. The necessary paraphernalia for that process is being explained by Me. You may take it up carefully." (*Bhāg.* 2.9.31)

In *Bhagavad-gītā* Kṛṣṇa tells Arjuna that He has revealed this most confidential knowledge to him because Arjuna is His very dear friend. That confidential knowledge is, *sarva-dharmān parityajya mām ekaṁ śaraṇaṁ vraja:* "Just surrender unto Me." (Bg. 18.66) Brahman realization is certainly confidential, and Paramātmā realization is still more confidential, but understanding Kṛṣṇa as He is, is the most confidential knowledge of all.

If one's mind and senses are completely absorbed in Kṛṣṇa consciousness, one is experiencing *bhakti. Bhakti* is not a sentiment but a practical science. One may engage in many activities, but in all cases, one's mind must be fully absorbed in Kṛṣṇa. Although a housewife is always busy working around the house, she always takes care that her hair is nicely combed. Regardless of her engagements, she never forgets to arrange her hair in an attractive way. Similarly, a devotee engages in many activities, but he never forgets Kṛṣṇa's transcendental form. This is the meaning of perfection.

CHAPTER SIXTEEN

The Pure Devotees' Spiritual Opulences

TEXT 37

atho vibhūtiṁ mama māyāvinas tām
aiśvaryam aṣṭāṅgam anupravṛttam
śriyaṁ bhāgavatīṁ vāspṛhayanti bhadrāṁ
prasya me te 'śnuvate tu loke

TRANSLATION

Thus because he is completely absorbed in meditation upon Me, the devotee does not desire even the highest benediction obtainable in the upper planetary systems, including Satyaloka. He does not desire the eight material perfections obtained from mystic yoga, nor does he desire to be elevated to the kingdom of God. Yet even without desiring them, the devotee enjoys, even in this life, all the offered benedictions.

PURPORT

The *vibhūti*, or opulences, offered by *māyā* are of many varieties. We experience different varieties of material enjoyment even on this planet, but if one is able to promote himself to higher planets like Candraloka, the sun or, still higher, Maharloka, Janaloka and Tapoloka, or even ultimately the highest planet, which is inhabited by Brahmā and is called Satyaloka, one will find immense possibilities for material enjoyment. For example, the duration of life on higher planets is far, far greater than on this planet. It is said that on the moon the duration of life is such that our six months are equal to one day. We cannot even imagine the duration of life on the highest planet. It is stated in *Bhagavad-gītā* that Brahmā's twelve hours are inconceivable even to our mathematicians. These are all descriptions of the external energy of the Lord, or *māyā*.

Besides these, there are other opulences which the *yogīs* can achieve by their mystic power. They are also material. A devotee does not aspire for all these material pleasures, although they are available to him simply by wishing. By the grace of the Lord, a devotee can achieve wonderful material success simply by willing, but a real devotee does not do so. Lord Caitanya Mahāprabhu has taught that one should not desire material opulence or material reputation, nor should one try to enjoy material beauty; he should only aspire to be absorbed in the devotional service of the Lord, even if he does not get liberation but has to continue the process of birth and death unlimitedly. Actually, however, to one who engages in Kṛṣṇa consciousness, liberation is already guaranteed. Devotees enjoy all the benefits of the higher planets and the Vaikuṇṭha planets also. It is especially mentioned here, *bhāgavatīṁ bhadrām.* In the Vaikuṇṭha planets everything is eternally peaceful, yet a pure devotee does not even aspire to be promoted there. But still he gets that advantage; he enjoys all the facilities of the material and spiritual worlds, even during the present life span.

According to Caitanya Mahāprabhu, Rūpa Gosvāmī in his *Bhakti-rasāmṛta-sindhu,* Nārada Muni in the *Nārada-pañcarātra* and Bhagavān Śrī Kṛṣṇa in *Bhagavad-gītā,* a pure devotee never wants anything from the Lord. He does not even want liberation, to say nothing of material things. Generally, people want *dharma, artha, kāma* and *mokṣa,* in that order. First of all, people want to become religious (*dharma*) in order to attain material opulence (*artha*). People want material opulence in order to gratify their senses (*kāma*), and when they are frustrated in their attempt to gratify their senses, they want liberation (*mokṣa*). In this way, *dharma, artha, kāma* and *mokṣa* are going on. However, a devotee is not interested in any of these. In the Christian religion, people pray, "Give us this day our daily bread," but a pure *bhakta* does not even ask for his daily bread. A pure devotee is kept in the hand of Kṛṣṇa just like a very precious jewel. When you hold something precious in your hand, you are very careful, and similarly, Kṛṣṇa holds the devotee and takes care of him.

One can just imagine his position if a very rich man says, "Don't worry. I will take care of everything for you." Kṛṣṇa, the Supreme Lord, is the proprietor of all opulence. There is no one more opulent than

Kṛṣṇa; therefore if Kṛṣṇa says that He will take care of His devotee, there is no question of poverty. Most people want material opulence, but they do not know that Kṛṣṇa is the proprietor of all opulence. That is their misfortune. Although the proprietor of all opulence says, "Just surrender unto Me, and I will take care of you," people do not do it. Instead, they say, "I will take care of my own business. I will maintain myself. I will take care of myself, my family, my friends and my country." Arjuna was very intelligent because he simply chose Kṛṣṇa, whereas Duryodhana took Kṛṣṇa's soldiers. It is not possible to conquer Kṛṣṇa, but the devotee can capture Kṛṣṇa with *bhakti*, love.

It is impossible for people to understand the great opulence of Śrī Kṛṣṇa. Therefore Caitanya Mahāprabhu tells us to abandon speculating about God. There is a story of a frog in a well being approached by a friend who says, "My dear frog, I have just seen a huge body of water." "What is that water?" the frog asks. "The Atlantic Ocean," the friend replies. "Oh, the Atlantic Ocean! Is it bigger than this well? Is it four feet? Ten feet?"

Our attempt to speculate about God is very much like this. If we want to understand God, we have to try to understand from God Himself. We may have a neighbor who is very wealthy, influential, wise, strong and beautiful, and we may speculate about his opulence, but if we make friends with him, we can understand his position by listening to him speak about himself. God cannot be subjected to our imagination. Our imagination is limited, and our senses are imperfect. The process of *bhakti-mārga* is the process of submission. There is no question of subjecting God to our imagination. We simply have to become very humble and submissive and pray to Kṛṣṇa sincerely, "Kṛṣṇa, it is not possible for me to know You. Kindly explain how it is I can know You, and then it will be possible." This is the way Arjuna approached Kṛṣṇa in the Eleventh Chapter of *Bhagavad-gītā*.

We can hardly understand or comprehend the innumerable universes. The word *jagat* refers to this universe, but there is more than one universe. Although we are seeing only one universe, there are millions of universes, and Kṛṣṇa is supporting all these millions of universes with a single fragment of Himself. This is also confirmed in many other Vedic literatures:

yasyaika-niśvasita-kālam athāvalambya
jīvanti loma-vilajā jagad-aṇḍa-nāthāḥ
viṣṇur mahān sa iha yasya kalā-viśeṣo
govindam ādi-puruṣaṁ tam ahaṁ bhajāmi

"Brahmā and other lords of the mundane worlds, appearing from the pores of hair of Mahā-Viṣṇu, remain alive as long as the duration of His one exhalation. I adore the primeval Lord Govinda, of whose subjective personality Mahā-Viṣṇu is the portion of a portion." (*Brahma-saṁhitā* 5.48)

This is the information given in *Brahma-saṁhitā*, the prayers offered by Lord Brahmā. This *Brahma-saṁhitā* was accepted by Śrī Caitanya Mahāprabhu, who copied it when He toured South India. Formerly there were no presses to print these literatures, and these important Vedic writings were written by hand. These literatures were not very cheap, and only highly qualified *brāhmaṇas* were able to keep them. They were worshiped in the temple as the *śāstra* Deity. It is not that they were available everywhere. Now, of course, the printing press has changed all this, but nonetheless we should always understand that the *granthas*, the scriptures, should be worshiped as God because they are the sound incarnation of God. One should not consider *Bhagavad-gītā* or *Śrīmad-Bhāgavatam* to be ordinary books, and one should take care of them just as carefully as one takes care of the Deity.

At any rate, when Śrī Caitanya Mahāprabhu returned from South India with a copy of *Brahma-saṁhitā*, He gave it to His disciples and told them that it was a summary of the *Vedānta* and the *Śrīmad-Bhāgavatam*. We therefore accept *Brahma-saṁhitā* as authorized scripture, for it was authorized by the Supreme Person, Caitanya Mahāprabhu. Just as Śrī Kṛṣṇa explains in *Bhagavad-gītā* in so many ways that the entire material creation is resting on one of His portions, *Brahma-saṁhitā* explains the same subject. It is stated that from the skin pores of the Mahā-Viṣṇu, all the universes are emanating. In each universe there is a Brahmā, a supervisor, who is the supreme creature and manager. These managers live only as long as the Mahā-Viṣṇu exhales. When He exhales, all the universes are created, and when He inhales, they all return into His body. In this way so many universes and Brahmās are coming and going. The durations of these breaths, which constitute a life of a Brahmā, are described in *Bhagavad-gītā* as many trillions of earth years. One may say that this is all fictitious and imaginary, but unless one believes it, one has no right to touch *Bhagavad-gītā.*

Generally people are interested in going to the higher planetary systems in order to become more opulent. This is the process of *karma-kāṇḍīya,* and people perform *yajñas* and pious activities in order to be elevated to higher planets. The idea is that one will be able to enjoy himself more, have a longer life span, more opulence, more beautiful women, nice gardens and so on. Actually this is the case, but a devotee is not at all interested in these things because he accepts Kṛṣṇa. In *Bhagavad-gītā* (8.16) Śrī Kṛṣṇa says, *ābrahma-bhuvanāl lokāḥ punar āvartino 'rjuna:* "From the highest planet in the material world down to the lowest, all are places of misery wherein repeated birth and death take place."

Even if we are promoted to the highest planet, Brahmaloka, the planet where Lord Brahmā lives, our situation there is still not eternal. So why should a devotee be interested in such a place? A devotee is simply interested in the supreme eternal, Śrī Kṛṣṇa. The Supreme Lord is the supreme leader of the *nityas,* the eternal living entities. We are all *nityas,* eternal, and Kṛṣṇa guides and plays with us. In the spiritual world, Kṛṣṇa and His devotees are friends, and they play together as cowherd boys. They are not interested in Brahmaloka or Candraloka, for these planets will ultimately be annihilated. There are some living entities that live only a few seconds, or, at most, a night. By the morning, they are all dead. Any life in the material world is comparable to that. Brahmā may live millions of years, but he ultimately has to die. Whether we go to the highest planet or the lowest planet, whether we are in the body of a Brahmā or a cat, we ultimately have to die. Kṛṣṇa presents Himself to atheists as death. He appeared in this way before Hiraṇyakaśipu, who said, "I am God. All the demigods are afraid of me. I am very powerful." Kṛṣṇa comes before such atheists as death and takes everything away—all power, opulence, money—everything. The theists worship God while they are living, and their only business in this life is serving God. After death, they render the same service; thus there is no difference between Vaikuṇṭha and a temple, for a devotee. In either case, his business is the same. Why, then, should he aspire to go to Vaikuṇṭha?

In the Vaikuṇṭha planets one attains opulence like Kṛṣṇa or Nārāyaṇa. There are five kinds of *mukti*, liberation, and one is *sārṣṭi*. This kind of liberation brings one opulence equal to the Lord. In the Vaikuṇṭha planets, everyone is four-handed like Nārāyaṇa, and everyone is equally opulent. In Goloka Vṛndāvana, Kṛṣṇa and the cowherd boys are equally opulent. In Vṛndāvana, the cowherd boys do not know that Kṛṣṇa is God. They look on Kṛṣṇa as an equal. This is the opulence of their devotional position.

Nonetheless, the devotees do not aspire for all this opulence. Their only aspiration is to engage in the service of the Lord. In this way, they get everything. Nor are the devotees interested in attaining the mystic *yoga siddhis*. They do not need to be able to create a planet, for they can create Vaikuṇṭha by worshiping Kṛṣṇa in the temple. The temple is *nirguṇa*, transcendental to the *guṇas*. In the *śāstras* it is said that the forest is characterized by *sattva-guṇa*, goodness, and the city is characterized by *rajo-guṇa*, passion, because in the city there is a great deal of illicit sex, intoxication, gambling and meat-eating. Formerly, when people were aspiring for spiritual realization, they left the cities and went to the forests. That was the *vānaprastha* stage. The word *vana* means "forest." Before taking *sannyāsa*, a man would leave his family and go to the forest to begin practicing austerities. *Vanaṁ gato yad dharim āśrayeta.*

Actually, superior to living in the forest is living in the temple because the temple is *nirguṇa*, above all the *guṇas*, even *sattva-guṇa*. The inhabitants of the temple are actually in Vaikuṇṭha.

Lord Kapiladeva next explains the nature of the special opulences of the devotees.

TEXT 38

na karhicin mat-parāḥ śānta-rūpe
naṅkṣyanti no me 'nimiṣo leḍhi hetiḥ
yeṣām ahaṁ priya ātmā sutaś ca
sakhā guruḥ suhṛdo daivam iṣṭam

TRANSLATION

The Lord continued: My dear mother, devotees who receive such transcendental opulences are never bereft of them; neither

weapons nor the change of time can destroy such opulences. Because the devotees accept Me as their friend, relative, son, preceptor, benefactor and Supreme Deity, they cannot be deprived of their possessions at any time.

PURPORT

It is stated in *Bhagavad-gītā* that one may elevate himself to the higher planetary systems, even up to Brahmaloka, by dint of pious activities, but when the effects of such pious activities are finished, one again comes back to this earth to begin a new life of activities. Thus even though one is promoted to the higher planetary system for enjoyment and a long duration of life, still that is not a permanent settlement. But as far as the devotees are concerned, their assets—the achievement of devotional service and the consequent opulence of Vaikuṇṭha, even on this planet—are never destroyed. In this verse Kapiladeva addresses His mother as *śānta-rūpa*, indicating that the opulences of devotees are fixed because devotees are eternally fixed in the Vaikuṇṭha atmosphere, which is called *śānta-rūpa* because it is in the mode of pure goodness, undisturbed by the modes of passion and ignorance. Once one is fixed in the devotional service of the Lord, his position of transcendental service cannot be destroyed, and the pleasure and service simply increase unlimitedly. For the devotees engaged in Kṛṣṇa consciousness, in the Vaikuṇṭha atmosphere, there is no influence of time. In the material world the influence of time destroys everything, but in the Vaikuṇṭha atmosphere there is no influence of time or of the demigods because there are no demigods in the Vaikuṇṭha planets. Here our activities are controlled by different demigods; even if we move our hand and leg, the action is controlled by the demigods. But in the Vaikuṇṭha atmosphere there is no influence of the demigods or of time; therefore there is no question of destruction. When the time element is present, there is the certainty of destruction, but when there is no time element—past, present or future—then everything is eternal. Therefore this verse uses the words *naṅkṣyanti no*, indicating that the transcendental opulences will never be destroyed.

The reason for freedom from destruction is also described. The devotees accept the Supreme Lord as the most dear personality and reciprocate with Him in different relationships. They accept the Supreme

Personality of Godhead as a dearmost friend, relative, son, preceptor, well-wisher or Deity. The Lord is eternal; therefore any relationship in which we accept Him is also eternal. It is clearly confirmed herein that the relationships cannot be destroyed, and therefore the opulences of those relationships are never destroyed. Every living entity has the propensity to love someone. We can see that if someone has no object of love, he generally directs his love to a pet animal like a cat or a dog. Thus the eternal propensity for love in all living entities is always searching for a place to reside. From this verse we can learn that we can love the Supreme Personality of Godhead as our dearmost object—as a friend, as a son, as a preceptor or as a well-wisher—and there will be no cheating and no end to such love. We shall eternally enjoy the relationship with the Supreme Lord in different aspects. A special feature of this verse is the acceptance of the Supreme Lord as the supreme preceptor. *Bhagavad-gītā* is spoken directly by the Supreme Lord, and Arjuna accepted Kṛṣṇa as his *guru,* or spiritual master. Similarly, we should accept only Kṛṣṇa as the supreme spiritual master.

When we speak of Kṛṣṇa, we include His confidential devotees; Kṛṣṇa is not alone. Kṛṣṇa includes His name, His form, His qualities, His abode, His associates, etc. For example, a king is always associated with his secretary, his commander, his servant and so much paraphernalia. As soon as we accept Kṛṣṇa and His associates as our preceptors, no ill effects can destroy our knowledge. In the material world the knowledge we acquire may change because of the influence of time, but nevertheless the conclusions received from *Bhagavad-gītā,* directly from the speeches of the Supreme Lord Kṛṣṇa, can never change. There is no use interpreting *Bhagavad-gītā;* it is eternal.

Kṛṣṇa, the Supreme Lord, should be accepted as one's best friend. He will never cheat. He will always give His friendly advice and protection to the devotee. If Kṛṣṇa is accepted as a son, He will never die. Here we may have a very loving son or child, but the father and mother, or those who are affectionate toward him, always hope, "May my son not die." But Kṛṣṇa actually never will die. Therefore those who accept Kṛṣṇa, or the Supreme Lord, as their son will never be bereft of their son. In many instances devotees have accepted the Deity as a son. In Bengal there are many such instances, and even after the death of the devotee, the Deity performs the *śrāddha* ceremony for the father. The relationship is never destroyed. People are accustomed to worship different forms of demigods, but in *Bhagavad-gītā* such a mentality is condemned; therefore one should be intelligent enough to worship only the Supreme Personality of Godhead in His different forms such as Lakṣmī-Nārāyaṇa, Sītā-Rāma and Rādhā-Kṛṣṇa. Thus one will never be cheated. By worshiping the demigods, one may elevate himself to the higher planets, but during the dissolution of the material world, the deity and his abode will be destroyed. But one who worships the Supreme Personality of Godhead is promoted to the Vaikuṇṭha planet, where there is no time, destruction or annihilation. The conclusion is that time cannot act upon devotees who have accepted the Supreme Personality of Godhead as everything.

Spiritual life is eternal; it cannot be destroyed. Whatever we have here in the material world is subject to destruction. In this material world we aspire for a nice house, good property, children, friends and riches, but ultimately all of these will be destroyed, including ourselves. Nothing here is permanent; therefore everything is called illusory. Actually we do not understand this; we take all this as permanent. The fact is, however, that only Kṛṣṇa is permanent. Kṛṣṇa's material energy is not permanent.

Māyāvādīs think that in the spiritual world there are no relationships. However, in the *śāstras* it is stated that in the spiritual world there is real life. Life in this material world is simply a shadow of that life. In the Fifteenth Chapter of *Bhagavad-gītā* this material world is likened to a banyan tree with its roots above and branches below. This means that it is like a shadow. When we stand beside a reservoir of water, we see the tree reflected upside down. We also have the experience of a mirage in the material world. We think that there is water, but actually there is none. Sometimes sailors at sea think they see land, but actually this is a mirage in the water. This material world is like that. In our lives we think we are enjoying some *rasa*, some relationship. Our children are calling us father, and we are enjoying our relationship with our wife, but all of these relationships are like shadows, although people have no information of this. The true enjoyment derived from these relationships can be attained in the spiritual world with Kṛṣṇa. Kṛṣṇa therefore comes in person to teach us that we can enjoy the same relationship with Him. We can enjoy Him as our master, our friend, our son, our father or our lover.

The Māyāvādī philosophers say that if Kṛṣṇa has become everything, there is no question of Kṛṣṇa as an entity or a person. This is a materialistic idea. If we tear up a piece of paper into small pieces and throw it away, the paper no longer has an existence. However, Kṛṣṇa is not like that.

advaitam acyutam anādim ananta-rūpam
ādyaṁ purāṇa-puruṣaṁ nava-yauvanaṁ ca

"I worship the Supreme Personality of Godhead, Govinda [Kṛṣṇa], who is the original person—absolute, infallible, without beginning, although expanded into unlimited forms, still the same original, the oldest, and the person always appearing as a fresh youth." (*Brahma-saṁhitā* 5.33) Kṛṣṇa has many millions of expansions, and He is also situated in everyone's heart. He is not only within human beings but within animals, trees, plants, aquatics and so forth. It is materialistic to think that Kṛṣṇa has no individual existence if He has entered into so many millions of hearts. Even though Kṛṣṇa has distributed Himself in many millions of parts, He is still present in the same strength. Kṛṣṇa is *sarvaiśvarya-pūrṇa.* He is never diminished.

There is an interesting story of a poor boy who was a student in school. During an annual Father's Day ceremony, the teacher requested the students to give some kind of a contribution. Formerly teachers would not earn a salary but would receive whatever the students would bring from their parents' homes or by begging. Generally the *brāhmaṇas* were teachers, and they could not charge anything. Thus some students brought the teacher rice, and some students brought other crops. This one student was so poor that he could think of nothing to bring; therefore he told his teacher that he would speak to his mother first. After school, the student told his mother, "My dear mother, all my classmates have promised to contribute something to the teacher. What shall I contribute?" The mother replied, "My dear son, we are so poor that we cannot give anything. However, Kṛṣṇa is the friend of the poor. If He gives you something, you can promise it to your teacher." "Oh, where is Kṛṣṇa?" the little boy asked. "Well, I understand that He is in the forest," the mother said. Therefore the little boy went to the forest and called for Kṛṣṇa. He then began to cry, and finally Kṛṣṇa came. When a devotee is very eager to see Kṛṣṇa, Kṛṣṇa is so kind that He comes. "So, what are you asking?" Kṛṣṇa said to the little boy. "You are the friend of the poor," the little boy said. "I am very poor, and what can I promise my teacher?" Kṛṣṇa then told him, "You can tell him that you will supply him some yogurt, some *dahī.*" The little boy was very satisfied with this, and the next day he went to his teacher and said, "I will supply you as much yogurt as you need." The teacher felt that this was very nice, and he was pleased with the boy. On the day of the ceremony, the boy again went to the forest and called for Kṛṣṇa. Kṛṣṇa appeared and gave him a quart of yogurt. The little boy took this yogurt to his teacher and said, "This is my contribution, sir." The teacher looked at the quart and said, "What is this? Hundreds of people will be coming, and you have only given this much yogurt?" The teacher became so angry that he spilled the yogurt out of the container. When he bent down to pick it up, he saw that the container was again full. He dropped it again, and it was again full. He could then understand that it was spiritual.

This is the nature of Kṛṣṇa. One can take everything, and yet the same will remain. In the material world, one minus one equals zero, but in the spiritual world, one minus one equals one. That is called *advaya-jñāna.* There is no duality in the spiritual world. One plus one equals one, and one minus one equals one. If we love Kṛṣṇa, that love will not be destroyed as love is in the material world. In the material world, a servant serves the master as long as the servant is pleased and as long as the master is pleased. The servant is pleased as long as the master pays, and the master is pleased as long as the servant renders good service. However, in the spiritual world, if the servant cannot serve under certain conditions, the master is still pleased. And if the master does not pay, the servant is also pleased. That is called oneness, absolute. A *guru* may have hundreds of disciples, hundreds of servants, but he doesn't have to pay them. They are serving out of spiritual love, and the *guru* is teaching without receiving a salary. This is a spiritual relationship. There are no cheaters and cheated in such a relationship. If we accept Kṛṣṇa as our son, friend or lover, we will never be cheated. However, we have to give up the false, illusory servant, son, father or lover, for they will surely cheat us. We may love our son with our heart and soul, but that very son may some day be our enemy. We may love our wife very much, but some day that wife may be such an enemy that she will kill us for her own interests. There are many instances of this in history. Māyāvādī philosophers are afraid of having such relationships because they have bitter experience with these relationships in the material world. They therefore want to negate all relationships, and therefore they say no more son, daughter, lover, master or whatever. Being disgusted with these things, they try to make everything void. Yet if we have the same relationship with Kṛṣṇa, we will never be cheated or disappointed. Our enthusiasm will increase more and more. Therefore Kṛṣṇa encourages us to accept Him as our son, as our friend and as our master. Then we will be happy.

TEXTS 39–40

imaṁ lokaṁ tathaivāmum
ātmānam ubhayāyinam
ātmānam anu ye ceha
ye rāyaḥ paśavo gṛhāḥ

visṛjya sarvān anyāṁś ca
mām evaṁ viśvato-mukham
bhajanty ananyayā bhaktyā
tān mṛtyor atipāraye

TRANSLATION

Thus the devotee who worships Me, the all-pervading Lord of the universe, with unflinching devotional service, gives up all aspirations for promotion to heavenly planets or happiness in this world with wealth, children, cows, home or anything in relationship with the body. I take him to the other side of birth and death.

PURPORT

Unflinching devotional service, as described in these two verses, means engaging oneself in full Kṛṣṇa consciousness, or devotional service, accepting the Supreme Lord as all in all. Since the Supreme Lord is all-inclusive, if anyone worships Him with unflinching faith, one has automatically achieved all other opulences and performed all other duties. The Lord promises herein that He takes His devotee to the other side of birth and death. Lord Caitanya, therefore, recommended that one who aspires to go beyond birth and death should have no material possessions. This means that one should not try to be happy in this world or to be promoted to the heavenly world, nor should he strive for material wealth, children, houses or cows.

How liberation is imperceptibly achieved by a pure devotee and what the symptoms are have been explained. The situation with a conditioned soul is different, however. If he is in the mode of goodness, he may be preparing for promotion to the higher planets; if he is in the mode of passion, he will remain here in a society where activity is very prominent, and if he is in the mode of ignorance, he may be degraded to animal life or a lower grade of human life. But for a devotee there is no concern for this life or the next life because in any life he does not desire material elevation. He prays to the Lord, "My dear Lord, it does not matter where I am born, but let me be born, even as an ant, in the house of a devotee." A pure devotee does not pray to the Lord for liberation from this material bondage. Actually, the pure devotee never thinks that he is fit for liberation. Considering his past life and his mischievous activities, he thinks that he is fit to be sent to the lowest region of hell. If in this life I am trying to become a devotee, this does not mean that in my many past lives I was one hundred percent pious. That is not possible. A devotee, therefore, is always conscious of his real position. Only by his full surrender to the Lord, by the Lord's grace, are his sufferings mitigated. As stated in *Bhagavad-gītā*, "Surrender unto Me, and I will give you protection from all kinds of sinful reaction." That is His mercy. But this does not mean that one who has surrendered to the lotus feet of the Lord has committed no misdeeds in his past life. A devotee always prays, "For my misdeeds, may I be born again and again, but my only prayer is that I may not forget Your service." The devotee has such mental strength, and he prays to the Lord: "May I be born again and again, but let me be born in the home of Your pure devotee so that I may again get a chance to develop my spiritual life."

A pure devotee is not anxious to elevate himself in his next birth. He has already given up that sort of hope. In any life in which one is born, as a householder, or even as an animal, he must have some children, some resources or some possessions, but a devotee is not anxious to possess anything. He is satisfied with whatever is obtainable by God's grace. He is not at all attached to improving his social status or the education of his children. He is not neglectful—he is dutiful—but he does not spend too much time on the improvement of temporary household or social life. He fully engages in the service of the Lord, and for other affairs he simply spares as much time as absolutely necessary (*yathārtham upayuñjataḥ*). Such a pure devotee does not care what is going to happen in the next life or in this life; he does not care even for family, children or society. He fully engages in the service of the Lord in Kṛṣṇa consciousness. It is stated in *Bhagavad-gītā* that without the knowledge of the devotee, the Lord arranges for His devotee to be immediately transferred to His transcendental abode just after leaving his body. After quitting his body he does not go into the womb of another mother. The ordinary common living entity, after death, is transferred to the womb of another mother, according to his *karma*, or activities, to take another type of body. But as far as the devotee is concerned, he is at once transferred to the spiritual world in the association of the Lord. That is the Lord's special mercy. Because He is all-powerful, the Lord can do anything and everything. He can excuse all sinful reactions. He can immediately transfer a person to Vaikuṇṭhaloka. That is the inconceivable power of the Supreme Personality of Godhead, who is favorably disposed to the pure devotees.

In these verses, Kapiladeva is describing the devotee's acceptance of Kṛṣṇa, the Supreme Personality of Godhead, as the most dear to us. If we want to love Kṛṣṇa as a son, Kṛṣṇa is prepared to be our son. Arjuna accepted Kṛṣṇa as his friend, and Kṛṣṇa was his best friend. Everyone can accept Kṛṣṇa in so many ways. We can love Kṛṣṇa as Arjuna did, or as mother Yaśodā did. Similarly, Parīkṣit Mahārāja simply heard about Kṛṣṇa and developed love. The first-class *yogī* takes Kṛṣṇa as everything—*priya, suta, sakhā, guru*, everything. This is real *bhakti*. If we want a son, Kṛṣṇa is prepared to be our son. If we want a lover, He is prepared to be our lover. If we want a friend, He is prepared to be our friend. Whatever relationship we want in the material world, we can have with Kṛṣṇa. We all have some loving propensity, and Kṛṣṇa is prepared to fulfill this propensity. Kṛṣṇa is not a person like ourselves. We occupy one body, but Kṛṣṇa is the owner of all bodies. The body is a machine given by Kṛṣṇa. In the material world, a father may give his son a car. Similarly, Kṛṣṇa gives the living entities bodies, 8,400,000 different types of bodies. The living entity gets into the body just as a person gets into a car, and he goes this way and that. We can drive this machine called the body for so many years; then it becomes old, and we have to change it for another machine. This is the process of birth and death. We drive one car for a while, and the car is finally broken, or it is smashed. We may have an accident or not, but eventually the car has to go to the junk yard. Then we have to get another car.

Actually our position is that we never take birth and never die, but why have we been put into this position of accepting these machines? This is our real problem. What is the cause of this? We want to enjoy this material world with its wealth and possessions. As long as we are after material possessions, we cannot transcend the cycle of birth and death. However, we have to give up all this and take shelter of Kṛṣṇa, the Supreme Personality of Godhead, and worship Him. Nor can we worship Him whimsically, but as He desires. If Kṛṣṇa says, "I want a glass of water," we must bring Him water. We cannot say, "Milk is better than water. I think I will bring Him milk." This is not favorable service. Some so-called *bhaktas* say, "I can worship the Lord in my own way." This is simply imagination. The Māyāvādīs say that Brahman has no *rūpa*, no form, and they suggest that we imagine some form. This is not the case with Kṛṣṇa. Kṛṣṇa is present in His original form, and He is described in Vedic literatures. We have recounted these descriptions before. If we want to attain a body like Brahmā's, we can get it. If we want a body like a worm in stool, we can get it. Or, if we want a body like Kṛṣṇa's, we can get that also. That is our real body of *sac-cid-ānanda*. We can also get a body like a demigod's and go to the heavenly planets. Or we can remain here in the middle planetary system. Our destination is our own choice. We are given full freedom through our activities. By pious activities, we go to the heavenly planets, and by Kṛṣṇa conscious activities, we go to Vaikuṇṭhaloka.

We are part and parcel of Kṛṣṇa, but somehow or other we have forgotten this. In *Caitanya-caritāmṛta* (*Madhya* 20:117) it is said:

kṛṣṇa bhuli' sei jīva anādi-bahirmukha
ataeva māyā tāre deya saṁsāra-duḥkha

"Forgetting Kṛṣṇa, the living entity has been attracted by the external feature from time immemorial. Therefore the illusory energy [*māyā*] gives him all kinds of misery in his material existence." Because we have forgotten Kṛṣṇa, Kṛṣṇa has given us all these *Vedas* and *Purāṇas*. Kṛṣṇa also comes into this material world in order to remind us of Himself. In this Kali-yuga, people are forgetting Kṛṣṇa more and more. They are not even interested in Him, but Kṛṣṇa is interested because we are His sons. A mad son may no longer be interested in his home, in his father or mother, yet the father never loses interest in his son. He is anxious because his boy has left home and is suffering. Similarly, Kṛṣṇa's son leaves the spiritual sky and takes up one material body after another and in this way travels from one planet to another in different species of life. Therefore Kṛṣṇa comes to rescue him.

CHAPTER SEVENTEEN

Taking Shelter of Kṛṣṇa, the Supreme Controller

TEXT 41

nānyatra mad-bhagavataḥ
pradhāna-puruṣeśvarāt
ātmanaḥ sarva-bhūtānāṁ
bhayaṁ tīvraṁ nivartate

TRANSLATION

The terrible fear of birth and death can never be forsaken by anyone who resorts to any shelter other than Myself, for I am the almighty Lord, the Supreme Personality of Godhead, the original source of all creation, and also the Supreme Soul of all souls.

PURPORT

It is indicated herein that the cycle of birth and death cannot be stopped unless one is a pure devotee of the Supreme Lord. It is said, *hariṁ vinā naiva sṛtiṁ taranti.* One cannot surpass the cycle of birth and death unless one is favored by the Supreme Personality of Godhead. The same concept is confirmed herewith: one may take to the system of understanding the Absolute Truth by one's own imperfect sensory speculation, or one may try to realize the self by the mystic *yoga* process; but whatever one may do, unless he comes to the point of surrendering to the Supreme Personality of Godhead, no process can give him liberation. One may ask if this means that those who are undergoing so much penance and austerity by strictly following the rules and regulations are endeavoring in vain. The answer is given by *Śrīmad-Bhāgavatam*

(10.2.32): *ye 'nye 'ravindākṣa vimukta-māninaḥ.* Lord Brahmā and other demigods prayed to the Lord when Kṛṣṇa was in the womb of Devakī: "My dear lotus-eyed Lord, there are persons who are puffed up with the thought that they have become liberated or one with God or have become God, but they are unintelligent." It is stated that their intelligence, whether high or low, is not even purified. With purified intelligence, a living entity cannot think otherwise than to surrender. *Bhagavad-gītā,* therefore, confirms that purified intelligence arises in a very wise man. *Bahūnāṁ janmanām ante jñānavān māṁ prapadyate.* After many, many births, one who is actually advanced in intelligence surrenders unto the Supreme Lord.

Without surrendering, one cannot achieve liberation. The *Bhāgavatam* says, "Those who are simply puffed up, thinking themselves liberated by some nondevotional process, are not intelligent because they have not yet surrendered unto You. In spite of executing all kinds of austerities and penances or even arriving at the brink of Brahman realization, they think that they are in the effulgence of Brahman. But actually, because they have no transcendental activities, they fall down to material activities." One should not be satisfied simply with knowing that he is Brahman. He must engage himself in the service of the Supreme Brahman; that is *bhakti.* The engagement of Brahman should be the service of Parabrahman. It is said that unless one becomes Brahman, one cannot serve Brahman. The Supreme Brahman is the Supreme Personality of Godhead, and the living entity is also Brahman. Without realizing that he is Brahman, spirit soul, an eternal servitor of the Lord, if one simply thinks that he is Brahman, his realization is only theoretical. He has to realize and at the same time engage himself in the devotional service of the Lord; then he can exist in the Brahman status. Otherwise he falls down.

The *Bhāgavatam* says that because nondevotees neglect the transcendental loving service of the lotus feet of the Personality of Godhead, their intelligence is not pure, and therefore they fall down. The living entity must have some activity. If he does not engage in the activity of transcendental service, he must fall down to material activity. As soon as one falls down to material activity, there is no rescue from the cycle of birth and death. It is stated here by Lord Kapila, "Without My mercy" (*nānyatra mad-bhagavataḥ*). The Lord is stated here to be Bhagavān, the Supreme Personality of Godhead, indicating that He is full of all opulences and is therefore perfectly competent to deliver one from the cycle of birth and death. He is also called *pradhāna* because He is the Supreme. He is equal to everyone, but to one who surrenders to Him He is especially favorable. It is also confirmed in *Bhagavad-gītā* that the Lord is equal to everyone; no one is His enemy and no one is His friend. But to one who surrenders unto Him, He is especially inclined. By the grace of the Lord, simply by surrendering unto Him one can get out of this cycle of birth and death. Otherwise, he may go on in many, many lives and may many times attempt other processes for liberation.

Presently we are so dull and foolish that we do not know what is *bhayam* and *tīvram.* The word *tīvram* means "very terrible," and *bhayam* means "very fearsome." We are entangled by a very terrible fear, but we have become so dull due to the spell of *māyā* that we do not care. At the time of death there are many troubles, and we become very fearful. Sometimes, when a person is dying, he falls into a coma and lies unconscious. We do not know what kind of fearful test this person is undergoing. He may be dreaming so many things, or he may be crying. He cannot express what is going on. Those who are very sinful especially die in that way. After death, one has to enter into the womb of another mother. That is also a very fearful stage. One becomes packed in a bag, and this bag is filled with stool and urine, and one has to remain packed in this airtight bag for nine months.

This is a horrible situation, but we have forgotten all about it. Therefore Kṛṣṇa says in *Bhagavad-gītā* that our real trouble is *janma-mṛtyu*—birth and death. When the living entity is packed in the womb, unable to move, he prays to God, "Please relieve me from this horrible condition. If You relieve me, I shall worship You." Finally, after nine months, the living entity emerges from the womb, and then he also undergoes so many troubles trying to adjust to the atmosphere of a new planet. As an infant, he cries and cries, and he is totally dependent on his mother's mercy. Sometimes a mother cannot understand what the child wants. Sometimes an ant may be biting the child, but the mother thinks that the child is hungry. There are bugs, worms, mosquitoes, stool, urine and so many things attacking the new body. These are the threefold miseries, yet we think that we have made such progress. We are being attacked moment after moment by one thing after another, yet people close their eyes to birth, old age, disease and death. The atheists want to forget these miseries, and therefore they like to think that there is no life after death. They are like ostriches, who stick their head in the ground when an enemy approaches.

Although the living entity in the womb promises to worship Kṛṣṇa, when he is delivered from the womb he does not fulfill his promise. As soon as he is born and grows up, he begins to acquire a good bank balance, a wife and children and then begins to think that his problems are solved and that he will live very happily. Actually his problems are not solved. He may have some temporary facilities, but the main problem is still there. Every minute, every second, people are dying and going to Yamarāja. Those who are living are thinking that they will not die. They see that their friends are dying, but somehow or other they think that they are eternal. Yudhiṣṭhira Mahārāja said that this was the most amazing thing in the world. No one thinks that he is going to die, although everyone else is dying.

The living entity thinks that he is very happy in whatever body he gets. He may get the body of a dog or the body of a cat, but he is happy in his body, and he does not want to lose it. This is called illusion. When an ant sees danger, he will run like anything. This is because he values his body and does not want to lose it. Once Lord Indra, the King of the heavenly planets, was cursed by Bṛhaspati to become a hog. He was going about on earth enjoying his hog body when finally Lord Brahmā came and told him, "My dear Indra, you have suffered enough. Now come with me and return to your heavenly kingdom." Indra in the form of a hog said, "Where shall I go?" "To the heavens," Lord Brahmā replied. It was then that Indra said, "No, I have my family and children. How can I go? I am very happy. Let me remain here." In this way, everyone is thinking that he is very happy, although he is in a horrible and fearsome condition. However, one who is actually intelligent can understand that he is not actually happy, that he is suffering. It is said that ignorance is bliss, but this is the bliss of a hog. When one actually comes to the understanding that he is not actually happy in the material world, he can begin to relieve his suffering.

There is no possibility of being liberated from suffering without taking shelter at Kṛṣṇa's lotus feet. People are thinking that they can relieve suffering through abortion, by killing the child within the womb. In this way they are committing one sin after another and becoming more and more entangled. Consequently the aborted living entity will have to enter into the womb of another mother in order to undergo the birth that he is destined to take. Then, when he enters the womb of another mother, he may again be killed, and for many years he may not be allowed to see the light of the sun. In this Kali-yuga, people are becoming so sinful that there is no possibility of rescue unless one takes to Kṛṣṇa consciousness. The entire human civilization is falling into the illusory fire of *māyā*. People fly into the fire just like moths. When there is a beautiful fire, moths come from a long distance, enter it and go pop, pop, pop. In this way one dies, takes birth and suffers and dies again.

Yet Kṛṣṇa and His devotees are so kind and compassionate that they are unhappy to see all the misery of this material world. Kṛṣṇa is the father of all living entities, and He is very unhappy to see His sons suffer. Kṛṣṇa therefore comes and canvasses: "Why are you captivated by this false, so-called happiness? Give up all of this and surrender to Me. Come to Me, and I will relieve you. You will then live happily, eternally and blissfully. You will not have any want, nor will you be troubled by anything." For this reason Kṛṣṇa comes. Actually He has no other business to carry out here because His agent *prakṛti* does everything. Nonetheless, out of compassion Kṛṣṇa comes in His original form or in an incarnation like Kapiladeva. Kṛṣṇa also sends His representative, who says, "You rascal! Simply take shelter of Kṛṣṇa and be happy."

Kṛṣṇa comes once in a day of Brahmā, and His incarnations also come, to educate foolish people who think that they are living happily on this earth. Kapiladeva comes to propound this Sāṅkhya philosophy, which is unalloyed devotion to the Lord. Herein Kapiladeva says that one is condemned to death unless he takes shelter of the Lord. There is no other way to be saved. We are all in a very fearful situation, but we do not understand this. Under the spell of *māyā*, we are thinking we are very happy, but this is not a fact. If we want relief from our dangerous situation, we have to surrender to the Supreme Personality of Godhead and revive our old connection with Him. What is that connection? We are all His eternal servants. We should not foolishly think that we can become one with God or equal to God. This is all the result of rascaldom. The beginning of knowledge is to understand that we are the eternal sons and servants of Kṛṣṇa. There is no difference between a son and a servant.

The son serves the father, just as the servant serves the master. There is affection between master and servant and son and father. The father also serves the son in so many ways; therefore the relationship is reciprocal. Caitanya Mahāprabhu has defined our original *svarūpa*, our original identity, as that of eternal servant. People are artificially thinking, "I am independent. I am no one's servant. I have become God. I have become Bhagavān. I am this, or I am that."

In the material world, it is not very pleasant to be a servant of anyone. We think that being God's servant is like this because we are materially infected. We are thinking that being a servant of God is like being a servant of some man, but in the spiritual world the servant and the served are the same. For instance, the *guru* is the servant of Kṛṣṇa, but he is accepted as Kṛṣṇa.

sākṣād dharitvena samasta-śāstrair
uktas tathā bhāvyata eva sadbhiḥ
kintu prabhor yaḥ priya eva tasya
vande guroḥ śrī-caraṇāravindam

"The spiritual master is to be honored as much as the Supreme Lord because he is the most confidential servitor of the Lord. This is acknowledged in all revealed scriptures and followed by all authorities. Therefore I offer my respectful obeisances unto the lotus feet of such a spiritual master, who is a bona fide representative of Śrī Hari [Kṛṣṇa]." (*Gurv-aṣṭaka* 7) This is the verdict of all *śāstras*. The *guru* never says, "I am Kṛṣṇa, I am God, I am Bhagavān." Rather, the *guru* says, "I am the most humble servant of the servant of the servant of God." He does not even say that he is the direct servant. Rather, he is the servant one hundred times removed. *Gopī-bhartuḥ pada-kamalayor dāsa-dāsānudāsa*. We should not try to become direct servants, for that is not possible. First of all we must become the servant of the servant. The *guru* is the servant of Kṛṣṇa, and if we become his servant, we become an actual bona fide servant. That is our real position. Therefore Caitanya Mahāprabhu prays:

ayi nanda-tanuja kiṅkaraṁ
patitaṁ māṁ viṣame bhavāmbudhau

"O son of Nanda Mahārāja, I am Your eternal servant, but somehow or other I have fallen into this ocean of birth and death." (*Śikṣāṣṭaka* 5) Caitanya Mahāprabhu addresses the Supreme Lord Kṛṣṇa as the son of Nanda Mahārāja. Kṛṣṇa is very pleased if one addresses Him as the son of Vasudeva, Yaśodā or Mahārāja Nanda. Kṛṣṇa likes to be named in relation to His pure devotees. Therefore He is called Yaśodā-nandana, Nanda-nandana, Vasudeva-nandana, Rādhikā-ramaṇa and so on. Thus Caitanya Mahāprabhu addresses Kṛṣṇa in this way. He says that although He is Kṛṣṇa's eternal servant, somehow He has fallen into the ocean of birth and death, accepting one body after another, dying and being born again, not only in this planet but throughout the whole universe, in many species of life. This is the situation with conditioned living entities, wandering from one life to another and from one planet to another for millions upon millions of years. We do not care about this because we say that we are brave and not afraid. We are very proud in this way, but this is a fool's pride. It is said, Fools rush in where angels fear to tread. In order to save ourselves from this fearful situation, we must take shelter of the Supreme Personality of Godhead. That is the verdict of all the *śāstras*, and Kṛṣṇa comes for this purpose and sends His devotees, who work day and night to propagate this Kṛṣṇa consciousness movement.

TEXT 42

mad-bhayād vāti vāto 'yaṁ
sūryas tapati mad-bhayāt
varṣatīndro dahaty agnir
mṛtyuś carati mad-bhayāt

TRANSLATION

It is because of My supremacy that the wind blows, out of fear of Me; the sun shines out of fear of Me, and the lord of the clouds, Indra, sends forth showers out of fear of Me. Fire burns out of fear of Me, and death goes about taking its toll out of fear of Me.

PURPORT

The Supreme Personality of Godhead, Kṛṣṇa, says in *Bhagavad-gītā* that the natural laws are perfect because of His superintendence. No one should think that nature is working automatically, without superintendence. The Vedic literature says that the clouds are controlled by the demigod Indra, heat is distributed by the sun-god, the soothing moonlight is distributed by Candra and the air is blowing under the arrangement of the demigod Vāyu. But above all these demigods is the Supreme Personality of Godhead, the chief living entity. *Nityo nityānāṁ cetanaś cetanānām.* The demigods are also ordinary living entities, but due to their faithfulness—their devotional service—they have been promoted to such posts. These different demigods, or directors, such as Candra, Varuṇa and Vāyu, are called *adhikāri-devatā.* The demigods are departmental heads. The government of the Supreme Lord consists not only of one planet or two or three; there are millions of planets and millions of universes. The Supreme Personality of Godhead has a huge government, and He requires assistants. The demigods are considered His bodily limbs. These are described in Vedic literature. The sun-god, moon-god, fire-god and air-god are working under the direction of the Supreme Lord. It is confirmed in the *Bhagavad-gītā* (9.10), *mayādhyakṣeṇa prakṛtiḥ sūyate sa-carācaram.* The natural laws are being conducted under His superintendence. Because He is in the background, everything is being performed punctually and regularly.

One who has taken shelter of the Supreme Personality of Godhead is completely protected from all other influences. He no longer serves or is obliged to anyone else. Of course he is not disobedient to anyone, but his full power of thought is absorbed in the service of the Lord. The statements by the Supreme Personality of Godhead, Kapila, that under His direction the air is blowing, the fire is burning, the sun is giving heat, etc., are not sentimental. The impersonalist may say that the *Bhāgavatam* devotees create and imagine someone as the Supreme Personality of Godhead and assign qualifications to Him; but actually it is neither imagination nor an imposition of artificial power in the name of Godhead. In the *Vedas* it is said, *bhīṣāsmād vātaḥ pavate/ bhīṣodeti sūryaḥ:* "Out of fear of the Supreme Lord, the wind-god and the sun-god are acting." *Bhīṣāsmād agniś cendraś ca/ mṛtyur dhāvati pañcamaḥ:* "Agni, Indra and Mṛtyu are also acting under His direction." These are the statements of the *Vedas.*

If the demigods are subject to fear, what of ordinary living entities? Material life is not very happy because we are always fearful of something. No one can say, "I am not afraid of anything." Everyone is afraid of something. There is not a bird, beast, human being or living entity alive that is not afraid of something. This is because we are absorbed in the bodily conception, thinking, "I am this body." Since everyone is thinking in this way, everyone fears bodily destruction. When there was an earthquake in Los Angeles, everyone ran out their houses screaming. Everyone was terrified, thinking, "Now death is coming!" This is material nature. There are many events in nature that cause fear. There are great cyclones and tornadoes. There is excessive heat and excessive rain. There is flood and famine and war. Yet people are thinking of being happy on this planet.

Modern scientists say that there are no demigods and that there is no God, that all events are being carried out by nature. It is true that nature is working, but nature, after all, is nothing but matter. Matter cannot work without being directed by a living being. We cannot say that matter works independently. In the ocean we always see that there are great waves moving. Water is dull matter, but the air is pushing these great waves and dashing them onto the earth. Scientists say that nature works in this way and that, but nature is not independent. We receive information from authoritative *śāstras* that nature is moving under the direction of the demigods. So we cannot say that these processes are automatically taking place. Scientists admit that nature is working in a wonderful way, but, after all, nature is not under their control. The scientists may accept or defy Kṛṣṇa, but they cannot defy the activities of nature. Everyone is subordinate to nature. Nature, however, is working under the direction of God; therefore everyone is subordinate to God.

The sun, oceans, land, space and everything else in material creation are but manifestations of Kṛṣṇa's external energy. Nothing is independent of Kṛṣṇa or His energy. In *Brahma-saṁhitā* (5.44) it is said that material nature is so powerful that it can create, maintain and destroy in itself: *Sṛṣṭi-sthiti-pralaya-sādhana-śaktir ekā.* However, material nature is working just like a shadow. If we place our hand before a light, we can see its shadow move on a wall. Similarly, material nature is working due to the touch of spirit soul. It is not possible for an automobile to drive itself. A person, a spirit soul, must be within to push certain buttons. Due to the touch of the spirit soul, the machine is moving. The entire universe is similarly moving due to the touch of God. According to the *śāstras*, the wind is blowing, the water is moving, the sun is shining and the earth is revolving under the direction of the Supreme Personality of Godhead. If the directors of the different material elements do not work properly, they are punished by their master, Kṛṣṇa.

When Kṛṣṇa was present on this earth, He saw that Lord Indra, the lord of the heavens and of rain, was somewhat puffed up. Kṛṣṇa therefore advised His father Nanda Mahārāja not to bother worshiping Indra. He told His father, "There is no need to offer sacrifices to Indra. It is better to worship Govardhana Hill, which is the representative of God. The cows receive their grass and grains from Govardhana Hill; therefore it is better to worship it." At first, Nanda Mahārāja was not willing to do this, but out of affection for Kṛṣṇa, he finally agreed. When Indra saw that Nanda Mahārāja was worshiping Govardhana Hill, he became very angry and sent vicious clouds to inundate all of Vṛndāvana with a flood. Kṛṣṇa then showed Indra that his power was not even competent to deal with the little finger of His left hand. Therefore Kṛṣṇa lifted Govardhana Hill with the small finger of His left hand and used it as an umbrella to save all the people of Vṛndāvana from Indra's torrents. All of this is related in *Śrīmad-Bhāgavatam.*

Thus everyone is a servant. No one can actually claim to be master. If we simply take shelter of Kṛṣṇa, we do not have to offer sacrifices to various demigods. If we water the root of a tree, we do not have to water the branches, twigs, flowers or fruits. If we supply food to the stomach, we do not have to feed the eyes, hands and legs separately. Similarly, if we worship Kṛṣṇa, the source of everything, no other worship is necessary.

Large amounts of wealth are necessary to perform sacrifices. In former ages, tons of food were offered in a fire as a sacrifice, but this is not possible in this age. Therefore *saṅkīrtana-yajña*, the chanting of the Hare Kṛṣṇa *mahā-mantra*, is recommended. Anyone can chant Hare Kṛṣṇa. There is no need for instruments, although Caitanya Mahāprabhu introduced the *mṛdaṅga* (drum) and *karatālas* (cymbals). Otherwise, clapping in itself is sufficient. Anyone can sit down with his family, clap hands and chant Hare Kṛṣṇa, Hare Kṛṣṇa, Kṛṣṇa Kṛṣṇa, Hare Hare/ Hare Rāma, Hare Rāma, Rāma Rāma, Hare Hare. This *saṅkīrtana* is very easy to perform. In the evening people go to restaurants and cinemas and waste time and money at clubs and dances. They are not aware of the fearful situation of birth, old age, disease and death. People are carried away by the waves of material nature, and they have submitted to its laws. We should not waste our time in this valuable human form but should begin to solve our problems.

Eventually everything on this earth will be annihilated. At present, three fourths of this earth is covered with water. In the beginning, the entire earth was covered with water, but gradually the water is drying up, and more land is emerging. Since the land has emerged, we have calculated that this is the Asian continent, this is North America, South America, Africa and so on. Eventually there will be no water but only land, and this means that there will ultimately be destruction. Since there will be no water, the heat will be scorching, and eventually the earth will be burned to ashes. Then again there will be rainfall, and everything will be mixed up again, and again there will be destruction. In this way things come into existence and are dissolved. Similarly, this body comes into existence, takes a nice form, and then is finally finished forever. We will then have to get another body. The body is like a bubble. It is present for one moment, then it bursts and is gone forever.

We simply take on one bubble after another, one body after another, and we think that we will become happy in this way because we are so foolish. Kṛṣṇa comes as a person like us, but we are such rascals that we think He is simply a man, and this is our misfortune. If we just surrender unto Kṛṣṇa, we will no longer be subjected to the *karma* of different bodies. Even if we attempt to render some devotional service to Him and fall down, we lose nothing and gain everything. A human life is guaranteed in our next birth. It is therefore to our benefit to accept Kṛṣṇa.

CHAPTER EIGHTEEN

Devotional Service: The Final Perfection

TEXT 43

jñāna-vairāgya-yuktena
bhakti-yogena yoginaḥ
kṣemāya pāda-mūlaṁ me
praviśanty akuto-bhayam

TRANSLATION

The yogīs, equipped with transcendental knowledge and renunciation and engaged in devotional service for their eternal benefit, take shelter at My lotus feet, and since I am the Lord, they are thus eligible to enter into the kingdom of Godhead without fear.

PURPORT

One who wants to be liberated from the entanglement of this material world and go back home, back to Godhead, is actually a mystic *yogī*. The words explicitly used here are *yuktena bhakti-yogena*. Those *yogīs*, or mystics, who engage in devotional service are first-class *yogīs*. They are described in *Bhagavad-gītā* as constantly thinking of the Lord, the Supreme Personality of Godhead, Kṛṣṇa. These *yogīs* are not without knowledge and renunciation. To become a *bhakti-yogī* means to automatically attain knowledge and renunciation. That is the consequent result of *bhakti-yoga*. In the *Bhāgavatam*, First Canto, Second Chapter, it is also confirmed that one who engages in devotional service of Vāsudeva, Kṛṣṇa, has complete transcendental knowledge and renunciation, and there is no further explanation for these attainments. *Ahaitukī*—without reason, they come. Even if a person is completely illiterate, the transcendental knowledge of the scriptures is revealed unto him because of his devotion. To anyone who has full faith in the Supreme Personality of Godhead and the spiritual master, all the import of the Vedic literatures is revealed. One doesn't have to seek separately; the *yogīs* who engage in devotional service are full in knowledge and renunciation. If there is a lack of knowledge and renunciation, it is to be understood that one is not engaged in full devotional service. The conclusion is that one cannot be sure of entrance into the spiritual realm—in either the impersonal *brahmajyoti* effulgence of the Lord or the Vaikuṇṭha planets within that Brahman effulgence—unless he is surrendered unto the lotus feet of the Supreme Lord. The surrendered souls are called *akuto-bhaya.* They are doubtless and fearless, and their entrance into the spiritual kingdom is guaranteed.

Devotional service is most important because there is danger in every step in this material world. At any moment, our life can be finished. We may be walking along very nicely, but at some moment we may slip and break our neck; therefore this planet is called Martyaloka, the planet of death, the place where death is a certainty. Regardless of how strong or healthy one may be, one cannot avoid death. One may exercise on the beach daily, but one may die at any moment. There is no guarantee. Everyone wants health and security, but actually there is no security. There is simply a struggle for existence. People are struggling for security, but in reality this is all foolishness. People are always fearful because they have forgotten or rejected Kṛṣṇa. We have forgotten that we are Kṛṣṇa's eternal servants, His eternal parts and parcels, and that we have a most intimate relationship with Him. In the material world we are situated in *asat,* a nonpermanent situation. When a child has lost his father and mother, he is always in a fearful condition. He cries in the street, "Where is my father? Where is my mother?" If we no longer want to be in such a fearful condition, we have to take shelter at the lotus feet of Kṛṣṇa. Kṛṣṇa is begging us to come to Him because we are all His sons. He says, "You are rotting here by repeatedly committing sins. You are changing from one body to another, and you are thinking that you are a human being, an American, this or that. The next moment you may become a dog or an insect." People are always thinking that they are secure, and this is called *māyā,* illusion.

Knowledge, *jñāna,* means understanding our relationship with Kṛṣṇa. A wise man asks, "What is my duty to Kṛṣṇa?" Once we understand our relationship with Kṛṣṇa and our duty to Him, we naturally become reluctant to engage in material activities. This is called *vairāgya*, detachment from material activities. *Jñāna* and *vairāgya* can be awakened by *bhakti-yoga. Bhakti* means surrender unto Kṛṣṇa. Without surrendering to Kṛṣṇa, we cannot understand our situation. Kṛṣṇa reserves the right of not being exposed to fools and rascals. He is simply meant for the devotees. We cannot understand Kṛṣṇa without becoming devotees.

Material life means sex. People work hard all day in order to have a little sex at night. In the material world everyone is suffering from the sharp arrow of Cupid. Madana, Cupid, shoots his arrow into men and women to make them mad after one another; however, when one actually sees Kṛṣṇa, he sees Madana-mohana, the charmer of Cupid. Then one is no longer pierced by Cupid's arrow. This means that one actually becomes fearless. One can then enter into *bhakti-yoga* and renounce this material world. According to the *śāstras*, there is *śreyas* and *preyas*. *Śreyas* is the ultimate goal. We should act in such a way that ultimately we will become happy. However, if we want immediate happiness and disregard the future, we want *preyas. Preyas* is for unintelligent people and children. A child enjoys playing all day; he does not want to be sent to school to be educated. Education is *śreyas*, the ultimate goal. No one is interested in this. The *śāstras* instruct us to aim for *śreyas* and not be captivated by *preyas*. The supreme *śreyas* is *bhakti-yoga*.

In the material world we are struggling for existence with the hope that someday in the future we will be happy. Yet we are bewildered. An animal in the desert sees a mirage, a shadow of water, and he runs after this shadow again and again. He runs further and further, and in this way, as he crosses the hot sands, he becomes more and more thirsty and he finally dies. Our struggle for existence is like this. We are thinking, "Let me go a little further. There will be water eventually. There will eventually be happiness." Yet there is no water in the desert. Those who are unintelligent, who are like animals, seek happiness in the desert of the material world. This false attachment has to be given up by the process of *bhakti-yoga*. This must be taken up very seriously, not artificially. Kṛṣṇa in all seriousness wants to see whether one has finished all his material desires. When Kṛṣṇa sees this, He is very pleased. We are actually busy with *dharma, artha, kāma* and *mokṣa*, but when we transcend these, *bhakti* begins.

If we study the history of the world, we see that it is simply a history of struggle. Mankind attempts to relieve its miserable condition, but it simply brings about another miserable condition. As we try to overcome one problem, another problem arises. Our determination to renounce our association with this material world is called *mukti. Mukti* means coming to the spiritual platform. Since we belong to the spiritual atmosphere, it is impossible for us to be happy in the material atmosphere. If a land animal is placed in water, he will simply struggle for existence, despite being an expert swimmer. We have come into this material world to gratify our senses, but our attempts will never be successful. If we actually want to attain a state beyond fear, we have to accept this *bhakti-yoga* process enunciated by Lord Kapiladeva.

TEXT 44

etāvān eva loke 'smin
puṁsāṁ niḥśreyasodayaḥ
tīvreṇa bhakti-yogena
mano mayy arpitaṁ sthiram

TRANSLATION

Therefore persons whose minds are fixed on the Lord engage in the intensive practice of devotional service. That is the only means to attain the final perfection of life.

PURPORT

Here the words *mano mayy arpitam,* which mean "the mind being fixed on Me," are significant. One should fix his mind on the lotus feet of Kṛṣṇa or His incarnation. To be fixed steadily in that freedom is the way of liberation. Ambarīṣa Mahārāja is an example. He fixed his mind on the lotus feet of the Lord, he spoke only on the pastimes of the Lord, he smelled only the flowers and *tulasī* offered to the Lord, he walked only to the temple of the Lord, he engaged his hands in cleansing the temple, he engaged his tongue in tasting the foodstuff offered to the Lord, and he engaged his ears in hearing the great pastimes of the Lord. In this way all his senses were engaged. First of all, the mind should be engaged at the lotus feet of the Lord, very steadily and naturally. Because the mind is the master of the senses, when the mind is engaged, all the senses are engaged. That is *bhakti-yoga. Yoga* means controlling the senses. The senses cannot be controlled in the proper sense of the term; they are always agitated. This is true also with a child—how long can he be forced to sit down silently? It is not possible. Even Arjuna said, *cañcalaṁ hi manaḥ kṛṣṇa:* "The mind is always agitated." The best course is to fix the mind on the lotus feet of the Lord. *Mano mayy arpitaṁ sthiram.* If one seriously engages in Kṛṣṇa consciousness, that is the highest perfectional stage. All Kṛṣṇa conscious activities are on the highest perfectional level of human life.

This verse marks the conclusion of *bhakti-yoga,* as described by Lord Kapiladeva to His mother. *Bhakti-yoga* is the business of one advanced in *jñāna-vairāgya,* knowledge and renunciation. Sārvabhauma Bhaṭṭācārya has explained *bhakti-yoga* as *vairāgya-vidyā-nija-bhakti-yoga. Bhakti-yoga* begins when we accept Kṛṣṇa's instructions:

sarva-dharmān parityajya
mām ekaṁ śaraṇaṁ vraja

"Abandon all varieties of religion and just surrender unto Me." (Bg. 18.66)

We have to renounce all material engagements and accept the lotus feet of Kṛṣṇa. We are making one plan after another to be happy in this material world, but this place is certified by the Supreme Personality of Godhead as *duḥkhālayam aśāśvatam,* a place of misery. This material world is actually *meant* for misery, just as a prison house is meant for punishment. Once we attain our constitutional position of *brahma-bhūta,* we can enter the kingdom of God, the spiritual world. By *karma-yoga* we attempt to get out of the gross body, and by *jñāna-yoga* we attempt to get out of the subtle body, but by *bhakti-yoga* we can directly transcend both the subtle body (mind, intelligence and ego) and the gross material body. Then we can be situated on the spiritual platform in our original, spiritual body. As long as we are in the subtle and gross bodies, we are suffering under the three modes of material nature. Once we enter into the devotional service of the Lord, we are immediately situated on the platform of *brahma-bhūta. Ahaṁ brahmāsmi* ("I am Brahman") is simply theoretical knowledge, but when one actually renders devotional service, one is situated in practical knowledge. Then one is no longer on the material platform but on the Brahman platform.

Prahlāda Mahārāja rendered the best service to his father, Hiraṇyakaśipu, by having him killed by Lord Nṛsiṁhadeva. Superficially it appeared that Prahlāda Mahārāja did not help his father, but this was not the case. In the *śāstras* it is said that if a person, even though a demon, is killed by God, he is immediately liberated. Prahlāda Mahārāja was thinking, "My father is so sinful and so much opposed to God consciousness that he might not be liberated." After Lord Nṛsiṁha killed Hiraṇyakaśipu, Prahlāda Mahārāja told the Lord, "My dear Lord, may I ask one thing from You? My father was a great atheist, and he committed many offenses at Your lotus feet. Now You have killed him. I request that he be excused and be given liberation." Actually Hiraṇyakaśipu was already liberated, yet his affectionate son was anxious to know whether he was liberated or not. It is confirmed by the Lord that not only does a Vaiṣṇava's father, but everyone for twenty-one generations before a Vaiṣṇava receives liberation. Thus by serving the Lord, one renders the best service to his family, because twenty-one generations are liberated if one becomes a pure Vaiṣṇava.

The *yogī's* real business is to focus his mind on Kṛṣṇa. That is the real *yoga* system. There are many gymnastics performed by *yogīs*, but all this is recommended for those who are overly concerned with the body. Rendering service to Kṛṣṇa twenty-four hours daily is called *bhakti-yoga*, and that is real *samādhi.* People are working hard day and night to enjoy some results. A person in *bhakti-yoga* works hard day and night but offers the results to Kṛṣṇa. There is a great difference between a *bhakti-yogī* and an ordinary *karmī.* Ordinary *karmīs* cannot understand that the *bhaktas* are on the transcendental platform.

As we have stated before, there are innumerable forms of God—Rāma, Nṛsiṁha, Varāha, Kṛṣṇa, Kapiladeva, Balarāma and so on. Sometimes foolish people ask, "You are worshiping Kṛṣṇa. Why don't you worship Rāma?" Actually there is no difference between Kṛṣṇa and Rāma, but everyone has his preference. For instance, Hanumān was particularly devoted to Lord Rāmacandra. The *gopīs* are exclusively devoted to Lord Kṛṣṇa. This does not make any real difference. The Lord appears in different forms, but in all cases He is the Lord. Once Kṛṣṇa left the *gopīs* and changed into His four-handed Viṣṇu form. The *gopīs* went out searching for Kṛṣṇa, and when they saw the four-handed Viṣṇu form, they did not offer much respect. They simply wanted to see Kṛṣṇa. Actually there is no difference between Kṛṣṇa and Viṣṇu, but every devotee has a particular inclination. In the Vaiṣṇava-sampradāya, some devotees worship Rādhā-Kṛṣṇa, and others worship Sītā-Rāma and Lakṣmī-Nārāyaṇa. Some also worship Rukmiṇī-Kṛṣṇa. All of these are the same, and all of the devotees are Vaiṣṇavas. Whether one chants Hare Kṛṣṇa or Hare Rāma, it is not very important. Worship of the demigods, however, is not recommended. In any case, *bhakti-yoga* begins with hearing—*śravaṇaṁ kīrtanam.* After one has heard from the right source and is convinced, one will automatically perform *kīrtana. Kīrtana* means glorification. *Kīrtana* is preaching, glorifying and speaking about the Lord. Parīkṣit Mahārāja attained perfection simply by listening to *Śrīmad-Bhāgavatam.* This is *śravaṇaṁ kīrtanam.* Parīkṣit Mahārāja was listening, and Śukadeva Gosvāmī was performing *kīrtana* by describing the glories of the Lord. Pṛthu Mahārāja simply worshiped the Lord, and Lakṣmīdevī massaged Viṣṇu's lotus feet. Arjuna made friends with the Lord, and Hanumān carried out the orders of Lord Rāmacandra. Bali Mahārāja offered everything he had to the Lord in the form of Vāmanadeva, and after he had offered all his possessions, he offered his body. There are many examples, but at the present moment, if we simply hear about Kṛṣṇa, that is sufficient. God has given us ears, and we need only go to a realized soul and hear about Kṛṣṇa from him. This is the process recommended for this age because people are very fallen and are uneducated.

Caitanya Mahāprabhu recommends that we search out a devotee regardless of our position. There is no need to change our position; it is better to remain where we are and simply hear about Kṛṣṇa. The Kṛṣṇa consciousness movement is meant to give everybody an opportunity to hear about Kṛṣṇa. Kṛṣṇa is within everyone's heart, and as soon as He sees that one is interested in Him, He helps. This is the beginning of *bhakti.*

Even if we do not understand this philosophy, we will be purified if we hear what Kṛṣṇa says. This is the whole process of *hari-saṅkīrtana.* One doesn't even have to understand what this Hare Kṛṣṇa is. One only has to hear to be purified. Unless one is purified, one cannot understand God. There are many contaminations within the heart, and the people in this age are engaged in many sinful activities—illicit sex, meat-eating, intoxication and gambling. The whole world is revolving about these things, yet despite this we have to spread this Kṛṣṇa consciousness movement. There may be many obstacles, but they can all be transcended by Kṛṣṇa's mercy. We only have to be determined in our devotion. The rest will follow. This is the essence of Lord Kapila's instructions to His mother.

Appendixes

About the Author

His Divine Grace A.C. Bhaktivedanta Swami Prabhupāda appeared in this world in 1896 in Calcutta, India. He first met his spiritual master, Śrīla Bhaktisiddhānta Sarasvatī Gosvāmī, in Calcutta in 1922. Bhaktisiddhānta Sarasvatī, a prominent religious scholar and the founder of sixty-four Gauḍīya Maṭhas (Vedic institutes), liked this educated young man and convinced him to dedicate his life to teaching Vedic knowledge. Śrīla Prabhupāda became his student, and eleven years later (1933) at Allahabad he became his formally initiated disciple.

At their first meeting, in 1922, Śrīla Bhaktisiddhānta Sarasvatī Ṭhākura requested Śrīla Prabhupāda to broadcast Vedic knowledge through the English language. In the years that followed, Śrīla Prabhupāda wrote a commentary on the *Bhagavad-gītā,* assisted the Gauḍīya Maṭha in its work and, in 1944, started *Back to Godhead,* an English fortnightly magazine. Maintaining the publication was a struggle. Singlehandedly, Śrīla Prabhupāda edited it, typed the manuscripts, checked the galley proofs, and even distributed the individual copies. Once begun, the magazine never stopped; it is now being continued by his disciples in the West and is published in over thirty languages.

Recognizing Śrīla Prabhupāda's philosophical learning and devotion, the Gauḍīya Vaiṣṇava Society honored him in 1947 with the title "Bhaktivedanta." In 1950, at the age of fifty-four, Śrīla Prabhupāda retired from married life, adopting the *vānaprastha* (retired) order to devote more time to his studies and writing. Śrīla Prabhupāda traveled to the holy city of Vṛndāvana, where he lived in very humble circumstances in the historic medieval temple of Rādhā-Dāmodara. There he engaged for several years in deep study and writing. He accepted the renounced order of life (*sannyāsa*) in 1959. At Rādhā-Dāmodara, Śrīla Prabhupāda began work on his life's masterpiece: a multivolume annotated translation of the eighteen-thousand-verse *Śrīmad-Bhāgavatam* (*Bhāgavata Purāṇa*). He also wrote *Easy Journey to Other Planets.*

After publishing three volumes of the *Bhāgavatam,* Śrīla Prabhupāda came to the United States, in September 1965, to fulfill the mission of his spiritual master. Subsequently, His Divine Grace wrote more than sixty volumes of authoritative annotated translations and summary studies of the philosophical and religious classics of India.

When he first arrived by freighter in New York City, Śrīla Prabhupāda was practically penniless. Only after almost a year of great difficulty did he establish the International Society for Krishna Consciousness, in July of 1966. Before his passing away on November 14, 1977, he guided the Society and saw it grow to a worldwide confederation of more than one hundred *āśramas,* schools, temples, institutes and farm communities.

In 1968, Śrīla Prabhupāda created New Vrindaban, an experimental Vedic community in the hills of West Virginia. Inspired by the success of New Vrindaban, now a thriving farm community of more than two thousand acres, his students have since founded several similar communities in the United States and abroad.

In 1972, His Divine Grace introduced the Vedic system of primary and secondary education in the West by founding the Gurukula school in Dallas, Texas. Since then, under his supervision, his disciples have established children's schools throughout the United States and the rest of the world, with the principal educational center now located in Vṛndāvana, India.

Śrīla Prabhupāda also inspired the construction of several large international cultural centers in India. The center at Śrīdhāma Māyāpur in West Bengal is the site for a planned spiritual city, an ambitious project for which construction will extend over many years to come. In Vṛndāvana, India, are the magnificent Kṛṣṇa-Balarāma Temple and International Guesthouse, and Śrīla Prabhupāda Memorial and Museum. There is also a major cultural and educational center in Bombay. Other centers are planned in a dozen important locations on the Indian subcontinent.

Śrīla Prabhupāda's most significant contribution, however, is his books. Highly respected by the academic community for their authority, depth and clarity, they are used as standard textbooks in numerous college courses. His writings have been translated into over fifty languages. The Bhaktivedanta Book Trust, established in 1972 to publish the works of His Divine Grace, has thus become the world's largest publisher of books in the field of Indian religion and philosophy.

In just twelve years, in spite of his advanced age, Śrīla Prabhupāda circled the globe fourteen times on lecture tours that took him to six continents. In spite of such a vigorous schedule, Śrīla Prabhupāda continued to write prolifically. His writings constitute a veritable library of Vedic philosophy, religion, literature and culture.

References

Bhagavad-gītā, 2, 3, 4, 5, 6, 8, 10–11, 15, 16, 18–19, 22, 24–25, 26, 27, 28, 29, 32, 33, 34, 35, 36, 37, 38, 43–44, 46, 52, 54, 58, 61, 63, 64, 66, 70, 71, 73, 74, 85, 86–87, 88, 89–90, 94–95, 95–96, 98, 100, 102, 108–109, 112–113, 113–114, 117, 120, 121–122, 127–128, 130, 131, 132, 133, 136–137, 139, 145, 148, 151–152, 153, 160, 161, 174, 177, 181–182, 190, 202, 203, 208, 211, 217, 218, 219, 225, 233, 238, 244, 253

Bhakti-rasāmṛta-sindhu, 24, 94, 121, 139

Brahma-saṁhitā, 25, 34, 35, 47, 52, 57, 69, 86, 113, 115, 125, 154, 162–163, 164, 178–179, 212, 224, 230, 245

Bṛhan-nāradīya Purāṇa, 3–4, 97

Caitanya-bhāgavata, 95

Caitanya-caritāmṛta, 16, 17, 30, 53, 59, 73–74, 87, 100, 109, 110, 120, 130, 139, 159, 164, 168, 172, 184, 199, 217, 236

Kaṭha Upaniṣad, 14, 73

Kṛṣṇa-karṇāmṛta, 194–195

Mahābhārata, 17

Muṇḍaka Upaniṣad, 33

Nārada-pañcarātra, 55, 106

Padma Purāṇa, 87, 141

Śikṣāṣṭaka, 70, 75, 183, 184, 186, 197, 204, 242–243

Glossary

A

Ācārya—a spiritual master who teaches by example.

Ādhibhautika miseries—miseries caused by other living entities.

Ādhidaivika miseries—miseries caused by natural disturbances.

Ādhyātmika miseries—miseries caused by the mind and body.

Akutobhaya—fearless.

Aṇimā—the mystic perfection of becoming smaller than the smallest.

Ārati—a ceremony for greeting the Lord with offerings of food, lamps, fans, flowers and incense.

Arcanā—the devotional process of Deity worship.

Āśrama—the four spiritual orders of life: celibate student, householder, retired life and renounced life.

Aṣṭāṅga-yoga—the mystic *yoga* system propounded by Patañjali in his *Yoga-sūtras.*

Asuras—atheistic demons.

Avatāra—a descent of the Supreme Lord.

B

Bhagavad-gītā—the basic directions for spiritual life spoken by the Lord Himself.

Bhagavān—one who unlimitedly possesses all opulences; a term of address for the Supreme Personality of Godhead.

Bhagavat-prasāda—*See: Prasāda*

Bhajana-kriyā—a regulated process of worshiping and rendering service to the Supreme Lord.

Bhakta—a devotee.

Bhakti-yoga—linking with the Supreme Lord by devotional service.

Brahmacarya—celibate student life; the first order of Vedic spiritual life.

Brahman—the Absolute Truth; especially the impersonal aspect of the Absolute.

Brāhmaṇa—one wise in the *Vedas* who can guide society; the first Vedic social order.

Buddhi-yoga—the practice of devotional service.

D

Dāsya—the servitorship relationship with the Lord.
Dharma—eternal occupational duty; religious principles.

E

Ekādaśī—a special fast day for increased remembrance of Kṛṣṇa, which comes on the eleventh day of both the waxing and waning moon.

G

Goloka (Kṛṣṇaloka)—the highest spiritual planet, containing Kṛṣṇa's personal abodes, Dvārakā, Mathurā and Vṛndāvana.
Gopīs—Kṛṣṇa's cowherd girl friends, His most confidential servitors.
Gṛhastha—regulated householder life; the second order of Vedic spiritual life.
Guṇa-avatāras—Viṣṇu, Brahmā and Śiva, the presiding deities of the three modes of nature.
Guru—a spiritual master.
Guru-kula—the school of Vedic learning; boys begin at the age of five and live as celibate students, guided by a spiritual master.

H

Hare Kṛṣṇa mantra—*See: Mahā-mantra*
Haṭha-yoga—the system of practicing sitting postures for sense control.

J

Jaya rādhe—"All glories to Śrīmatī Rādhārāṇī."
Jīva-tattva—the living entities, atomic parts of the Lord.
Jñāna-yoga—the process of approaching the Supreme by mental speculation.

K

Kacaurīs—a deep-fried pastry made of flour filled with mashed dahl beans or a vegetable.
Kali-yuga (Age of Kali)—the present age, characterized by quarrel; it is last in the cycle of four and began five thousand years ago.

Kapha-pitta-vāyu—phlegm, bile and air, the three humors of the body.

Karatālas—hand cymbals used in *kīrtana.*

Karma—fruitive action, for which there is always reaction, good or bad.

Karma-yoga—(1) action in devotional service; (2) action performed by one who knows that the goal of life is Kṛṣṇa but who is addicted to the fruits of his activities.

Karmī—a person satisfied with working hard for flickering sense gratification.

Kathā—an account or story.

Kīrtana—chanting the glories of the Supreme Lord.

Kṛṣṇaloka—*See:* Goloka

Kṣatriya—a warrior or administrator; the second Vedic social order.

L

Laghimā—the yogic power to become light as a feather.

M

Mādhurya—conjugal love relationship with the Lord.

Mahā-bhāva—the highest stage of love of God.

Mahā-mantra—the great chanting for deliverance:

Hare Kṛṣṇa, Hare Kṛṣṇa, Kṛṣṇa Kṛṣṇa, Hare Hare
Hare Rāma, Hare Rāma, Rāma Rāma, Hare Hare.

Maṅgala-ārati—an early-morning ceremony in which various articles of worship are offered to the Deity of the Lord.

Mantra—a sound vibration that can deliver the mind from illusion.

Mathurā—Lord Kṛṣṇa's abode, surrounding Vṛndāvana, where He took birth and later returned to after performing His Vṛndāvana pastimes.

Māyā—illusion; forgetfulness of one's relationship with Kṛṣṇa.

Māyāvādīs—impersonal philosophers who say that the Lord cannot have a transcendental body.

Mṛdaṅga—a clay drum used for congregational chanting.

O

Oṁ tat sat—three transcendental syllables indicating the Supreme Absolute Truth, the Personality of Godhead.

P

Paramparā—the chain of spiritual masters in disciplic succession.
Paravyoma—the spiritual sky.
Pradhāna—the total material energy in its unmanifest state.
Prāpti—the yogic perfection of being able to attain anything one desires.
Prasāda—food spiritualized by being offered to the Lord.
Priya—loved one.

R

Rasagullā—a Bengali sweet made of milk.

S

Sac-cid-ānanda-vigraha—the Lord's transcendental form, which is eternal, full of knowledge and bliss.
Sakhā—friend.
Sakhya—friend relationship with the Lord.
Śaktyāveśa-avatāras—empowered incarnations of the Supreme Lord.
Saṁsāra—the cycle of repeated birth and death.
Saṅkīrtana—public chanting of the names of God, the approved *yoga* process for this age.
Sannyāsa—renounced life; the fourth order of Vedic spiritual life.
Santaḥ—saintly or devoted.
Śānta-rasa—a neutral relationship with the Supreme Lord.
Śāstras—revealed scriptures.
Sat—eternal.
Sattva—the quality of goodness.
Śrāddha—ceremony performed to release one's forefathers from hellish conditions of life.
Śravaṇaṁ kīrtanaṁ viṣṇoḥ—the devotional processes of hearing and chanting about Lord Viṣṇu.
Śūdra—a laborer; the fourth of the Vedic social orders.
Surabhi—spiritual cows, in the spiritual world, which yield unlimited quantities of milk.
Suta—son.
Svāmī—one who controls his mind and senses; title of one in the renounced order of life.
Svayam-avatāras—*See: Viṣṇu-tattva*

T

Tapasya—austerity; accepting some voluntary inconvenience for a higher purpose.

Tilaka—auspicious clay marks that sanctify a devotee's body as a temple of the Lord.

Tulasī—a tree sacred to worshipers of Lord Viṣṇu.

V

Vaikuṇṭha—the spiritual world.

Vaiṣṇava—a devotee of Lord Viṣṇu, Kṛṣṇa.

Vaiśyas—farmers and merchants; the third Vedic social order.

Vānaprastha—one who has retired from family life; the third order of Vedic spiritual life.

Varṇa—the four occupational divisions of society: the intellectual class, the administrative class, the mercantile class, and the laborer class.

Varṇāśrama—the Vedic social system of four social and four spiritual orders.

Vātsalya—parental relationship with the Lord.

Vedas—the original revealed scriptures, first spoken by the Lord Himself.

Viṣṇu, Lord—Kṛṣṇa's expansion for the creation and maintenance of the material universes.

Viṣṇu-tattva—the original Personality of Godhead's primary expansions, each of whom is equally God.

Vṛndāvana—Kṛṣṇa's personal abode, where He fully manifests His quality of sweetness.

Vyāsadeva—Kṛṣṇa's incarnation, at the end of Dvāpara-yuga, for compiling the *Vedas.*

Y

Yajña—an activity performed to satisfy either Lord Viṣṇu or the demigods.

Yogī—a transcendentalist who, in one way or another, is striving for union with the Supreme.

Yugas—ages in the life of a universe, occurring in a repeated cycle of four.

Guide to Sanskrit Pronunciation

Throughout the centuries, the Sanskrit language has been written in a variety of alphabets. The mode of writing most widely used throughout India, however, is called *devanāgarī*, which literally means "the city writing of the *devas*, or gods." The *devanāgarī* alphabet consists of forty-eight characters, including thirteen vowels and thirty-five consonants. The ancient Sanskrit grammarians arranged the alphabet according to concise linguistic principles, and this arrangement has been accepted by all Western scholars. The system of transliteration used in this book conforms to a system that scholars in the last fifty years have almost universally accepted to indicate the pronunciation of each Sanskrit sound.

The short vowel **a** is pronounced like the **u** in **but**; long **ā** like the **a** in **far**; and short **i** like the **i** in **pin**. Long **ī** is pronounced as in **pique**, short **u** as in **pull**, and long **ū** as in **rule**. The vowel **ṛ** is pronounced like the **ri** in **rim**. The vowel **e** is pronounced as in **they**; **ai** as in **aisle**; **o** as in **go**; and **au** as in **how**. The *anusvara* (**ṁ**), which is a pure nasal, is pronounced like the **n** in the French word *bon*, and *visarga* (**ḥ**), which is a strong aspirate, is pronounced as a final **h** sound. Thus **aḥ** is pronounced like **aha**, and **iḥ** like **ihi**.

The guttural consonants—**k, kh, g, gh,** and **ṅ**—are pronounced from the throat in much the same manner as in English. **K** is pronounced as in **kite**, **kh** as in **Eckhart**, **g** as in **give**, **gh** as in **dig hard**, and **ṅ** as in **sing**. The palatal consonants—**c, ch, j, jh,** and **ñ**—are pronounced from the palate with the middle of the tongue. **C** is pronounced as in **chair**, **ch** as in **staunch heart**, **j** as in **joy**, **jh** as in **hedgehog**, and **ñ** as in **canyon**. The cerebral consonants—**ṭ, ṭh, ḍ, ḍh,** and **ṇ**—are pronounced with the tip of the tongue turned up and drawn back against the dome of the palate. **Ṭ** is pronounced as in **tub**, **ṭh** as in **light heart**, **ḍ** as in **dove**, **ḍh** as in **red-hot**, and **ṇ** as in **nut**. The dental consonants—**t, th, d, dh,** and **n**—are pronounced in the same manner as the cerebrals but with the forepart of the tongue against the teeth. The labial consonants—**p, ph, b, bh,** and **m**—are pronounced with the lips. **P** is pronounced as in **pine**, **ph** as in **uphill**, **b** as in **bird**, **bh** as in **rub hard**, and **m** as in **mother**. The semivowels—**y, r, l** and **v**—are pronounced as in **yes**, **run**, **light** and vine respectively. The sibilants—ś, ṣ and s—are pronounced, respectively, as in the German word *sprechen* and the English words **sh**ine and **s**un. The letter **h** is pronounced as in **h**ome.

Index of Sanskrit Verses

The teachings of Lord Kapiladeva, as found in this volume, are derived from the *Śrīmad-Bhāgavatam*, Third Canto, Chapter Twenty-five. All the original Sanskrit verses of this chapter are found in *Teachings of Lord Kapiladeva*. The following index constitutes a complete listing of the first and third lines of each of these verses, arranged in English alphabetical order. The first column gives the Sanskrit transliteration, and the second and third columns, respectively, list the verse reference and page number for each verse.

General Index

Api cet sudurācāro
verse quoted, 132
Ārādhanānāṁ sarveṣāṁ
quoted, 141
Arcanam defined, 103
See also: Deity form, worship of
Arcanaṁ vandanaṁ dāsyaṁ
verse quoted, 22
Arcā-vigraha defined, 69, 210
See also: Deity form
Arcāyām eva haraye
verse quoted, 216
Arjuna
acted for Kṛṣṇa, 122, 151
Kṛṣṇa sided with, 190
submissive to Kṛṣṇa, 171
Artha defined, 194, 222
Ārto jijñāsur arthārthī
verse quoted, 160
Āruhya kṛcchreṇa paraṁ padaṁ tataḥ
quoted, 47, 116
Asad-grāhān defined, 78
Asat defined, 23, 78, 159
Asat-saṅga defined, 159
Asat-saṅga-tyāga,—ei vaiṣṇava-ācāra
quoted, 139, 159
Asito devalo vyāsaḥ
verse quoted, 38
Aśocyān anvaśocas tvaṁ
verse quoted, 174
Āśramas defined, 27
Association with devotees. *See:* Devotees, associating with
Asuras defined, 61, 209
See also: Demons
Ataeva māyā tāre deya saṁsāra-duḥkha
verse quoted, 109, 236
Ataḥ pumbhir dvija-śreṣṭhā
verse quoted, 151–152
Ataḥ śrī-kṛṣṇa-nāmādi
quoted, 200
verse quoted, 94
Atha me deva sammoham
verse quoted, 79
Athāpi te deva padāmbuja-dvaya-
verse quoted, 187
Athāto brahma-jijñāsā
quoted, 57, 173
Athavā bahunaitena
verse quoted, 114
Atheists
compared to ostriches, 240
fear punishment, 169
See also: Demons; Impersonalists; Kapila, atheist; Materialists
Ātmā defined, 34, 84
Atoms, Lord in, 125
Attachment
causes bondage, 138
material vs. spiritual, **105**, 128–129
redirected vs. stopped, 149–151
Austerity (penance)
painful at first, 153
transcendental result of, 8–9
Authorities (*mahājanas*), twelve listed, 42, 192
Avaiṣṇavo gurur na syād
verse quoted, 87
Avajānanti māṁ mūḍhāḥ
quoted, 4, 10
verse quoted, 85
Avatāras defined, 23
Avyaktād aṇḍa-sambhavaḥ
quoted, 116
Avyaktā hi gatir duḥkhaṁ
verse quoted, 218
Avyakto 'kṣara ity uktas
verse quoted, 19
Ayi nanda-tanuja kiṅkaraṁ
quoted, 242
verse quoted, 70
Āyuṣaḥ kṣaṇa eko 'pi
quoted, 110

B

Bahūnāṁ janmanām ante
quoted, 98, 138
verse quoted, 6
Bali Mahārāja, 255
Bāṇaḥ defined, 178

D

E

F

I

J

L

N

Q

R

U

V

W

KEEP IN TOUCH . . .

If YOU find this book interesting, you might like one of these publications — at reduced prices — which will help you experience the pleasure of spiritual life. Just indicate the appropriate boxes, remove these pages from the book, enclose your payment and mail to one of the addresses given on the last page of this special offer section. (If you'd prefer not to remove these pages, you may photocopy them or write out your order.)

All prices include postage and handling in the USA or Europe.

US $	UK £		
Free	Free	❒	**Free Information Package**
1.00	1.00	❒	**Śrī Īśopaniṣad**
3.20	2.50	❒	**The Mantra Meditation Kit**
11.60	8.95	❒	**The Hare Krishna Book of Vegetarian Cooking**

Śrī Īśopaniṣad

Biochemists tell us our thoughts, our feelings, and our very consciousness are simply patterns of electromagnetic impulses flashing briefly in the vast void of space and time. But something deep within us refuses to be analysed into lifeless blips of energy. *Śrī Īśopaniṣad,* the most confidential of the 108 *Upaniṣads,* explains that personality is the unifying principle of our existence.
160 pages, paperback.

The Mantra Meditation Kit

Meditation — an essential part of your survival plan for the nineties. Try Hare Kṛṣṇa meditation for yourself. It works! Here's all you need to get started . . .

Meditation beads
Indispensable for the serious mantra meditator. For thousands of years in India, great *yogīs* and sages have chanted on *japa-mala* just like this; a string of 108 hand-carved beads of sacred neemwood.

Bead Bag
Fashioned from homespun Indian cotton, this handy bag will protect your mantra meditation beads from dirt and damage.

Counting Beads
This short string of sliding beads helps you keep track of how many times you chant round your 108-bead *japa-mala.*

"The ability to handle stress increases with the practice of meditation. In a culture like ours, in which inner spiritual growth is totally neglected in favour of materialistic results, we might have something to learn from the Hare Kṛṣṇa devotees' meditational practices."

Daniel Goldman, Ph.D., associate editor of Psychology Today, *and author of* The Varieties of Meditational Experience.

The Hare Krishna Book of Vegetarian Cooking

A colorfully illustrated, practical cookbook that not only helps you prepare authentic Indian dishes at home, but also teaches you about the ancient tradition behind India's world-famous vegetarian cuisine.

130 kitchen-tested recipes, 300 pages, hardback.

US $	UK £	
3.90	3.00	❒ paperback
10.30	7.95	❒ hard
18.10	13.95	❒ De-Luxe

Bhagavad-gītā As It Is

The World's Most Popular Edition of a Timeless Classic

Throughout the ages the world's greatest minds have turned to the *Bhagavad-gītā* for answers to life's perennial questions. Renowned as the jewel of India's spiritual wisdom, the *Gītā* summarizes the profound Vedic knowledge concerning man's essential nature, his environment, and ultimately his relationship with God. With more than fifty million copies sold in twenty languages, *Bhagavad-gītā As It Is*, by His Divine Grace A.C. Bhaktivedanta Swami Prabhupāda, is the most widely read edition of the *Gītā* in the world. It includes the original Sanskrit text, phonetic transliterations, word-for-word meanings, translation, elaborate commentary and full-color illustrations.

US $	UK £	
495.-	295.-	❒

Śrīmad-Bhāgavatam

The Ripened Fruit of the Tree of Vedic Wisdom

If you've enjoyed this book and are eager to learn more about the complete science of self-realization and God-realization, then this magnificent set of 18 encyclopedic volumes is for you.

The *Śrīmad-Bhāgavatam* was compiled some fifty centuries ago by the exalted sage and *yogī* Śrīla Vyāsadeva, who lived in an ashram high in the Himalayas. It was the beginning of the winter of the universal cycle, the Age of Kali, when the strength, intelligence, and spirituality of human beings would slowly diminish. Able to see the future, Vyāsadeva felt great compassion for those who would live in the spiritually dark ages to come. He therefore penned a vast eighteen thousand verses, drawing on the immense resource of his accumulated wisdom and mystical realization. The result of his labour is the *Śrīmad-Bhāgavatam.*

For thousands of years this sacred literature was concealed in the Sanskrit language, carefully passed down from spiritual master to disciple throughout India. It was not until 1965, when the great scholar and guru His Divine Grace A.C. Bhaktivedanta Swami Prabhupāda came to the West and began distributing his newly-published three-volume edition of the *Bhāgavatam's* first canto, that the English-speaking world began to discover this spiritual masterpiece on a wide scale. Over the next twelve years, while developing his Kṛṣṇa Consciousness Society and traveling extensively worldwide, Śrīla Prabhupāda produced twenty-seven more volumes of the *Bhāgavatam.* He carefully rendered the original Sanskrit text into English and then added his own purports, which were based on his vast realized knowledge of Kṛṣṇa and the commentaries written by great scholarly saints of past centuries. After Śrīla Prabhupāda passed away in 1977, his disciples completed the remaining chapters and consolidated the whole work into 18 volumes.

Great sages of antiquity declared the *Bhāgavatam* to be "as brilliant as the sun," able to illuminate the spiritual path of any soul inquisitive enough to study its profound words.

The Bhaktivedanta Book Trust invites readers interested in spiritual development of any kind to discover the unique wisdom contained in the *Śrīmad-Bhāgavatam.*

18 hardback volumes, each with approximately 900 pages and 16 full color plates.

Readers in North America please send to:
The Bhaktivedanta Book Trust,
3764 Watseka Ave.,
Los Angeles, CA 90034
USA

For the UK and Europe send to:
The Bhaktivedanta Book Trust
P.O. Box 324,
Borehamwood,
Herts. WD6 1NB, UK

Please, don't forget your full name and address, including post/zip codes, **in block capitals.**